# Steven
# GERRARD
### *My Story*

**RED FOX**

STEVEN GERRARD: MY STORY
A RED FOX BOOK 978 1 862 30438 3

First published in Great Britain by Bantam Press,
a division of Transworld Publishers
A Random House Group Company

Bantam Press edition published 2006
Bantam edition published 2007
Red Fox abridged edition published 2007

1 3 5 7 9 10 8 6 4 2

**Mixed Sources**
Product group from well-managed
forests and other controlled sources
www.fsc.org  Cert no. TT-COC-2139
© 1996 Forest Stewardship Council

FSC

Set in 11/17.5 pt Sabon
by Falcon Oast Graphic Art Ltd

Red Fox Books are published by Random House Children's Books,
61–63 Uxbridge Road, London W5 5SA

www.kidsatrandomhouse.co.uk
www.rbooks.co.uk

Addresses for companies within The Random House Group Limited can
be found at: www.randomhouse.co.uk/offices.htm

THE RANDOM HOUSE GROUP Limited Reg. No. 954009

A CIP catalogue record for this book is available from the British
Library.

Printed in the UK by CPI Bookmarque, Croydon, CR0 4TD

# Contents

# Acknowledgements

This book is for the people who make my world go round: for my wonderful partner Alex, and my precious daughters Lilly-Ella and Lexie, for my loving parents Julie and Paul, who have always been there for me, and for Paul, the brother I idolize. Struan Marshall has always been a good friend as well as my trusted agent, and his assistant, Kathryn Taylor, has been fantastic.

I'm eternally grateful to everyone at Liverpool Football Club for giving me the chance to live my dream. I know I'll never walk alone.

I'm grateful to Henry Winter of the *Daily Telegraph* and Paul Joyce of the *Daily Express* for listening to my story and recording it so faithfully. The Transworld team have been terrific, led by editor Doug Young and his assistant Emma Musgrave. I'd also like to thank other members of the Transworld team: publisher Bill Scott-Kerr, copy-editor Daniel Balado-Lopez, publicist Alison Barrow and jacket designer Steve Mulcahey. Many thanks also to Ged Rea and Dave Ball for supplying the statistics of my career with Liverpool and England.

# Picture Acknowledgements

All uncredited images are © Steven Gerrard.

FIRST SECTION
*Page 1*
Portrait: © Alan Clarke.

*Pages 4 and 5*
Dave Shannon and Liverpool youth team; training at Melwood; SG with Liverpool trainees and Steve Heighway, Dave Shannon and Hughie McAuley; SG in changing room with Dave Shannon, Hughie McAuley and Michael Owen: all courtesy of Liverpool Football Club Academy. SG and Michael Owen in England blazers: © Steven Gerrard.

*Pages 6 and 7*
SG with Lilly-Ella at Anfield; SG and Gérard Houllier; SG and Jamie Carragher: © Empics.

*Page 8*
SG and Stan Lazaridis; SG scores against Alaves: © Empics. SG, Danny Murphy and Robbie Fowler with FA Cup: © Action Images/ Darren Walsh. Robbie Fowler, SG and Sami Hyypia during a parade: © FP/MC Reuters, picture supplied by Action Images.

SECOND SECTION
*Page 1*
SG scores against Olympiakos; SG scores first goal against AC Milan: © Empics.

*Pages 2 and 3*
SG lifts Champions League trophy; SG scores his side's 3rd goal against West Ham United during the FA Cup final; SG lifts FA Cup: all © Empics.

*Pages 4 and 5*
SG and Kevin Keegan; SG and Sven-Goran Eriksson; SG and Michael Owen; SG scores against Germany: all © Empics.

*Pages 6 and 7*
SG scores his side's 2nd goal against Trinidad and Tobago; SG and Wayne Rooney in Germany: © Empics. SG celebrates his goal: © Stephane Reix/For Picture/ Corbis. SG at England v. Ecuador: © Action Images/Reuters/Alex Grimm. David Beckham celebrated by his team-mates after scoring against Ecuador: © Empics.

*Page 8*
SG and Ecuador's Luis Valencia: © Empics. SG and Portugal's Cristiano Ronaldo; SG dejected: both © Action Images/Tony O'Brien Livepic.

# Dedication

Every time I drive into Anfield, I slow to a crawl as I pass through the Shankly Gates. My eyes are drawn towards the Hillsborough Memorial. I see the tributes to the ninety-six Liverpool fans who never returned from that FA Cup semi-final in 1989. I see the scarves left by visiting fans, signs of respect that lie alongside wreaths placed by families whose tears will never dry. I see the flame that burns always, reminding the world that the ninety-six will never, ever be forgotten.

As my car inches past the memorial, I look down the names of those who fell on the Leppings Lane End, never to rise again. My eyes stop at one name. Jon-Paul Gilhooley, ten years old, the youngest of those who never came home from Sheffield. A fan who died following the team he loved. I knew

Jon-Paul. He was my cousin. A shiver runs down my spine. I make the sign of the Cross and drive on. I park the car and step into Anfield still thinking of Jon-Paul, his parents, and how lucky I am. I was nearly nine when Hillsborough took Jon-Paul from us. I had just started at Liverpool's Centre of Excellence and training was cancelled for a while after the tragedy. When we finally resumed, I could tell from the shocked look on the coaches' faces that this was a disaster that affected a whole club and a whole city. Hillsborough was the talk of my family for months afterwards.

Whenever I saw Jon-Paul's parents during my Youth Trainee Scheme days at Anfield, it gave me an extra determination to succeed. Just before I made my Liverpool debut, they said, 'Jon-Paul would be so proud of you.' During that match, I felt Jon-Paul was looking down on me, pleased I was fulfilling a dream we both shared. In the thrill of victory, I always think of Jon-Paul and about how buzzing he would be over a Liverpool win. It breaks my heart every day just to think Jon-Paul is not here any more.

Liverpool were brilliant with Jon-Paul's family. They were so caring and helpful towards all the people who lost loved ones at Hillsborough. They still are. Liverpool are a compassionate club with roots that go deep in the community. I remember Jackie, Jon-Paul's mum, once telling Dad how well the club treated them. Every year, on the anniversary of Hillsborough, Liverpool hold a service at Anfield. It's compulsory for players to attend. Rightly so. The team must show their respects to the ninety-six. In 2005 I felt really fluey, but I went. No way would I miss the Hillsborough service. It is part of my life.

Hillsborough must never be allowed to happen again. No one should lose a life or a relative at a football match. Every time I see Jon-Paul's name cut into the cold marble outside the Shankly Gates, I fill with sadness and anger. I have never let anyone know this before, but it's true: I play for Jon-Paul.

# 1
# Born to Be Red

Cut my veins open and I bleed Liverpool red. I love Liverpool with a burning passion. My determination to reach the heights at Anfield intensified when poor Jon-Paul passed away. Also fuelling my drive to succeed was an accident I suffered during my school days. My career was nearly destroyed before it started. All my dreams of starring for Liverpool and England, of lifting European Cups and shining in World Cups, rested on the skill of a surgeon when I was only nine.

Anfield was already my first love and my second home. I'd been there a year, training with Michael Owen, when a calamity hit me that left me in hospital fearing for my future. Even now, I shudder at the memory of what took place on a patch of grass near my house on the Bluebell Estate of Huyton, Merseyside.

It was just a field, surrounded by bushes, a mess really. The type of place where people threw their rubbish without a second thought. Me and my mates didn't care. All that mattered to us was the grass was half-decent for a game of footy. We were on it night and day, summer and winter. To us kids, that scrap of wasteground was Anfield, Goodison and Wembley rolled into one – a heaven on earth. One Saturday morning, I was kicking about on the strip with a kid from our street, a boy called Mark Hannan. We'd sorted out the pitch. It wasn't exactly the Bernabéu, but it was home. A mate nicked some nets from his Sunday League team, cut them in half, and rigged up two seven-a-side goals. Perfect.

So there was me and Mark, having a dead good kickabout, when the ball flew into some nettles. No problem. I ran across to fetch it. 'I'm not putting my hands in there,' I shouted to Mark. 'I'll get stung.' I couldn't see the ball. The nettles were too thick. 'I'm going to have to kick it out.' So I pulled my footy socks up and put my leg into the nettles to kick the ball out. It wasn't coming. I gave it a really good welly with my right foot, the one I shoot and pass with. I kicked fast and deep into the nettles.

Agony. Total agony. My foot hit something. Jeez, the pain was merciless. I nearly had a heart attack. I fell down, screaming for help. In my career I've broken bones and pulled muscles, but honest to God, I have never felt pain like this. Like poison from a needle, it shot up my shins. Mark sprinted over.

'I don't know what it is, Mark,' I yelled. 'I can't see it. My leg won't come out of the nettles.'

Mark looked and all the blood drained from his face. I thought he was going to throw up. I looked down and couldn't believe my eyes. A garden fork was embedded in my big toe. Straight through my trainer and into my foot, no stopping. Some idiot had tossed this rusty fork away, and it got lodged in the nettles. The handle wasn't there, just the metal prongs, and I had kicked right into them. I felt the prong go in, burrowing into the bone.

'Go and tell someone!' I shouted, and Mark ran off to get my mum and dad.

I just lay there on the grass, tears spilling down

my face and fears spinning through my head. Would I ever kick a ball again?

Mum and Dad arrived sharpish. Immediately, Dad realized how serious this was. 'He's going to lose his foot,' I heard him tell Mum. I couldn't believe it. My Liverpool career was being buried in a bed of nettles.

Finally, the ambulance nosed its way into the field. It had taken only ten minutes but it felt like ten hours. The medics took one look at the foot and even they understood they couldn't yank the fork clear. So they lifted me into the ambulance and off we went, bells and lights going crazy, racing to the hospital.

The journey was torture. Every time we drove over a bump, I screamed at the ambulance driver. Whenever I moved, I took the load of the fork in my bone, bending my toe. Tears followed every movement. I was shaking. One of the medics tried to hold the fork to stop it digging further in. The pain was horrific. I kept shouting at the driver. 'It's not his fault,' Mum and Dad told me. I just wanted the pain to stop. Stop. Please stop. As we sped through the streets, they pumped me with gas and air.

At the hospital, I was rushed straight into Accident and Emergency on the trolley – straight through, no waiting. Everyone could see how bad it was. And hear. Mum was hysterical, and I screamed the hospital down.

Only when a painkilling injection took hold did my howling stop. I was all dazed and weak but not quite unconscious. Through the clouds, I heard the doctor say, 'The fork is rusty, there's a chance of infection. We might have to take the toe off to stop it spreading.'

'Wait,' Dad intervened. 'Steven plays football, you must speak to Liverpool before you do any operation. They must know what is going on.'

My dad quickly called Steve Heighway, Liverpool's Academy director, who drove over sharpish. Steve's the strong type, and he immediately took control. 'No, you are not bloody well taking his toe off,' Steve told them.

The doctor replied, 'We have to operate. The decision will be made by the surgeon.'

Steve was adamant. 'No. Don't take his toe off.'

Steve won the argument. Thank God. The

surgeon numbed the whole foot and tugged the fork out. The hole was huge, as big as a 20p coin and an inch and a half deep. It was a mess, but at least the surgeon saved my toe and my career. 'You are a very, very lucky young man,' Steve said. The doctors all agreed. 'We have never seen anything like this before,' they said. Even my brother, Paul, looked worried when he came to see me, and Paul usually winds me up over anything.

The one half-decent thing about the accident was that I missed three weeks of school. The doctors insisted, so who was I to argue! School sent homework round but it never got done. No chance. I was too busy milking my injury. My family spoiled me rotten. I lay there on the couch, being waited on hand and bandaged foot, and watching Liverpool videos. Fantastic. All my heroes parading their skills on the screen: John Barnes, Kenny Dalglish and Ian Rush. This was my sort of medicine, guaranteed to quicken recovery. Every day, a nurse came round to clean the hole with antiseptic, pack it with cotton-wool balls, put a mesh around it. She then bandaged the foot up to the ankle. As the wound healed, the nurse put less and less cotton-wool in. Soon I could go to school on crutches. But I was not able to play in the yard. Nor could I go to train with Liverpool. For the first time in my life, I was prevented from doing what I love most.

That accident, and the weeks of recuperation, reminded me how important football was in my life. I started watching football seriously on the telly. I sat on the couch juggling the ball on my head, or with my left foot. I held the ball tight, almost for reassurance. I never wanted to be apart from a ball again. I was still getting twinges of pain, but after five weeks I was able to kick the ball cleanly. Thank God. Without football, my life would have been empty. I never forget that utter desolation of being separated from a ball.

When I think back to the accident, the pain still goes right through me again, like an electric shock. I still see the fork sticking out of my trainer, still sense it grating against the bone. Once or twice, I spoke about the incident with my dad. He wasn't the type to take credit. Dad just says, 'You were fortunate, Steven.' We all knew if I had lost the big toe of my right foot, any chance of Liverpool and England would have ended right there, impaled on a rusty garden fork on a council wasteland in Huyton.

I lived at No. 10 Ironside Road on the Bluebell Estate. Ironside was known as the Happy Street. I arrived there on 30 May 1980, straight out of Whiston Hospital and into a football-mad house. Bluebell's quite a big estate, a warren of roads with four pubs, one on each side: the Swan, Bluebell, Rose, and Oak Tree.

I loved life on the Bluebell – my kingdom, my playground. Two youth clubs offered the usual attractions, but mostly we were outside, playing. Me and my brother Paul would come home filthy with mud. Mum went crazy, Dad just smiled. Ironside was always alive with activity. In the summer, families sat out, chatting away, sharing a drink while the kids played. Ironside had many distractions. Two girls my age, Lisa and Caroline, lived either side of our house and I knocked about with them, crawling around the square, playing in the mud. Girls fascinated me. I had no sisters myself. I thought Lisa and Caroline were well fit. I flirted with them. Lisa and Caroline had one fault, though: they couldn't play football.

Didn't matter really. I never had far to look for a game. Bluebell was full of lads up for some footy action, always has been. The town is crammed with Sunday League sides. Football is the local religion. On the Bluebell, I joined forces with seven or eight lads my age and we all became good mates, playing football every hour until our mums shouted us in. One problem bugged me: I never got a really decent game out of them. I was better than them, simple as that. I preferred games with my brother, who is three years older. Paul had around fifteen mates and their matches were full-on brilliant. At six, I could hold my own with Paul and the other nine-year-olds. Most of Paul's mates wanted me on their side. I loved competing against them. They accepted me because I didn't look out of place. Paul's mates were good players as well. They played in a local league for an Under-10s team called Tolgate, run by two fellas from the Huyton area. One day, I followed Paul down to a Tolgate match and asked the organizers if I could join in.

'How old are you?' they asked.

'Seven,' I replied.

'Too young,' they said.

I burst into tears. 'You're wrong, I'm good enough,' I said, but they didn't listen and the feeling of rejection burned hard inside me.

The concrete patch outside my house on Ironside and the back-field on the Bluebell were breeding grounds for competitive players. A good touch and a tough streak were needed to survive, and I quickly developed both. I had to. Paul and his mates never held back in tackles on me, even though I was three years younger. Bang. Knock me over. No mercy. That's how I liked it. Do it again. That's why they used to let me play. I hobbled back into No. 10 all the time, covered in cuts and grazes from slide tackles on the concrete. I still have a scar on my face after being shoulder-charged into a fence. A nail nicked my skin. No fuss. No bother. I went in to see Granddad Tony across the road at No. 35 Ironside. He put three butterfly stitches in, and I charged back to the game. 'Hurry up!' they shouted at me. Bang. Back into battle.

I have since bought 35 and 10 Ironside. Those houses will always be in our family. My brother lives in No. 10. There will always be Gerrards in Ironside. My brother Paul is my best mate. Always has been. Always will be. He had the bigger bedroom at Ironside, which really annoyed me at the time; my room was tiny. Paul had the heater, the biggest bed, all the trimmings. I didn't really mind. Paul was my hero. I just wanted to hang around with him and his mates. 'Get away,' Paul shouted at me, 'go home.' He didn't mind me joining in his football games, but didn't want me about when he and his friends were sitting around, talking. Me and Paul had some real toe-to-toe fights, steaming into each other, no holds barred. 'I hate you!' I'd shout at Paul after another scrap, rubbing my face or ribs where he whacked me, but I soon forgave him. Even if Paul gave me a real hiding, or wouldn't let me play with him and his mates, an hour later he would come back in and say, 'Stevie, do you want a game on the computer?' 'Yeah,' I'd reply en-thusiastically, grateful to be back in Paul's world again. We'd then play a computer game as if no punches had been thrown. Storms passed quickly between Paul and me. I worshipped my brother. Looking at Paul now, he seems younger and smaller than me. No-one would ever cotton on he was my older brother. Strange.

Paul was a decent player, but short of aggression – something I've never lacked. Paul never wanted to be a footballer. He played for a laugh with his mates. 'Get more involved,' Dad yelled at Paul. 'It's cold,' Paul responded. 'I'd rather be at home.' Paul would never have made a living out of football, but he knows tactics, and can spot a good player. I speak to Paul after matches and we are on the same wavelength.

Family friends and relatives tell me Dad was a good player. So does he! 'That's where you get your football skills from, Steven!' Dad laughs. Sadly, he damaged his knee as a kid playing on Astroturf, and his footballing dreams were over. Dad's brother, Tony, was meant to be decent, and played Huyton Boys. Between ten and fifteen, people thought Tony had a chance of making it as a professional. Football runs deep in my family. I've got loads of cousins, who often came down Ironside for a game. One of them, Anthony Gerrard, was good enough to be signed by Everton. He's at Walsall now after being released by Goodison. Sunday League football around here

**18**

has always been packed with my cousins and uncles.

A love of football ran through my family like letters through a stick of rock. Anfield and Goodison were regular weekend haunts. Walk into any of my relatives' houses and I guarantee there is a match on. Everyone crowds around the telly. Grab a drink, pull up a chair, watch the game. It's brilliant. On Saturday nights, Dad headed down the pub, but he was always back for *Match of the Day* on the BBC. You could almost set your watch by Dad, stepping back through the door of our house in time for *Match of the Day*. Dad, me and Paul squeezed onto the sofa for our Saturday-night ritual. I'd be buzzing with excitement as the programme came on. All of us sang along to the music. The Gerrards never missed *Match of the Day*. Never. It was the high point of the week.

Now and again, as a treat, Dad took me and Paul down the local to watch the live Sunday match on a big screen, or for a game of darts. I'd have a glass of Coke, chuck a few darts, and watch the match. Dead grown-up, I felt. Shortly before six p.m., the fun was over and we headed home with heavy hearts. School loomed in the morning like a dark cloud on a sunny day.

Still now I hate Sunday nights. Still! It's impossible to blank out the memory of getting ready for school, a ritual torture that ruined the final moments of a glorious weekend. According to the calendar most people use, a weekend lasts two days. Not at No. 10 Ironside. Not with Mum. A weekend is a day and a half with her. She demanded we be home by six p.m. to be scrubbed, bathed and ready for school the next morning. We ran in at six and the uniform was there, on the ironing board, all pristine and pressed, glaring at us. Just seeing the uniform made me sick. It resembled prison clothes after the freedom of the weekend. It was not that I hated school; I just loved my weekends roaming around Bluebell. Mum took school more seriously than Paul and I ever did. A proud woman, she made sure our uniforms were absolutely spotless. She polished our shoes so hard you could see your grimacing face in them. Poor Mum! She had her work cut out. If I left the house with a clean uniform, it was guaranteed to come home dirty. The same with shoes. Scuffed and muddy. Every time. Mum went up the wall.

My journey through the Merseyside school

system was straightforward and undistinguished. I looked on schools as fantastic playing fields with boring buildings attached. My first stop was St Michael's. Though it was only a short walk from Ironside, Mum still insisted on driving me to St Mick's and picking me up. I enjoyed the infants and junior school, just messing about. When I was naughty, the teachers made me stand by the wall, looking at the bricks for five minutes as punishment. I never bullied anyone. I never hurt anyone or swore. I was just cheeky and mischievous. My crimes were petty ones: answering back or going on muddy grass when we were told to stay on the yard. Usual kids' stuff.

School held limited appeal. I sat in class, longing for play-time because there was always a match on in the playground. I loved dinner-time because it lasted an hour, which meant a longer match. I abandoned hot dinners because they wasted precious minutes. Queuing for my meal, I'd shout, 'Come on, there's a big game going on out there.' Eventually, I asked my mother for packed lunches. 'You should be on hot dinners,' she screamed, 'or come home if you don't like school food.' We compromised on packed lunches: sandwich, bar of chocolate and drink. And some fruit. The fruit always came home untouched. Apples, bananas and oranges weren't me. Butties weren't even me at that age. It would be bread off, meat out, quick bite, on with the game. 'Stevie, you haven't eaten your butty,' Mum would say, 'you've only eaten your chocolate.' Mum didn't understand. Speed was vital at dinner-time. I ate the packed lunch while playing or wolfed it down running back into class. Same with my tea. If there was a match going on outside Ironside, a game of chase, or my mates were waiting for me, I slipped my food in my pocket, sprinted out the door, threw the food to the neighbour's dog and raced on to the match. I returned home starving, picking at biscuits, crisps and chocolate.

Back at St Mick's, the teachers watched me scribbling away busily in my school-book. Steam almost rose from my pencil I wrote so furiously. The teachers must have thought I was focusing really hard on the lesson, but I wasn't, I was busy working out the teams for dinner-time. In the back of my school-book, I wrote down the names. When the bell for break rang, I dashed out to organize all the boys. The pitch was marked out with bags and tops for goals. They were right serious battles at St Mick's. Wembley Cup finals have been less intense. Defeat was unthinkable. The winners milked it loudly while the losers got caned for the next lesson.

Me and Barry Banczyk were the best players at St Mick's. Barry and I were good mates, but our playground rivalry was something else, real physical. We picked the sides, Barry's team against mine, always dead competitive. Barry was a decent player. He turned out for Denburn Under-13s, a side my dad helped run. Denburn were good: and I turned out for them briefly, helping them win the Edgehill Junior League, until Liverpool stopped me playing. Barry and I were the main men in the school team. One year, we helped St Mick's win a local cup which gave us a chance of playing at Wembley. First we had to beat sides from different districts in a tournament. The prize was huge. Wembley! Just the thought of the famous old stadium had me lying awake in bed, thinking of what it would be like to step out onto the best-known pitch in all the world. Wembley! What a dream come true that would be! I was certainly up for the tournament. In one match I went in for a slide tackle with my usual determination. I caught my knee on the sharp ring-pull of a Coke can, which sliced open my leg. It was only five stitches but it cost me my chance of joining the team at Wembley. I cried my eyes out. That was typical of my luck. My mates were off to Wembley and I was off to hospital. The scar on my knee faded but the pain of missing that trip to Wembley remains.

The time came when I had to leave St Mick's. For secondary school, a difficult choice awaited. Most of my class were going either to Bowring Comprehensive School or Knowsley High. Paul was at Bowring so I wanted to go there, just to be with my brother. Bowring and Knowsley High had serious problems, though: football was not high on the agenda. Everyone knew I was mad keen on football so only a school which improved me as a player would do. My teacher at St Mick's, Mrs Chadwick, gave me some sound advice. 'You should go to Cardinal Heenan, Steven,' she told me. 'It will be better for your football.'

Along with a reference from Mrs Chadwick that I

was half-decent in class, my ability on the ball carried me through the gates of Cardinal Heenan. My career demanded I go there. Enrolling at Cardinal Heenan brought eligibility for Liverpool Boys rather than Knowsley Boys, and that was key. Liverpool Boys teams were better run. The scouts at Liverpool and Everton knew that and always went talent-spotting at Liverpool Boys games. Cardinal Heenan was the only place for me.

Having picked my secondary school for foot-balling reasons, I still had to endure lessons there. Cardinal Heenan was massive – more than 1,300 boys. I didn't want to go at first, even with the know-ledge that the football would be good. Night after night, I cried. The idea of moving among so many strangers horrified me. Cardinal Heenan was three miles from home – another country in my mind. But Mum and Dad persuaded me it would be best for my football. Reluctantly, I went. I needed time to settle, for it to become a familiar scenario in my life.

By the third year, I was on the back of the bus from the Bluebell with the boys, the whole atmos-phere buzzing, loving it. For this was the first time

Mum let me go to school on my own. I was thirteen and it was brilliant. I left Ironside with my bus money and dinner money jangling in my pocket, feeling like a king, strutting down the Bluebell streets. I'd knock on the door of a couple of mates, Terry Smith and Sean Dillon, and the three of us would head on to the bus-stop, striding along like the top gang in town. Sean was a nightmare, late every day. Terry and me chucked stones at Sean's bedroom window to get him up at quarter to nine. Sometimes we got so annoyed we threw the stones really hard. A few shards of broken glass around Sean's bedroom would sort out his lousy time-keeping. When we finally got Sean out of his house, there would be a mad dash to the bus. All three of us, school-bags dangling, legs racing, sprinting down the road, laughing our heads off. Great times. Sean is a bricklayer now, doing well. I see Terry often. He's a huge Everton fan. So we have some banter.

When Sean, Terry and I reached Cardinal Heenan, the day revolved around waiting for the two play-times of twenty-five minutes each and the hour-long dinner-time. I spent all day thinking about football. I loved PE with Mr Chadwick. Unfortunately, we never did football all the time and I used to get a cob on if it was rugby, gymnastics or cricket. I wanted football, indoor or on the field. Or tennis. I was quite warm at tennis. At Cardinal Heenan we played short tennis, with a smaller net and these wooden bats. We decorated our bats with the Nike Swoosh or Adidas stripes to see who had the tastiest bat. But football remained the main subject on my personal curriculum.

Cardinal Heenan wasn't rough. Just a few fights in the playground now and again, a few big boys who were the so-called Cocks. I had my own gang and we looked out for each other. The odd fight erupted and I would be in the midst of it, throwing punches, standing my ground. No-one was going to push me around. Older boys, bigger boys, no-one. I suffered the occasional split lip from a punch I failed to dodge, but my uniform tended to be more spattered with mud than blood. I was always throwing myself around on the pitch, covering myself in dirt. I lived for those moments. Lessons were just the dead time between games.

When it came to class-work, though, I wasn't

thick. All the way through Cardinal Heenan, I was in the middle academically. Different subjects provoked different moods. If I wasn't doing well at maths, I despised it and hated going to the lesson. But if I was flying in English, and our brilliant lady teacher helped me, I wouldn't mind it. I enjoyed creative writing, making up stories. I wrote about how one day I'd win the World Cup. I liked messing about with words. Reading, too. My favourite book at school was *Of Mice and Men*. It's quite a sad story when you get to know the characters. I read *Of Mice and Men* from cover to cover so many times the book almost fell apart. We watched the story on video, did a project on it, and an exam on it. When GCSEs arrived I got a C in English, six Ds and two Es.

But above all this I had only one ambition, one dream, one target – football.

# 2
# Growing Up and Toughening Up

I never bunked off school. Never. Dad wouldn't have any of that. The consequences of bunking off, sneaking a ciggy, or fare-dodging, were unimaginable. Dad gave me a few clips round the ear and bollockings, but nothing too damaging. He never hit me. Dad showed his disappointment in a different way. He had a stare that could break my heart. What stopped me messing about was I feared losing the great relationship we had. Dad didn't need to use violence or to raise his voice to teach Paul and me right and wrong. Dad would not have his kids disrespecting anyone or doing wrong. He wouldn't tolerate having police coming round to our house. Loads of people banged on the door to complain about Paul and me throwing stones at their windows, but we never had the police round. Never.

I messed up once. Just once. I went robbing and got caught. Me and a mate were mucking about in the centre of Liverpool, as eleven-year-olds do, just being stupid in Woolies. We had five quid between us to get home and grab a Maccies or Wimpy at Lime Street on the way. The problem was I needed some stationery for homework, just graph paper and pens – usual school nonsense. The plan was sorted with Woolies the target. We snuck in and went up and down the aisles putting pens in our pockets and paper up my coat. Confidently, we walked towards the exit. The plan seemed to be working. Brilliant. I could feel the money in my pocket for a burger and a Coke at Lime Street. Easy, easy. Step through the door, onto the pavement, turn left, ready to leg it . . .

A shout stopped us in our tracks. 'Oi!' came a voice that froze our blood. 'Stop!' The Woolies security man was standing there. I couldn't move, I was so scared. He grabbed us both by the collars. It was the worst day of my life. 'That's it,' I thought, my heart and mind racing. 'I have blown everything. Liverpool is finished. The club will go crazy. Dad's going to disown me.'

This security guard marched us back into Woolies, into an office, and took the stationery off us. He then gave us a massive telling off. 'What school are you at?' he screamed. 'Where do you live? Give us your phone number now.'

My head was spinning. 'We've not got a phone,' I lied.

The security guy went red in the face. 'Give me your address then.'

I couldn't mention our house. Dad would go mental if the police went round. Think. The guard asked again, so I gave the address of my auntie's house. He wrote that down, gave us another rollicking, and kicked us out of Woolies.

My head in a mess, I ran to Lime Street. Woolies would phone school, then get hold of Dad, and that would be it, me grounded, no football for ages. When I jumped off the train at Huyton, I couldn't face going home. 'Dad will definitely kill me for robbing,' I thought. Home was out of the question, so I sprinted round to my auntie Lynn's. She let me in, sat me down, and listened me out. 'Will you go and see Dad?' I pleaded with her. 'Please? Make sure he's all right.'

Auntie Lynn went round to our house and explained to Dad how terrible I felt. Too late. Dad already knew about my shoplifting. Bad news travelled fast. Woolies had been on to St Mick's, who phoned Dad, and he was on the warpath. Dad came round, dragged me back home and slaughtered me, big-time. He looked me in the eye and just massacred me. 'Why did you do that?' he shouted. 'Why go robbing? Why didn't you pay for it? Why didn't you ask me or your mum for money? Why? Why? We can't tolerate stealing in this family. You'll get another telling off at school. They'll want to know why you were nicking things.'

Dad then hit me with another killer thought: 'If Liverpool find out, you are in even more trouble, Steven,' he said. 'What the hell is Steve Heighway going to think of you? You might have messed up everything at Liverpool. They could kick you out.'

Those words smashed into me like a wrecking ball. I felt so small. I love Dad. I hated letting him down. I love Liverpool. The idea of them giving me the elbow horrified me. Football was all I dreamed about. Why had I gone robbing? Jeez, what a mess.

Robbing was stupid. I had money, and if I hadn't, I could have just done without. Idiot that I was, I went robbing and now faced the consequences. Dad sent me to my room and grounded me for three nights. It felt like six months.

I got no sympathy off Paul. Just the opposite. My brother laughed his head off at me being locked up in my room. There'd be a knock on my door and I'd hear Paul whispering, 'Stevie, I'm going into town. It's going to be brilliant. Come on.' Thanks. He wound me up something rotten. 'The computer's on down-stairs,' Paul said through the door, 'do you fancy a game?' Paul knew I couldn't come out. It was only banter but it cut me to pieces. I heard Paul running outside and organizing a game of football. He called out to all the other Ironside boys in a really loud voice, 'Who wants a game? Let's go.' It was torture. I heard the game going on, listened almost in tears to the screams of delight, the jokes, the noisy celebrations. I couldn't escape. My room was in the front. My mates shouted up to my window. 'Stevie, Stevie, this is a bril-liant game, it's such a pity you can't join in. You'd love it.' Cruel laughter followed their words up to my window. My mates! My bloomin' brother! They knew I could hear. They knew it would kill me. When they stopped calling up, I sneaked a look out the window to watch them enviously. It was my fault. I deserved my spell in solitary confinement.

Normally, I behaved myself, certainly by the standards of some boys I knocked about with. Mates of mine robbed shops and garages, nicking sweets and drinks, when I was with them. I never got involved, but I was there. I watched friends pull ciggies out of pockets at play-time at school. They'd light up and blow smoke in people's faces. They didn't care. A few were on the road to nowhere, but I enjoyed hanging out with them. I could have gone off the rails. Temptations abounded, dangerous ones. Fortunately, Dad kept me straight. Without his guidance, I wouldn't be where I am today.

Dad was always the boss of No. 10 Ironside. Dad's word was law, but he was never a dictator. Me and Paul have never been scared of our parents. Sometimes we were spoiled brats wanting more – too much more, given our modest circumstances. But Paul and I had unbelievable respect for our parents. We are a very close family – as close as it gets. We ate breakfast together, tea together, sat in every night, watching telly and chatting. The atmosphere was class. Paul and I couldn't have asked for more loving, caring parents.

Money was tight. Holidays abroad were a distant dream. Every year we went to Butlin's, in Skegness, or to a holiday park in Devon. My auntie and uncle would come with their kids, Nan and Granddad too. The whole family. What an adventure! The trip dominated my thoughts for months in advance. Mum was always planning, always squirrelling away money throughout the winter to pay for the holiday. She knew how much Skegness meant to the family, and particularly Paul and me. Sometimes, if Paul and I were lucky, a mate was allowed along. I let Paul pick the lucky guest. I would be buzzing to be with them, to hang out and play football with older boys. Skegness was great. 'Make sure you do the soccer schools,' Dad told me on the drive to the Lincolnshire coast. As if I needed reminding! Even when we mucked about on the beach, hitting balls around with bats or bombing down the slides in the water park, one thought occupied my mind: when can I get to the soccer school? Even when I was on the go-karts, chasing Paul round the track, I was thinking about getting to the soccer school. 'Is it time to go now?' I'd ask Dad. 'Come on. Must be time.' Skegness was luxury. Of a night, we would go into the local club where there would be singers on, bands, and karaoke. The next morning, I would wake early and say, 'When can I get to the soccer school?' Skegness felt like heaven.

Me, Paul and Dad talked football all the time. Dad was daft about Liverpool. He bought me Liverpool videos and we watched them together, admiring the way Graeme Souness thundered into challenges, Alan Hansen's coolness and Kenny Dalglish's class around the box. One day, Dad came home with a massive picture of Dalglish. He climbed the stairs to my room and handed over the picture. 'Kenny Dalglish is the best player who ever played for Liverpool,' Dad said. 'He's The Man. Get him up on your wall.' Dalglish's picture was up on my wall for years. It was like a shrine. I was lucky enough to see King Kenny live at Anfield when I was very young, only about six or seven. I even have one of Kenny's shirts in my trophy room at home now. Back then, I loved standing on the Kop, bewitched by Kenny, Ian Rush, John Barnes and Steve McMahon. Great players. I saw some amazing championship moments. I was on the Kop in 1989 when Michael Thomas broke Liverpool hearts with that amazing last-minute goal for Arsenal. It denied us the title. I remember the following year when Hansen lifted the title. What a brilliant sight. I set my heart on following Hansen and bringing that trophy back to Anfield again.

Only when I began training with Liverpool at the age of eight did I become a hard-and-fast Kopite. Before then, I didn't understand who to support. I would be in the Panini enclosure at Goodison Park one week, singing and swaying on the Kop the next week. My heart was taken by football, not by one tribe. Other people didn't see it that way. With Dad, you were either Red or Dead. 'Liverpool, Liverpool, Liverpool,' he drummed into me, like a religious chant. As with many families on Merseyside, there were mixed loyalties. Mum's brother, Leslie, was crazy about Everton – season-tickets, scarves, flags, the lot. Leslie was always coming back from games with Everton kit for me, trying to turn me into a Blue.

A quick search on the Internet will reveal a photo of me as a schoolboy in a full Everton strip. Blue shirt, shorts, socks, the works. When I became big news with Liverpool, some enterprising Everton fanzines discovered the picture and printed it. They must have loved that! The *Mirror* heard about it, tracked down the picture and published it when I was becoming famous at Liverpool. A huge debate broke out. Was the picture real or not? Many people thought it was a fake. It isn't. It's a genuine photograph, taken in 1987. That is me, dressed as an Evertonian, and it wasn't at a fancy-dress party or for a bet. Leslie took me to Goodison when I was six and I saw some of Everton's games on the way to their league championship. I won a programme competition to have my picture taken with the league trophy and Charity Shield at Goodison. Uncle Leslie was buzzing. He knew it would send Dad through the roof, and it really did. Dad went ballistic at the thought of his son, all in blue, standing proudly in the Goodison trophy room. 'He's not going,' Dad kept telling Leslie. 'You're not going,' Dad kept telling me. But I did. I was so keen.

I was seven by that time, mad about football, not that clued-up in those days about the intense rivalry between Everton and Liverpool. It didn't seem wrong at the time. Leslie came over to Ironside with a brand-new kit. All excited, I ripped open the wrapping, put the crisp blue strip on and headed off for Goodison with Leslie, leaving an enraged Dad behind. Disowning me must have crossed his mind. Leslie guided me into the trophy room at Goodison, all smiles, and the photographer snapped away. Now that my heart belongs to Liverpool, I look back on the incident and wonder what the hell I was doing.

Everton, Liverpool or whoever – at the time, just the chance to own a new football kit thrilled me. Collecting different strips became a massive hobby. Every Christmas I got two kits. Every birthday, more kits. I had a face like thunder if I never got replica gear for presents. Mum and Dad were superb. They knew how much shirts from different clubs meant to me. With Granddad's help, they saved up to buy the kits. I had Tottenham, Man City and, of course, Liverpool and Everton. Panini sticker books were scoured intensively. Every page checked out, every kit assessed.

'Mum,' I'd shout downstairs, 'I want this new Spurs top. Please?' Catalogues and sports-shop windows were not the only ways of feeding my addiction. *Match of the Day* was a catwalk for kit. What a parade! It became an obsession. If Tottenham met Everton on the TV on a Sunday, I would be out on the street after the final whistle, wearing the kit of who- ever won, imagining myself to be the hero of the game. I had stars in my eyes, and the star's shirt on my back.

That jersey was often Neville Southall's. His Everton goalie kit was a real favourite. Days went by when I never took it off. I copied Southall perfectly: socks rolled down, so you could see the tops of his shin-guards. Big Nev wore Hi-Tec boots so I badgered Mum and Dad for a pair of those. I loved Southall. When I didn't fancy playing out, I donned my goalie kit and pretended I was the great Neville Southall, throwing myself around on the grass, diving at my mates' feet, making brave and athletic saves like the real Everton master. Neville was a real character and I loved his committed approach to football. It was always a special moment when I opened a Panini sticker and found Neville Southall. Fantastic. I would be buzzing for hours. Running around Ironside, holding the sticker aloft like some great trophy.

Stickers, kits, going to games, playing matches – my life, as I said, revolved around football. And that passion was channelled through Liverpool Football Club.

# 3
# Clocking on at the Dream Factory

Joining Liverpool was like starting a love affair you know will never, ever end. It's true: You'll Never Walk Alone at Anfield. Of course, I could have gone to another top club. Loads pursued me: Man United, West Ham, Everton, Spurs, you name it. Nice letters dropped through the letter-box, detailing how much they wanted me and how I would flourish under their care. But only one destination beckoned – Anfield. Dad insisted. He was spot-on, as usual. Anfield just felt right, going to the club I adored and being coached by people whose trademark is trust. Good, honest footballing men ran the Liverpool School of Excellence. Meeting Steve Heighway, Dave Shannon and Hughie McAuley for the first time, I instinctively knew they would look after me. Even aged eight, I knew. Steve, Dave and Hughie inspired me from the first handshake and conversation. Steve is a Liverpool legend, a fantastic player from the seventies. Dave was friendly with Ben McIntyre, the manager of my Sunday League team, Whiston Juniors, and it was a simple step from there to Anfield. I carried on with Whiston, and got my first international experience in an U-12 competition against teams from all over the world, but my main focus was Liverpool.

I couldn't wait to get started. Come on! Give me the ball! Let me learn. Let me show you what I can do. My dream was gathering pace. Heighway, Shannon and McAuley held these brilliant training sessions down the Vernon Sangster Sports Centre every Tuesday and Thursday – special times of the week. I counted down the hours, minutes and seconds before we burst out into that sports hall – our Anfield, our Wembley. As well as being in good hands, I was also in good company. Michael Owen and Jason Koumas were in my year at Liverpool and we quickly fell in together.

The three of us soon realized how to get the best out of the Vernon Sangster. On arrival, we shook hands with the staff, all very respectful – the Liverpool way. Skills, drills and possession work occupied us for an hour. The best bit was yet to come. Michael, Jason and I knew there would be half an hour at the end of five-a-side. 'All those in Liverpool tops this end,' Dave Shannon would shout, 'and all the rest put bibs on.' Kids wore all types of tops. But me, Michael and Jason came prepared: we agreed in advance which strip to wear. Come the five-a-sides we were always in the same team. 'Right,' Michael said, 'let's all wear the Liverpool away kit next week.' Jason and I made sure we came in with the right Liverpool top on. If my extensive collection of strips did not contain the proposed outfit, I'd be on Mum and Dad's case in the car all the way back home. 'Mum, Dad, I must have this kit. If I don't, Jason and Michael will be on a different team. Please?' Poor Mum and Dad. I pressured them badly. I sat in the back of the car and explained the humiliation if I didn't have the right kit. Mum and Dad usually relented and got me sorted. Thank God. The thought of letting Michael or Jason down made me almost sick.

Jason was a good player. Really good. He was

always going to make it as a pro. But Michael stood out most. Even aged eight he was obviously special, a star in the making. Everyone knew it. Michael was put on this world to destroy goalkeepers. Those five-a-sides in the Vernon Sangster was the first time I ran into Michael and I was gobsmacked by his unbelievable talent. He played his schoolboy football over the Mersey, on Deeside. When he breezed into the Vernon Sangster, it was like a whirlwind visiting. The moment I saw him running at the keeper, killing him with his pace and touch, I appreciated his extraordinary gifts. Michael's talent didn't just talk; it shouted. From first glance, I understood his game was goals. A natural. Michael realized I was a good passer, so we quickly teamed up. Everyone thought we wanted to be on the same side because we were best mates and wanted to talk. Rubbish. Michael and I just wanted to win. Simple as that. That's always been the way with Michael and me. We chatted after the game, but the main line of communication was footballing: me transferring the ball to Michael in places where he could inflict most damage. Michael and I still joke about our days in Liverpool's U-12s when we battered teams. Michael always says, 'Every time Stevie got the ball he would pass to me.' To which I reply, 'And every time I did, Michael scored!'

My parents were very aware of the qualities Liverpool sought in a player. One day, I heard Dad tell Mum, 'Steve Heighway and Dave Shannon are always checking on how their players present themselves. Steven must represent Liverpool well.' Standards count at Liverpool. Be tidy. Be on time. Mum and Dad wouldn't let me go to training or do any activity associated with Liverpool Football Club unless my hair glistened, my face shone and my clothes were spotless clean. Sometimes I wanted to go to the Vernon Sangster in my comfy shoes, a pair of trainers full of holes, battle-hardened from games on Ironside. I loved them. 'You are not going in those,' Dad would insist. 'We'll get you a new pair.' Mum even ironed my kit for training. Ironed! I watched in amazement as she put creases in the shirt with her iron. Those neat lines in an uncrinkled shirt summed up Mum's desire for me to look smart always. No-one irons football kits! My mum did. The kit had to be all matching as well. I couldn't wear a Liverpool home top with away shorts. Or Spurs shorts with a Liverpool shirt. Mum would not let me. 'You must show respect for Liverpool,' she said. My parents were so proud their son was involved with Liverpool Football Club. They wanted to make sure I gave it my best shot.

Under the guidance of Steve and Dave, I rose steadily through the Liverpool ranks. Towards the start of every season, I worried whether I would be kept on by Steve. Impatiently, I waited for the letter of confirmation from Liverpool. 'Tell Steven not to worry,' Heighway always told Dad. 'He will be in. Here's a pair of boots for him.' I was doing well, building a reputation, enjoying the training. When I was fourteen, Steve called four of us into his office: me, Michael, Stephen Wright and Neil Murphy. Wrighty eventually played for Liverpool before joining Sunderland. Murphy was a very good right-back who made the reserves and now coaches at the Academy. Steve had big news for the four of us: 'You've all been invited to trials for Lilleshall.'

Lilleshall! The National School! I couldn't believe it. Lilleshall was the business, the place to be if you wanted to make it as a footballer. Only the very best got in. This was serious. Lilleshall meant everything, a springboard to success. The trials would be incredibly competitive, I knew that. Everyone wanted to go to the National School. At the first trial there were hundreds of hopefuls, good players drawn from across England, all dreaming of a place at Lilleshall. A series of trials gradually reduced the numbers and destroyed the ambitions of many. Soon there were only fifty boys left, then thirty, then twenty-four. It was brutal. Few survived. Every time I got through a trial, a letter popped through the door at Ironside saying 'Congratulations . . . you have been selected for the next trial'. I was flying. Lilleshall beckoned.

The quality was high, the competition intense. As well as Michael Owen and me, there were good players like Michael Ball, the left-back who did so well at Everton before heading up to Rangers, and Kenny Lunt, the midfielder from that impressive youth set-up at Crewe Alexandra. I still fancied my chances of getting the final call from Lilleshall. I looked around the pitches during the trials and checked out my rival midfielders. No-one was better than me. Honestly, no-one. I never hid in the trials. I was right in there, hard in the tackle, clever in the pass. Lilleshall's officials must have been impressed. I was my normal self: driven by a will to win so powerful it almost hurt. I had the ability. No doubt. No-one could pass the ball better. Liverpool were my club, and Liverpool took on only the best kids. Lilleshall must pick me. The one nagging doubt in the back of my mind was that my rivals were bigger. I was really small and facing some tall, strong units in my position. Michael Owen was tiny as well, but he had so much pace he made big fellas look like dustbins. Midfield is different.

It did not seem to matter. I progressed to the penultimate trial and an invitation to Lilleshall seemed inevitable. I thought of the two years there, learning to become an even better player, on the fast-track to fame and fortune. Every morning, I annoyed the postman as I ambushed him outside Ironside. 'Where is it? Where's my letter from Lilleshall?' The final trials were just around the corner, so I knew the letter was imminent. Family life almost stopped as we sweated on this one letter. One morning, it fell through the letter-box. I was upstairs, still in my room. Dad was first to the post. He picked up the letter, which he knew from the writing came from the National School. He opened it, knowing how much it meant to me. I could hear him downstairs by the door, shuffling the letter and envelope in his hands. The silence killed me. Why the pause? Bad news? Must be. If I had been accepted, my old fella would have shouted 'YES!' by now. Instead, Dad just called up, 'Post's here.' The disappointment in his voice rang like a church-bell at a funeral. As I walked downstairs, I saw him standing in the hall with the letter in his hand, a crushed look on his face. Lilleshall had rejected me.

I tore straight back upstairs. It felt like the end. It was bad. Dad climbed the stairs slowly. He knew I was beyond consoling. He knew how much I wanted the chance of going to Lilleshall. He walked into my room and saw I had the pillow over my head. I was completely gone, in floods of tears. My dream of a life in football seemed wrecked. I felt I was not good enough. Me! Captain of Liverpool Boys! Rated by Liverpool Football Club! Big clubs like Manchester United chased me. If those people from Lilleshall had been there in that room, I'd have killed them. How could they do this to me? I knew I was good enough. Never before had someone dared tell me I was not up to scratch. Never. My first setback hurt like hell. I dreaded the news circulating within Liverpool. Michael was a dead cert to go to Lilleshall. Jamie Carragher and another Liverpool kid, Jamie Cassidy, were already there. I just wanted so much to join them.

In their letter, the Lilleshall people gave a vague explanation. 'You are a great player, don't give up,' they wrote. 'Sometimes it is not just on football why we select certain people to go further than you. It's for other reasons.'

I heard the whispers: Huyton was looked down on by those smart blazers from the National School. Did Lilleshall feel I might be a jack the lad and disrupt life at their nice school? That wasn't me, though. Honest. At the trials I was quiet, well behaved and well presented. I always did the right thing. Before the trials, Steve Heighway warned us the Lilleshall staff watched how we ate, whether or not we were polite. I tried my best.

What were these 'other reasons'? I knew Lilleshall

held meetings during the trials and Mum and Dad were quizzed about me. 'What's Steven like? Is he doing well at school? Could he handle being away from home?' Mum and Dad spoke well of me. I know that. They always backed their sons 100 per cent. Maybe Lilleshall felt I couldn't cope away from home, being separated from the family I adore. I certainly hated being away from home. Even now. In my heart, I don't know whether I would have gone to Lilleshall anyway. Maybe I would have done simply through Dad forcing me. But, for all the whispers about Huyton and homesickness, I still feel it was my lack of height in those days that brought rejection from Lilleshall.

No reason could ease the grief, though. My anger at Lilleshall's cold shoulder has never subsided. The insult was personal, one that remains in my mind, needling away at me. It never dims, that memory of rejection. Of course, I never chucked football in. Dad talked me round. Still, the sense of frustration, humiliation and bitterness lingered. But life went on. 'Prove them wrong, son,' said Dad.

With a heavy heart, I resumed Liverpool training.

Steve Heighway was waiting for me. He pulled me into his office, sat me down, and went behind his desk. 'I am absolutely ecstatic you didn't get into Lilleshall,' Steve said.

'I didn't want you to go, I don't want Michael to go. I'm selfish. I want you here at Liverpool. Steven, I know you are upset but, trust me, I can make you a better player than Lilleshall can.'

At the time, I didn't believe him. Michael was packing his bags for a new adventure, and supposedly the best coaching in the country. Michael deserved it. Good luck to him. 'I'm buzzing for you,' I told him when he came to say goodbye. Secretly, I was gutted. I just wanted to be setting off to Lilleshall, walking in there shoulder to shoulder with Michael. I didn't want to be left behind, staring at Michael's empty place in the dressing-room. I loathed the taste of failure. I thought that if Steve had pushed me, I could have got into Lilleshall. It took me a long time to understand Steve's motives.

In my opinion Lilleshall messed up, and I hoped and prayed every day they would recognize their mistake. I dreamed of a letter coming through with a

Shropshire postmark apologizing for their terrible oversight and telling me to get down there now. But the call never came.

Seven months later, my anger with Lilleshall found a fantastic outlet. The National School came to Melwood, where us Heighway kids were based at the time, for a fixture. Thank you, God! I prepared an ambush. I was steaming for this game like nobody's business. The night before the game I was cleaning my boots, making sure the studs were nice and sharp for those pretty boys from Lilleshall. I was burning inside. I stayed awake all night before the game, as if I feared sleep might soften me, lessening the fury inside. In the morning, I stormed into Melwood on a wave of adrenalin and resentment.

And when I saw those Lilleshall boys marching into the pavilion at Melwood, all smart and smiling in their England blazers, the fire raging within me turned into an inferno. Even now, I don't know how I restrained myself from nailing them in the corridor. 'Huyton v. Lilleshall, now. We'll see who's better!'

The first whistle made the same impression on me as a bell in a prize fight. A call to arms, the signal for battle. I smashed Lilleshall's midfield to pieces. Absolutely shredded them. No mercy. Into every tackle I poured all my frustration at being ignored by the National School. I loved the thought of their coaches standing helplessly on the Melwood touchline as I tore into their chosen ones. 'This will show them what they rejected,' I thought as I crunched another set of shin-pads. 'This will make them see how wrong they were,' I told myself as I sent another of their precious boys flying. 'Calm down,' the ref kept shouting at me. No chance. Those Lilleshall boys were getting it big-time. Nothing was going to stop me.

Lilleshall fielded some good players, like Michael Ball, Wes Brown and, of course, my mate Michael Owen, who inevitably struck his usual hat-trick. The score was 4–3 to Lilleshall, but I settled a personal score. My performance was so good that all their players ran over at the end to shake my hand. I had battered them, but they still wanted to show their respect. Fair play. I admired them for that. 'How you never got into Lilleshall was a joke,' Michael remarked as we walked off, the battle over. 'You are well better than these.' The England staff all strolled across to congratulate me. I just turned and ran to the dressing-room. I was so upset inside. There was no way I could shake hands with those who gave me so much heartache. They snubbed me. Here was some of their own medicine. Take that.

Lilleshall's rejection deepened my love for Liverpool. They wanted me, and I was determined to deliver for them and prove Lilleshall wrong. In the long run, failing to get into the National School worked in my favour. In my opinion, those national coaches would never have developed me as well as Steve Heighway did. Steve used to come round Ironside, see how we were, or call on the phone. Steve always had Mum and Dad into the Academy, checking everything was OK. Steve gave me boots on the sly. 'How's your family?' he often enquired. 'What's the money situation?' He knew we never had much. He used to help. Steve likes to bond with families, assist people. He's a top guy. Genuine. Obviously, it was in Liverpool's interests to keep me happy, but Steve's commitment to me was not merely professional. He really cared. I was not a piece of meat, or an investment opportunity, to Steve and

Liverpool. I was flesh and blood, fears and dreams, and Steve looked after me like a son. I will never forget Steve Heighway's immense involvement in shaping me as a man and as a footballer.

Steve knew how many clubs circled around me. Manchester United kept sending letters to Ironside, and the postman also brought regular offers from Crystal Palace, Manchester City, Everton and Spurs. One day, Dad spoke to Steve. 'Look, Steven is getting all these offers,' he said. 'Can we sort out his future here?'

Steve was laid-back, perhaps deliberately so. 'If Steven wants to go and have a look at what Manchester United and the rest have to offer, then let him,' he said. 'If he wants to have a look at the facilities at Spurs or City, no problem. We won't think anything different of him. We won't fall out with Steven.'

So I did. Everton showed me around, attempting to woo me. I played a trial game for Tranmere Rovers. I wore the claret and blue of West Ham when we took Cambridge United apart 6–2. At fourteen, the red of Manchester United even enveloped my small frame in two trial matches. After doing well in those games, United offered me a three-year pro contract. I even met their legendary manager, Sir Alex Ferguson. A group of us triallists had dinner with Mr Ferguson, as he was then. Michael Owen was meant to be at the meal, but he didn't turn up. We sat and listened in awe to one of the managerial greats. Mr Ferguson was top man. I knew all about him, obviously. He was masterminding United's re-emergence. He had heard about me and desperately wanted me to sign. Mr Ferguson told us how well we would do at Old Trafford and that he was committed to promoting good youngsters. Ryan Giggs and the David Beckham generation were beginning to break through around then. I enjoyed the meal, and listening to Mr Ferguson, but I was never going to sign for United. No chance. I looked around other clubs partly to pressure Liverpool into giving me a Youth Training Scheme contract.

When I returned to Liverpool after those games, I sought out Steve Heighway. 'I really enjoyed playing for those teams,' I said with a smile. I soon got a promise of a Youth Trainee Scheme contract out of

Liverpool! Towards the end of the U-16 season, all the schoolboys went one by one into this room at Melwood to learn whether a YTS place was on offer from Liverpool. I never went in. I already knew. I couldn't click on to anyone that I had this deal with Steve, all in black and white. But it was there: £50 a week. Michael Owen had one off Steve as well.

Steve always looked after us, like getting us tickets for the Kop for me, Paul and our friends. He took me to Wembley three times to watch FA Cup finals and Coca-Cola Cup finals. We travelled south on the train, with Steve, Hughie, Dave and their wives looking after me like a son. We saw Liverpool's 2–0 FA Cup defeat of Sunderland in 1992, and that brilliant Steve McManaman performance against Bolton Wanderers in the Coca-Cola Cup three years later. Michael was also in the party heading down to Wembley. Michael was Liverpool's prized junior, so I thought I must be the second best if I was also being taken down to Wembley.

Steve was always good to me. I will never forget receiving a phone call from him early one morning in May 1996. I was just about to head out of the door to catch the bus to school when the phone went. Steve came quickly to the point. 'Steven, we've got the FA Youth Cup final against West Ham in two days' time and we have one or two injuries, so we need you on stand-by. Be on your toes.' I was buzzing, floating on a cloud all the way to Cardinal Heenan. Injuries and illnesses had plagued the youth team, but I never dreamed they might turn to me. I wasn't required in the end – a real pity. Liverpool had some youth side, with David Thompson, Jamie Carragher and, of course, Owen, the real star of the show. They won the final against the likes of Rio Ferdinand and Frank Lampard comfortably. But I was grateful to Steve simply for considering me.

Steve even organized it so I did my work experience at Liverpool. I sat in the classroom at Cardinal Heenan, listening to all the boys talking of where they were going on work experience. Stacking shelves at Asda or Kwiksave was not for me. As the forms were going round, someone mentioned that a few Cardinal Heenan boys wangled work experience at Melwood in the past. That was me sorted. No chance was I going to a supermarket. Not with a chance of Melwood.

Sharpish, I was into Steve Heighway's office. 'I will mop as many floors, clean as many boots as you want, so long as I can do my two weeks' work experience at Melwood,' I told him. Steve agreed, and set it up with Cardinal Heenan. Liverpool obviously thought a lot of me. While the rest of my year worked with their dads, brick-laying, labouring or helping out in shops, I joined Liverpool's first team for a fortnight. I could not believe my luck. Nor could my schoolmates. I was the envy of everyone at Cardinal Heenan.

Those boys who had done work experience at Melwood just trained with the reserves. When I reported for duty, I was informed I would be training with legends like John Barnes and Jan Molby. My idols! The pair of them, I swear, were so good. It was a privilege just to watch them at close quarters. Standing on the touchline at Melwood, my mouth open in amazement at their skills, seemed the closest I would get. Work experience involved washing floors, cleaning boots, pumping balls up, putting cones out, and collecting balls. But Roy Evans, the manager at the time, invited me to join in the five-a-sides. I was sixteen and passing a ball to John Barnes and Jan

Molby! They kept passing to me, making me a better player. They made me look like Diego Maradona.

Those two weeks deepened my passion for football and my desire to make it as a pro with Liverpool. I never changed with the first team those two weeks. I was put in with the young pros like Jamie Carragher, Jamie Cassidy, David Thompson and Gareth Roberts. Their banter was just pure quality. So funny. I was so jealous of them. Carra and the rest were in at Melwood every day, having the time of their lives, and I was heading back to a boring classroom after a fortnight. I was spewing. It was not for long. I had that promise of a YTS. That last term, I did most of my homework and had a go in my exams, but I wasn't really focused. I knew two months down the line was Liverpool.

On my last day at Cardinan Heenan, I faced a two-hour RE exam. I sat in the exam hall thinking hard over one important question: exactly how I would burn my uniform. The clock showed barely an hour before I sprinted out the room. I have never run so quick to a bus-stop. I wanted to get back to Ironside, get into my normal clothes, ditch my uniform, have six weeks off and then start football full-time.

'How did your exams go?' Mum asked.

'Yeah, fine,' I replied, knowing I had done badly. I handed her my uniform. 'Just pop that in the bin, please, Mum.'

A new uniform awaited me: Liverpool FC.

# 4
# Teenage Kicks

And so began the best days of my life, my two years as a Liverpool apprentice, a time of banter and dreams, dressing-room fights and glorious wind-ups. Laughter all the way. As I swapped the dour school uniform of Cardinal Heenan for the bright red strip of Liverpool Football Club, my character changed as well. Gone was the shyness that accompanied me through school. At Cardinal Heenan, I always avoided getting into trouble. I hated being told off, being sent out of classrooms, or being ordered home to face Dad. I loathed the thought of getting a telling-off or a little belt from my old man. So I behaved at school. But a mischievous streak emerged the moment I set foot in Melwood as an apprentice.

At Cardinal Heenan, I never had many mates.

Liverpool was different. Everyone was a friend. We all shared this unbelievable passion for football. My partners in crime were known as Boggo, Greggo, Wrighty, Bavo and Cass. John Boggan soon became a close ally in the wind-up business. Boggo, a real funny character, could talk for England. Neil Gregson was another real character, and like Stephen Wright and Matty Cass, he was always up for some banter. Ian Dunbavin, a Knowsley lad, was also in the group; Bavo now keeps goal for Accrington Stanley and to this day is a really good friend of mine. And of course there was Michael Owen, the Boy Wonder, who mucked in brilliantly with us mortals. None of us could believe our luck. After the drudgery of school we were actually getting paid to live the dream of becoming footballers. It wasn't riches. As an apprentice, I got only £50 a week; Mum was paid £160 a month to feed me. Compared to what I make now it was peanuts, but I felt on top of the world every day. The sun seemed to shine just on us Liverpool apprentices.

Because the new Academy at Kirkby was not ready until my second year on the YTS, we spent the first twelve months at Melwood, seeing all the stars. We heard the banter bubbling around the first-team dressing-room at Melwood, so we copied them. So this was the way to become a Liverpool professional: work hard, train hard, laugh hard. Boy, did we muck about. Liverpool's staff slaughtered me for all kinds of minor offences, but it was completely different from being coated by the teacher or Dad. I made amends in the next training session.

Pure madness reigned in the apprentices' dressing-room. As soon as I came through the door, I started wars simply by flicking the lights off. That would be the signal for all the lads – Greggo, me, Bavo, Wrighty, Cass, Michael and everyone – to batter each other with towels in the dark. That room staged many an ambush.

One of us YTS boys' favourite dressing-room games was Chinese Whispers. The lights went off and the maulings were verbal not physical. We'd sit around in a gang, the lights extinguished, and the whispers began. I might quietly tell my neighbour, 'Greggo's got some shocking gear on.' Caning people was the aim of the game, and I was a master. Whispers went round the room, everyone trying to remember all the abuse. The last man switched the lights back on and recited every whisper. 'Tell Stevie to sort his trainers out. Tell Greggo he dresses like a tramp.' I loved Chinese Whispers. It was a brilliant chance to slaughter someone without them knowing.

No-one was safe. Even tough guys like me were targeted. Whenever I came in with a new pair of trainers on, the other apprentices plotted their demise. The moment I headed off to the showers, the lads would cut right through the laces or tie them in unbelievable knots. One time, it took me an hour to get my trainers back to normal. Frequently, I pulled a sock on and my foot went straight through the end, which my team-mates had kindly cut off. I sat there in the dressing-room, with my toes sticking out the sock, as all the boys fell about laughing. They were so bloody sneaky. I never knew they had planned any skit against me until it was too late.

Revenge was had, though, big-time. I was one of the ring-leaders, inflicting loads of grief on others. Sometimes it stepped over the line. Fights broke out in training through bad tackles, pushes and snarls. The changing-room was no different. If someone couldn't take the banter or a prank, arguments would erupt. Rucks were part of my daily life. If I ruined someone's trainers and they weren't happy, I reacted. Pushing and shouting broke out. 'Can't you take a joke?' I'd scream at Greggo or Wrighty as they stood there, steaming, holding a pair of wrecked trainers. Emotions ran high at times. Training was so exhausting, I would be knackered, short-tempered, my head gone. A confrontational streak occasionally seized me in the dressing-room, but I never, ever got nasty violent.

We all stuck together though, and loyalty was an unbreakable code in Liverpool's YTS dressing-room. Whatever happened, however ruined your trainers were, nobody complained to the staff. If there was a fight, it would be split up. 'Shake hands,' came the order from all the other boys. If two lads wrestled and one got cut, everyone else shouted, 'So what? Get on with it.'

But the happy days at Melwood couldn't last for ever, and one day, the management announced that us YTS boys were moving to Liverpool University's grounds, before we eventually settled at the new Academy at Kirkby. Liverpool's staff almost had to drag us kicking and screaming from Melwood. We loved it there, but Liverpool decided it would be best if the YTS lads and first-year pros were kept separate from the first team. It really annoyed me as I wanted to be at Melwood, showing what I could do in front of the Liverpool management. Melwood was the gateway to Anfield. Instead, we were packed off to some student pitches. I came back from the university on the first day and Dad immediately asked what the set-up was like there. 'Rubbish,' I replied. 'The pitches and facilities are rubbish.' It was only for six months, before Kirkby opened, but I felt like I had stepped on a snake after climbing so many ladders.

But even away from the first teamers I loved it all. All clubs have banter, but people say the atmosphere at Liverpool is unique. The dressing-room games of sock-ball, where we'd kick around balled up footy socks, Chinese Whispers and battering each other with towels was passed down the generations. It was a Liverpool thing. Sadly, that special spirit may be going. I look at the current YTS boys when they come over from the Academy to Melwood and they seem quiet and shy. They don't have the banter we did. I wish everyone was together, as we were for that first wonderful year at Melwood, Liverpool's first team and apprentices living side by side.

Back then, Liverpool's first team were known as the Spice Boys. People used the tag as a derogatory one for the likes of Jamie Redknapp, Robbie Fowler, Steve McManaman, Jason McAteer and David James. I never considered the label offensive. I was steaming to be a Spice Boy. Let me be in your team! Let me be your mate! Every day, I went out of my way to be nice to Redknapp, Fowler, McManaman, McAteer and Jamo. After every encounter, I told myself, 'Hopefully, I will be in with these one day. Some day, we will be on the same level.' I am not a Spice Boy type, certainly not flash or obsessed with fashion, but I admired Jamie, Robbie and the rest. The image was false anyway. Nobody used to say, 'Oh, we're the Spice Boys. Let's all go off on modelling assignments.' No chance. The Spice Boy label was a media creation. Jamo, McManaman and the boys didn't take any notice of it. Those 1996 FA Cup final suits, where the players looked like ice-cream salesmen, didn't help, but the perception that the Spice Boys weren't professional is a myth. During my work experience and YTS, I trained with the Spice Boys and played with some of them in Liverpool's A and B sides. They worked so hard. None of the Spice Boys took the mickey in training. None of them eased off. It wouldn't happen.

People claimed our manager Roy Evans wasn't strong enough, but that's rubbish. Roy and Ronnie Moran, his assistant, had a relationship with the players where they could have a real go at them. Some managers were stricter than Roy and Ronnie, but the standard of training was really good. John 'Digger' Barnes was an absolute joke in training; I couldn't get the ball off him. It was pointless closing Digger down. Redknapp too. When I was a YTS and invited to train with the seniors, I couldn't get near any of them. If I gave the ball away, Ronnie or Roy were immediately on my case. 'Look after the ball!' Everyone else did. Possession was the Liverpool creed. All the Spice Boys treated the ball as their best friend. They never surrendered it cheaply. When I got told off, I just wanted the ground to open up and swallow me.

'Wow, this is real pressure,' I thought as I chased McManaman or Digger around Melwood. It did my head in. I walked off the pitch at the end, having looked a fool trying to tackle some of the Spice Boys. They had so much skill. I would sit in the changing-room, heaving with frustration. 'How am I going to get to this level?' I would ask myself. 'Some of these players are frightening.' Even when our YTS sessions finished, me, Boggo, Greggo, Wrighty and Cass would sit spell-bound watching the first team doing shooting or pattern of play. The Spice Boys were so talented. Forget all the rumours about Jamie and the rest being playboys first, players second. These were proper professionals.

Fowler and McManaman were my main heroes. Part of my YTS duties involved standing outside the first-team dressing-room and getting shirts, balls and pictures signed by the first-team stars. These items were then sent to hospitals, schools or charity auctions. Whenever Fowler and McManaman walked past, I was in awe. They were local heroes. Some banter went on between the YTS and first-teamers, but I made sure I never said the wrong thing or was too cheeky. I was not intimidated, but I looked up to Fowler and McManaman so much. I never wanted them to think I was a idiot. If they had caned me, I would have been devastated. The sad truth is that they probably were not even aware of me, Steven Gerrard, an unknown kid with a huge desire to copy them.

Another Liverpool legend was John 'Digger' Barnes, the skipper. England international. Twice Footballer of the Year. Awesome. Talking to Digger scared the life out of me. If I walked into a room at Melwood and Digger was there, I tried to get out quickly. When I did pluck up the courage to speak to him, though, he was incredibly friendly, putting his arms around me, giving me advice. We used to have pretend fights, with John shaping up to punch me, shadow-boxing with me, sometimes wrestling me. Just mucking around with stars like John Barnes was the business. I was being noticed! Suddenly my dream of playing for Liverpool did not seem so unreal.

I had so much to prove to myself, and to everyone at Liverpool. I never thought established stars like Jamie Redknapp realized I existed until one day after training. 'You are a player,' Jamie said to me. 'I love the way you pass and shoot. Keep doing that.' I went home on cloud nine. Jamie Redknapp, England international, spoke to me! Not only that, Jamie Redknapp rated me. He only talked to me for a few seconds, it was only a few words, but they meant the world. Jamie was different class with the young lads. Unbelievable. After the first few words of encouragement, he was always offering advice. I will never forget how Jamie helped me climb the ladder to Liverpool's first team. When he came back from injuries, Jamie regained his sharpness in the A or B teams and I was lucky enough to play alongside him. What a privilege. I felt like a king being named on the same team-sheet as Jamie Redknapp. He talked to me more and more. In games, he explained which positions I should take up, when to make runs. I was an apprentice learning from a master. What an education. He often called me over in the dressing-room and said, 'How are you? What have you been up to, Stevie?' Jamie Redknapp knew my name! Jamie talked to me as if I had played with him in the first team for five years! I felt so honoured just to be in the same room with him, let alone talking to him. Maybe it was because I played in the same position as Redknapp that he took me under his wing. Maybe it was because he was simply a nice bloke who cared about other people.

'Hey, Stevie, what size are you?' Jamie shouted one day.

'Same as you,' I replied. I cleaned Jamie's boots, so I knew his size. He was actually a size bigger, but I pretended to be the same.

'Well, these will fit you then,' said Jamie, throwing me some boots.

Christmas came flying through the air in the shape of those beautiful boots. Jamie often gave me boots, moulded and studs, brand-new Mizunos. They were the boots at the time.

The British players in the first team were so generous. Me and all the YTS boys loved Redknapp, McManaman and Fowler. We would leave training, swapping stories of which star had given us what. Dom Matteo, the defender who played for Scotland, was brilliant as well. Looking after Dom's boots was also my job, and he really looked after me. Before Christmas one year, Dom walked past me, stopped and turned round. 'Stevie, come here,' he said. He put his hand in his pocket, handed me what seemed like small bits of folded paper, and strolled off. I couldn't believe it. I looked at the paper and counted out £200. Some Christmas tip! I worked hard for Dom and Jamie. They massacred me if their boots weren't done properly. I would sometimes come into training knackered and think, 'It's ten o'clock, I haven't done Dom's boots.' So I'd get busy, washing and brushing all the mud off his boots, making sure they were polished properly. I knew how I liked my boots, so I made sure Dom's and Jamie's boots were perfect. With their big tips and helpful advice, Dom and Jamie were worth the extra effort.

Only one thing annoyed me as an apprentice at Liverpool: injuries. In my first year, I was plagued with them. A vicious circle trapped me: one step forward, playing really well; strain a muscle, hobble one step back. My ankle always played me up. When my back was wrong, I didn't look forward to training or playing because I knew it would be only a matter of time before something else would be sore. Injuries first began impeding my development towards the end of my time at school. If I played two or three games in a week, my back would be really stiff. The medical term for my problem was Osgood-Schlatter's, a bone disease tied up with the growth spurts that took me from a fifteen-year-old the same height as Michael Owen to a gangly six-footer. My back hurt. My knees were sore. Every physio and doctor I went to see just examined me and said, 'It's because you are growing.' I wanted to be tall, but it was a pain getting there.

Fortunately, I was in the down-to-earth hands of Liverpool manager Roy Evans. Whenever I look back now, I thank God I had such a caring person as Roy helping me in the early days of my career. One day, Roy called me into his office. His assistants, Doug Livermore and Ronnie Moran, were already in the room. 'How are you, Steven?' Roy asked kindly. 'How are the injuries?'

'It's so frustrating, boss,' I replied.

He knew. Roy had picked up signals that I was gloomy. 'Steven, keep your chin up,' he said. 'We've noticed you are down. Steve Heighway thinks so highly of you, and you are definitely going to play for the first team. Get your injuries right. Keep working.

Don't be getting involved in messing around. We think the world of you here. As soon as you are right, you will sign your first pro contract.'

I was really grateful to Roy. But that's the way Liverpool are as a club. They look after players. We're family to them.

My development was still stop-start. At seventeen, and back from a broken wrist, I went flying into a tackle in training and damaged my ankle. Typical me, never holding back. I was told to calm down millions of times by Liverpool coaches. Ronnie Moran pulled me aside once and said, 'Steven, the staff are telling me you are getting injured because you go into stupid tackles. You try to kill people in training. These are your mates, Steven. Relax. Save it for the games.' I couldn't help it. It's the way I train, the way I play. Full on. No pulling out. No messing. Of course, I was also trying to impress, to catch the eye of the coaches. But it's my nature to go in hard. I couldn't go into a session thinking, 'I'll take it easy today, I'm not going to tackle.' It's a waste. Pointless. I got loads of warnings off Dave Shannon and Hughie McAuley. Actually, Hughie loved it. If you tackled hard, you were in

Hughie's Academy team, especially against Everton and Man United! Because of the rivalry, those matches were like blood sports. Boys tackled like men. When the final whistle blew, I felt like a boxer who had been the distance – bruised, and sometimes bloodied.

For all my passion for big, bruising matches against Everton and Man United, my body struggled to withstand the pressure. Injuries held me back. I soon arrived at the age when pro contracts were being handed out. Lads younger than me were going in to see Roy and coming out with pro contracts. Naturally, I got the hump. Roy promised me a contract but it never came at the right time because of injuries. Liverpool were clever. They wanted me back fit a while before giving me the contract. That made sound financial sense to Liverpool. They did not want to give someone a three-year deal and then see his body pack up. So Liverpool delayed. It drove me mad with anxiety. Roy told me I was in his long-term plans but the doubts kept crowding in with every passing week without a hint of a contract. I lay in bed at night at Ironside, staring at the ceiling with one thought bouncing around in my head: 'Do Liverpool think these injuries are never going to go away?' Doubts affected me as much as the injuries. I felt my whole career was on a knife-edge. My dream was to make it with Liverpool. Did they really believe my body was too frail? I felt my head was about to explode.

One day, after training, I'd had enough. I stormed home, mind all over the place. 'Dad,' I said, 'you had best get in to Liverpool and talk to Steve and Roy. I can't go on with this uncertainty. Do they really want me?'

Dad was brilliant, as usual. 'Don't worry, Steven, we know they rate you,' he said. 'I'll go and talk to them.'

That calmed me down a bit. 'Dad, just tell them I want to sign pro because I am not having lads in the year below signing pro before me.' Dad got the message!

He went to see Steve. 'Look,' said Dad, 'Steven's head has gone. He needs that deal. He's sick with worry.' Dad had a bit of a moan. Steve listened and appreciated how important the contract was for me. He realized it would give me peace of mind about my future. I soon had my deal. Three years – £700 a week for the first year, then £800, then £900! It was some jump from my apprentice cash of £50 a week. I thought I had won the lottery! I could not believe my luck. For Steve to offer me that deal, to go to Roy and say, 'I am going to offer this Gerrard kid this amount of money,' meant Liverpool thought something of me.

Anfield's appreciation of my potential was more important to me than the money. I was so grateful to Roy, Steve and Dad for sorting it out. It was like emerging from a dark tunnel. I could see the way ahead now. I was nearing my first-team destination.

# 5
# Liverpool Heaven

Gérard Houllier turned me from a boy into a man but he can't take all the credit for the player I am today. Liverpool had always backed me, giving me a six-year contract taking in schoolboy forms and YTS, and then that fantastic three-year pro, before Gérard even arrived. Academy coaches Steve Heighway, Dave Shannon and Hughie McAuley were the ones who worked so hard at improving my game from an early age. They helped shape me as a player from the moment I set foot in the Vernon Sangster. Steve has been a massive influence on me. He still is. Even now, when I get the chance, I talk to Steve and he makes useful points about my game. After Gérard took full charge, he did a lot for me, I know, and I am incredibly grateful. He looked after me, protected me and built up my game. But everyone at Anfield assisted my development into an England international. I have a good relationship with them all – Steve Heighway, Gérard and his coaches Phil Thompson and Sammy Lee. I never fell out with any of them. Gérard was definitely brilliant for me, but I made it because of my own efforts, because of fantastic coaching at the Academy, and because of the love and support of my parents. Gérard opened the door to the first team, but I had been banging loudly on it.

People talked about me at Melwood, Anfield and outside. Premiership clubs tried to buy me. When I played my first game for Liverpool U-19s, against Tottenham Hotspur in August 1998, Spurs certainly knew all about me. The match was at Spurs' Chigwell training ground in Essex and we were buzzing. Me, Boggo, Wrighty and the other lads felt like proper pros, proudly wearing our Liverpool tracksuits. We travelled south the night before, doing it in style, like the first team. The whole trip was quality. Luxury coach. Smart hotel. I roomed with Wrighty, and we almost didn't get to sleep we were so busy discussing what our first U-19 match would be like. I loved everything about the whole experience. Before the game, we ate a proper meal with all the right food: pasta and chicken. Tottenham fielded a good side at Chigwell. Peter Crouch and Luke Young both played; they went on to represent England, and Crouchy is now my team-mate at club and international level. So it was a tough old battle. Quite a few people were watching, including Alan Sugar, then the Spurs chairman rather than the firer of apprentices from TV. I played really well, and smacked one in from long-range. The game finished 1–1, and as I walked off the pitch I noticed Sugar in conversation with Steve Heighway. Sugar even put his arm round Steve's back as they chatted. When I got into the changing-room, Boggo said, 'They were talking about you.'

'How do you know?'

'Because I heard them mention your name. I don't know exactly what they said, but Alan Sugar was talking a lot about you.'

I didn't think anything more of it. I got showered, changed and jumped on the bus back to Liverpool. A week later, I heard Sugar tried to buy me. For £2 million! Not bad for an 'unknown'. Liverpool turned Spurs' offer down. 'Don't be ridiculous,' Steve told Alan Sugar. They obviously did rate me.

A month or two after that Spurs game, I got fined for messing about by Dave Shannon. As crimes go, it was a minor offence: not taking my plate back after a meal. Trivial. It was only a fiver, but I had just come off YTS money and it felt a decent sum – plus I was innocent. I was raging. I went in to see Dave, one-on-one. Straight in. Slammed the door.

'What's the fine for? I'm not happy.'

'You never took your plate back.'

'I did take it back.' I had. Some of the lads I was with left their plates everywhere. Not me. Mum and Dad brought me up to show respect. I was upset Dave didn't believe me. 'You are not taking a fiver off me.'

Dave refused to budge. 'No, it's done. You're fined, and I want it Friday.'

I knew I'd lost. 'I'll take the fine, but you are out of order, Dave.'

Everyone bantered with Dave. He was a terrific bloke, the one who got the team spirit going. Anyway, while he was getting that fiver off me, we got talking about football and the season. 'Dave, do us a favour, give us another fixture list for the reserves and nineteens,' I asked. 'Someone has nicked mine.'

Dave looked at me and smiled. 'You won't need those fixtures. You'll be needing these.' He put his hand into his bag and pulled out the fixtures for the first team.

The firsts! I was stunned. I walked out of Dave's office thinking he would not have given me the first-team list without the coaches deciding I had a chance. That gave me the biggest boost I ever needed. My fury over the fiver disappeared immediately.

Gérard said he came down to watch me training at the university one afternoon, but it wasn't him. It was his number two, Patrice Bergues, a top fellow. Patrice checked me out before Gérard did. I will never forget that day. In the morning, Steve Heighway pulled me into his office. 'Steven, we've got company today,' he said. 'Gérard Houllier, Phil Thompson, Sammy Lee and Patrice Bergues are coming down from Melwood to look at you in training.' Steve didn't need to say any more. I knew. This was it. This was my chance to force my way into the first-team squad.

Before training started, the whisper went round the dressing-room that only two were coming down from Melwood. It didn't matter to me how many; it just mattered to me that I was being assessed by the management. I must take this chance to impress. I always trained hard, but this session was my ticket to fame. I was itching to get cracking. I sprinted out of the door, onto the pitch, and looked around. No-one there! Maybe Gérard and his coaches decided they weren't coming after all. Maybe they felt I wasn't ready. I thought nothing of it and got on with training.

After a while, I became aware there were people walking around. They stayed well back from our pitch, but they were definitely watching us. I looked closer. It was Patrice and Sammy. Brilliant. Time to step up a gear. We trained for an hour and forty-five minutes, doing possession, then had a game. I was everywhere. First to every ball, hardest in the tackle, strongest in the shooting. I treated it as a trial for the first team. I sweated buckets. I could see them looking at me. Sammy did the pointing, and wrote little notes. Patrice just studied me and the other lads.

When the session ended, Steve introduced us to Sammy and Patrice. We all knew Sammy anyway. He was superb with the young lads. Everyone liked Sammy. Sammy certainly appreciated who I was. 'Well done,' he said. I was buzzing to hear those words. As the group broke up, Patrice strolled across. I had never met him before. None of us had. Gérard had only just taken over fully with Patrice. It was a big moment. Patrice shook my hand. 'You are looking sharp,' he said. That was it. He strolled away. I walked away on air.

Another audition needed passing. Gérard had not seen me yet. The story of Gérard 'discovering' me came about because a couple of weeks after that training session watched by Patrice and Sammy we had an U-19 game against Man United. It was a November Saturday, and I was dying to play. By then I was starting to push for a reserve-team place full-time, but there were special reasons for wanting to start that U-19 fixture. The opponents were United and I love piling into them, always have done and always will do. It was also my first game back after an injury. I broke my wrist and had been playing with a cast on. I was meant to play in a reserve/YTS match against the first team, but the doc stopped me. He took one look at the cast and said, 'You're not ready.' I was devastated, particularly as the word was that Patrice was going to watch me again. The wrist got better by the time Man U were in town. I couldn't wait to launch myself into them.

All my U-19 mates were playing, boys like Boggo and Greggo. A decent crowd gathered, around 200, which is good for an Academy match. Dad was there, giving me the support I prize so highly. All our normal staff were present, too, like Steve and Dave, and I spotted Gérard standing near them. I took control. I bossed the game from start to finish, smashing into United players left, right and centre-midfield. I really should have been shown the red card for bad tackles. 'One more and you're going off,' warned the ref. 'One more and you are coming off,' warned Steve. I ignored them both. I just wanted to rip Man United to pieces. They were a good team, as well, with players like John O'Shea in their ranks. It felt similar to when the

Lilleshall boys swanned into Melwood. I wanted to crush them. We drew 1–1, but I scored, and I knew I had shone. As I walked off the pitch, feeling like a king, I glanced around to check Gérard's reaction. He'd gone. But he must have been impressed. When I reached Ironside, Dad was already home.

'The manager was there, you know,' Dad said.

'I know,' I replied with a smile. 'I saw him.'

Dad's next comment filled me with pride. 'You never did yourself any harm there, Steven.' That was lavish praise from my dad. I went up to bed feeling on top of the world.

Sunday passed slowly. My impatience for Monday was massive. I wanted to get into training to find out if there had been any word from Gérard. Nothing happened on the Monday. Nor Tuesday. But on the Wednesday, I was walking down a corridor in the Academy and there, coming towards me, were Gérard and Roy Evans. Roy had called time on 12 November, and was going round saying his goodbyes. Typical Liverpool – even dismissals are done in a civilized fashion. Roy stopped me. I didn't know what to say. I shifted from one foot to the other, slightly embarrassed. Here was Roy Evans leaving as joint-manager standing next to the man who was taking over fully, my new boss whom I'd never met before.

Roy was brilliant. 'How are you, Steven?' he asked. 'Keep going, you've got a great chance of making it.'

Gérard then interrupted. 'You've got a very good chance,' he said.

I looked at him, looked at that face that was to become so familiar to me over the next few years.

'Keep doing what you are doing,' he added. 'I watched you last week against Manchester United and you were very good.'

'Thank you,' I said to Gérard, and turned back to Roy. 'Sorry to hear about what happened.'

'Don't worry, Steven, I'll be OK. You just make sure you keep doing what you are doing.'

I felt sorry for Roy. I wanted him to stay manager. He was always first-class with me, and I knew how much he wanted me in the first team. Whenever I saw Roy, he always said, 'Just get rid of your injuries and you will be with me.' Now I wondered what would happen. Would Gérard really want me in the first team? He didn't really know who I was. Roy had known me since I was twelve. Roy leaving really felt like a huge blow. I heard from people at Melwood that no-one enjoyed training any more. Gérard was really strict. A lot of negative vibes came down from the reserves, too. On first impressions, Gérard seemed a nice guy. But I was scared of him. Definitely. He was the boss, the man who could decide whether to keep me or bomb me out. It seemed inevitable under Roy that I would progress to the first team. It was a matter of when, not if. But then Roy got shown the door.

Two days later, on the Friday, Steve Heighway called me and Wrighty into his office. Dave Shannon was already there. 'Important news, lads,' Steve announced. 'Gérard and Phil want you at Melwood now.' Wrighty and I looked at each other. Fantastic. This was it, the news we'd craved. 'You start on Monday,' Steve added. 'Gérard wants to put you on a programme, and get you to train with the first team. Go on, lads, this is your big chance to leave us behind.' Steve paused, and then gave us some really important advice. He knew our Academy days were over. 'Never forget where you've come from,' he told me and Wrighty. 'Never forget what we've done for you and that we are still here for you. We don't want you to change as people. Keep your feet on the ground. Blank out all the big-heads. And you are leaving good mates behind, so make sure you come back and see them.' It was good advice, as usual from Steve, but he need not have worried. I would never have raced out of the Academy, glanced briefly over my shoulder and never again looked back. I know my roots. I know the names of those who guided me along the road to the first team: Steve Heighway, Dave Shannon and Hughie McAuley.

I drove home, parked up outside Ironside, and nodded to the young lads kicking the ball about, as I used to. My world was spinning fast, faster than even I had dreamed of when it was me playing shootie out there. I walked through the front door, my head still in a daze. Dad was sitting in the front room, flicking through the paper. He looked up and saw the glint in my eye.

'What is it?' he asked.

'I'm at Melwood now!' I said.

Dad was so proud. 'This is where it starts,' he said.

That weekend passed by in a blur. All I could think of was Monday and Melwood. That Sunday night, as the clock ticked towards our move towards the big time, Wrighty stayed at Ironside. The two of us were really close, and spent a lot of time together off the field. We were both buzzing and could hardly sleep. Me and Wrighty just talked and talked. We felt as if we had made it as pros. But before I left the house and embarked on the next stage of my career, Dad pulled me aside. 'This is the beginning,' he reminded me. 'You are going into a room full of England players. Full of internationals. Remember, Steven, you've achieved nothing yet. Know your place, but take your chance.' Dad's words acted like a wake-up call. I was very focused.

And nervous. Going into Melwood that day, I was filling my pants. Wrighty and I arrived ridiculously early. Those big steel gates were open, but few cars were inside. We went in, and walked cautiously towards the pavilion. Wrighty and I knew where the dressing-room was, but we stood outside it for a few minutes, plucking up courage. Eventually, I turned the handle and went in. The room was empty. The kit-man had been in, laying out each player's training stuff. Wrighty and I looked along the pegs to see if there was any spare kit for us. None. Our hearts dropped.

'Wrighty, they don't know we're coming,' I said.

We felt like trespassers.

I looked at Wrighty and said, 'The first team are going to come in and say, "What are youse doing here?"'

We were just about to make a break for it when the door opened and the stars began rolling in. Robbie, Macca, Jamie. Thank God for friendly faces. Wrighty and I knew them and they had always been brilliant with us.

'You down here for good now?' said Jamie. 'Well done.'

Macca laughed. 'About bloody time!'

Robbie joined in. 'Bit late, aren't you?'

Wrighty and I relaxed. Maybe they were expecting us after all. 'Get your kit, and get in next to me,' said Jamie. 'Wow, I've arrived,' I thought, as I sat down next to one of the country's most famous footballers. But then one of the coaches came in and signalled for me and Wrighty to sit down at the far end, with all the fringe players and the old guys. No pegs, hardly any room. We folded our clothes up and bundled them together on the bench. So what? I didn't care that my spot in the dressing-room was cramped. This was it, lift-off, time to train with the first team. Get on with it. Get out there.

On the training pitch, Gérard called us all together in a circle. He stood in the middle and pointed at me and Wrighty, the new boys. 'These lads are here now,' said Gérard. 'I have moved them up from the Academy.' That was it! Introductions over. On with training.

For all my fears about what training would be like under Gérard, I loved it. It wasn't as strict as I expected. The pattern-of-play work was enjoyable. The practice games were brilliant. Afterwards, as Jamie, Macca and the others were heading off to the dressing-room, all laughing and shouting, Gérard kept me and Wrighty back. Neither of us had had a proper one-on-one with him yet. This was the first time he had addressed us. 'You are here now,' Gérard began. 'This is where it starts. We are not happy with how you look. We want you bigger and stronger. You are very thin. Look around the first-team dressing-room and they are a lot bigger than you. You must get to their level. We are going to put you on a different training regime from them. Don't complain. Get on with it. If you are told to stay back, or get in early, make sure you do as you are told. Eat what we tell you. Drink what we tell you. We want you physically ready for the first team. You are not far away.'

Things moved fast. A dietician spoke to us. He checked me over and ordered me to cut out fast food. My eating habits weren't too bad before, but I knew I had to get fitter. No more burgers. 'Live like an athlete' became my motto. A fitness guy worked hard on me and Wrighty, keeping us in the gym four afternoons a week for two hours of weights. I sweated loads, pushing myself to the limit to inch closer to the first team. Every time I bench-pressed some more iron, I told myself the effort hastened the date of my Liverpool debut. I imagined touching the 'This Is

Anfield' sign as I ran out to the roar of the Kop. That image made the pain worth it.

Gérard often put his head around the door to check on my progress. After one afternoon in the gym, I was called into his office. 'Steven,' he said, 'you've got a great chance. You have the ability. It is whether you have the mentality. We are going to watch you closely.' Gérard really cared. 'I want to have a meal with your mum and dad,' he added. So we went for a quiet meal, somewhere nice on the Allerton Road. Gérard didn't talk much about football. He wanted to know my background, so we all just chatted. My parents came away very impressed, pleased that their son was being looked after by a genuine guy.

Football had suddenly become big-time serious for me. All my banter from the YTS days was gone. Now I was just a little boy in the first-team dressing-room. Joining in with the banter was impossible – I was that scared. I would have died if I had got hammered by Robbie, Jamo or any of the established boys. Keep quiet, work hard, I told myself. Gérard had introduced so many rules that I had to be on my toes the whole time. There were fines for everything. I was fined a few times for being late, for turning up in the wrong T-shirt through being nervous. I knew from the first day not to mess about with the French regime or with Gérard. He made it very clear that anyone who didn't abide by the rules would be out. Simple as that. Some players found it hard because Liverpool had been more relaxed under Roy Evans. Some couldn't adapt. Macca was going on a free to Real Madrid. Phil Babb was training on his own, seeing his contract out. Everyone understood: don't mess with Gérard.

Despite my trepidation, I began to win favour with Gérard. On 23 November, Liverpool flew out to Celta Vigo for a UEFA Cup third-round first-leg tie. Wrighty and me were on the plane! We had not been at Melwood a month and there we were, checking in for a flight to Spain with the first team! I was awestruck, travelling with the other players, the coaches and directors. I sat next to Wrighty on the plane and told him, 'We are just here to help with the kit. We'll not get a kick.' Wrighty agreed. The lack of pressure made the trip even more enjoyable. I was just buzzing to be there: sitting with the first team during meals, getting changed with them for training at the stadium that night, mingling with them around the hotel. I was a kid fresh out of the Academy talking to players who had graced World Cups. Awesome.

When it came to sorting out the hotel rooms, Gérard split me and Wrighty up. I shared with Jamie. 'Watch him,' Gérard advised me. 'Watch how Jamie behaves around the place. How he eats, trains, conducts himself, how he plays. You can learn off him.' Jamie was, as usual, first class. He treated everyone the same. He talked to me as if he were talking to Jason McAteer, Phil Babb or anyone he had played with for years.

I still didn't expect to get closer to the pitch than the stands. But then I walked into the dressing-room and found a shirt with my name and number on, 28. My own shirt. I belonged. I was now part of the fabric of Liverpool FC. It hit me then that I had crossed the threshold into an exclusive new world. Gérard named me and Wrighty as subs. European ties allow seven on the bench, so Wrighty and I had our chance.

We sat there that night and watched Liverpool being given a lesson in possession. Celta were a useful side with players like Claude Makelele, who went on to prove such a formidable player for Real Madrid and Chelsea, and the clever Russian attackers Valeri Karpin and Alexander Mostovoi. Celta were too good for Liverpool and we lost 3–1. Neither me nor Wrighty made it off the bench. No problem. It was unbelievable simply to experience European combat close up, in a noisy stadium containing 24,600 fans, scarcely a month after playing in an U-19 game at Liverpool University in front of 200 people. Some change.

When we got back to England, I was dying to find out whether I had kept my place in the match-day squad. I was at full throttle in training. In our first session back from Vigo, I absolutely took the mickey out of Paul Ince. He couldn't get near me, I was that up for training. Incey was only interested in matches, not practice, but he could turn it on when he wanted. A lot of people claimed when Incey came to Liverpool from Inter Milan that he wasn't as good, but there were certain training sessions and games when he was awesome. I swear it. I never knew there was any tension between him and Gérard, but I did know

Incey was one of the main men in Liverpool's dressing-room. Everyone knew it. Incey made sure we all knew it. Rule number one at Melwood: don't get on the wrong side of Incey. Training was different. I was busting to make a point, to prove myself. Towards the end of the session, Incey started to step it up, but he still couldn't touch me. The players wound Incey up something rotten. 'That's the end of you, Incey,' Fowler shouted. 'Watch your back!' Redknapp teased Incey. I wasn't showing off. I was just doing everything right. Deep down, I thought, 'I want Incey's place. End of story.' I was on fire that session.

Gérard obviously noticed. He named me in his eighteen-man squad for Liverpool's next Premiership game, against Blackburn Rovers, on 29 November. My heart went out to Wrighty, who wasn't included, but privately I was overjoyed for myself. 'I have a chance of being on the bench here,' I told myself. Two got left out of the squad, but I was picked among the subs. Gérard selected his subs on covering positions and he appreciated I could do a number of jobs: central midfield, right midfield or at right-back. 'The boss must have an idea of putting me on,' I thought.

Magical is the only way to describe the whole experience that day at Anfield. The memory is so strong it feels like yesterday. I left the dressing-room, lined up in the corridor and religiously touched the 'This Is Anfield' sign on the steps leading to the pitch. This is Anfield. This is it. I came out and heard the noise of the 41,753 fans. Absolutely deafening. During the game, Gérard sent the subs down the touchline, towards the Kop, to warm up. I was scared stiff.

With five minutes left, I thought, 'I'm not coming on. I'm sound. I'm safe. Just relax.' Liverpool led 2–0, with goals from Incey and Michael, and the lads were just seeing out the game. It was all over. Then Phil Thompson turned round and said, 'Go and do a warm-up.' I put in a big professional warm-up, actually believing I might now get a minute or two. I was sixty yards away from the dug-out, doing my stretches in front of the Kop and waiting for Phil to wave at me. I didn't want to look back, as if I was being busy. I leant down to do some stretching and sneaked a glance back. Phil was standing up and beckoning to me. Me! I sprinted back to the dug-out.

Veggard Heggem, our Norwegian right-back, came off and I was told to slot in there. 'Keep the ball for us,' Gérard ordered, 'keep the position, see the game out.' My heart beat crazily fast. I tried to keep my cool. 'Get on, get the job done, get off,' I told myself as I ran into the fray. Despite my nerves, I was desperate for the ball. I didn't want to come on and not get a touch. Touching the ball just once would feel like I'd arrived. The ball soon came my way. I controlled it, looked around and passed to another red shirt. Nothing fancy, nothing risky. Thank God. I didn't want to see the ball again. My job was done. I looked at the ref. Blow the flipping whistle!

Then the ball got switched and I was down the right. Incey played me in, the ball gagging to be crossed into the box. It was set up perfectly. I had been in this situation so many times before and always delivered. As I brought my right foot down into the ball, one aim raced through my mind: 'Just whip it in, put it in the danger area.' But the occasion got to me. I must have been too keen. With 41,000 pairs of eyes burning into me, I overhit the cross disastrously. The ball went twenty yards over the last defender's head and almost cleared the Centenary Stand.

Liverpool won, so the atmosphere was good in the dressing-room afterwards. Everyone shook my hand, patted me on the head and gave me hugs. Wrighty came over and said, 'Well done – you've now played for Liverpool.' I really appreciated that, because it must have been hard for Wrighty. For all his frustration at not yet getting a game, Wrighty was buzzing for me. Everyone was. I just wanted to get my clothes on and go and see my family in the players' lounge. That was another massive thing. Mum, Dad and Paul mingling with the other players' families. It was a long way from shivering on the touchline at Liverpool University.

Games kept coming. On Friday, 4 December, I was down at Melwood getting ready with the rest of the squad for the journey down to White Hart Lane. It was a big game, and I was hopeful of a place as Liverpool had been hit by some injuries and suspensions.

After dinner at our hotel on the edge of London,

Gérard called me to his room. 'Steven, you are starting,' he said. My first start! I floated out of Gérard's room, got back to my room, lay down on my bed but never slept a wink I was so nervous.

The next morning, Gérard ran through the formation: 3–5–2. 'Steven, you're on the right,' the boss said. The implication sank in like a dead weight. Starting on the right meant one thing: David Ginola. I knew Ginola was good. I'd seen him on TV many times, but he couldn't be that good, could he? French international, darling of the Spurs fans, on his way to being voted Footballer of the Year. Just give it your all. Adrenalin will get you through.

Before leaving the dressing-room, Gérard took me to one side. 'Get stuck into Ginola,' he ordered. 'Don't let him do his turns.' Gérard really wanted me to nail Ginola. There was history between the pair. Make that bad blood. He and Ginola were not the best of friends after their falling-out when Gérard coached France. Gérard claimed a mistake by Ginola cost France the chance of qualifying for the World Cup in America in 1994. He wanted Ginola sorted out here.

No chance. Ginola was on fire. He took the mickey out of me. He was so strong. I stumbled through a nightmare. Ginola was awesome that afternoon. Within five minutes, he had done seven step-overs running at me and put six crosses into the box. He was just knocking balls into Steffen Iversen and Chris Armstrong for fun. It was an onslaught. I was a bag of nerves, terrified when the ball came near me. I panicked. I gave a few passes away, and Incey was on to me straight away. 'Get a grip!' he screamed. 'How can this get worse?' I wondered. 'Incey is on at me. Ginola is taking the mickey. I am out of position, and out of my depth. Get me out of here!'

Liverpool got battered first half. I actually had a half-chance to score but couldn't take it. What a disaster. Players I really respected rallied behind me. Thank God for good team-mates. Fowler was on to me all game, helping me. Jamie said, 'Carry on, you are doing all right, keep the ball for us.'

In the first half, I was on the far side of the pitch from the bench, so I got no encouragement or advice from Gérard, Phil Thompson or Sammy Lee. Actually, that was probably a blessing. That far away, maybe Liverpool's coaches couldn't tell the excruciating level of my discomfort. Still, every second I expected my number to go up. I could imagine Gérard's thoughts: 'Gerrard, you're off. Sharpish. You've been found out.' I wouldn't have blamed him for the early hook. All the Spurs players were miles too good for me. On the day, Ginola was The Man, but even when I was bumping into Iversen and Armstrong, they were just so much bigger and stronger.

My first start ended in a 2–1 defeat for Liverpool and humiliation for me. Everyone was polite enough afterwards. 'You did OK,' said Gérard. 'Well done,' said Thompson. All the lads were all right with me, yet I knew deep down I hadn't done myself justice. Some words of my dad's crept into my head: 'Just take your chance, Steven, just take your chance.' I hadn't.

The trip home was long. I sat next to Wrighty but couldn't bring myself to say more than a few words. Family and friends phoned and enquired, 'How did it go? How long did you play?' I gave them the bare details, and hoped they would be out when *Match of the Day* came on. Dad called. I could be honest and open with him. 'It was really hard, Dad. I hope I haven't blown it.' Sammy Lee knew I would be hurting. He came down the bus and was brilliant with me, trying to lift my spirits. But my depression was beyond even Sammy's motivational powers of curing. When the bus arrived back in Liverpool, I didn't want to get out. I thought it wouldn't be long before I was out permanently, sent back to the U-19s with a note marked 'Not Good Enough'.

Somehow, I survived. Liverpool's next game was the return with Celta Vigo at Anfield on 8 December – a big game, even though we trailed from the first leg. I was surprised to discover I was actually starting – amazing, given that I was convinced Ginola had dug a grave for me in North London soil. Incey was suspended in Europe after getting sent off against Valencia, so Gérard turned to me. A rumour gathered pace that I would be used in my normal position. The stories were right. I started in the middle, and immediately felt comfortable. I played a couple of nice balls early doors and confidence flooded through me. This was it! I was showing people what I could do, thumping into tackles, pinging balls about. Back on the dirty old tarmac of Ironside, I had dreamed of this. The fans' songs and applause lifted me higher. Liverpool supporters have always loved home-grown players and they were right behind me, cheering whenever I did something right. I was even voted Man of the Match.

In a way, there was no pressure. Everyone knew Liverpool were up against it that evening, because of what happened over in Spain. Our team was really weak, too. Injuries and suspensions took their toll, claiming important players like Incey, Redknapp, Heggem and McManaman. No-one really gave us too much hope of overturning the deficit against Celta. The Spaniards were a tidy outfit. For their goal, by the Israeli Haim Revivo, me and Danny Murphy got turned inside out, embarrassingly so. We were made to look like schoolboys. But that mistake never got mentioned in the changing-room afterwards. Everyone came over and congratulated me. Gérard was made up. Liverpool had lost 1–0, but the look in the manager's eyes told me how pleased he was with me. All the staff and players were going, 'Flipping

heck, your first home start and you did really well.'
When I first entered the dressing-room that night, my
mind was racked with doubts about whether I could
cut it as a top player after my Trial by Ginola. When
I walked out of the dressing-room at the end of the
evening, I knew I belonged. 'I can handle this,' I told
myself as I left Anfield.

First thing next morning, I almost broke the
world 100m record getting down the newsagent's. I
bought all the papers to see what they had written
about me. I checked the player ratings. Only nine out
of ten. Eff off! Where's my picture? Back page. Magic.
I craved being recognized. Walking down the street
and having people asking for my autograph was such
a buzz. Having my family make a fuss over me spread
my smile even wider. Fame was new to me, and I
couldn't get enough. More please! In the Liverpool
programme, there were pages on Steven Gerrard – 'the
new kid on the block'. I must have read the piece a
thousand times. Arrogance wasn't the reason; I just
loved all this recognition. If I got noticed in the street
or written up in the papers, I was delighted because it
meant I was doing all right on the pitch.

The praise didn't go to my head. I had the right people around me. Dad was brilliant, always making sure my new-found celebrity did not soften me or make me slacken off in training. 'Don't read all that,' Dad said when he saw me lounging around on the settee, flicking through newspapers. 'You've got training tomorrow. Make sure you play three or four games. You have done nothing.' Dad had one special piece of advice, which he kept reminding me of: 'Don't copy those players who have played 300 games and are starting to relax. Train and play as if it's your first ever game. Train and play as if it's the World Cup final. Learn. Never ease off.' Established players like Incey, Redknapp and Fowler would never have let that happen. If this new boy fresh from the Academy had got above his station, Incey would have hammered me straight back down.

I began to receive more and more attention in the papers – 'The local lad in the Liverpool engine room', 'Huyton's Hero', that sort of thing. Jamie, Robbie and Michael helped me handle the fame, and gave me tips on how to deal with dodgy questions in interviews. I just kept stressing how much I had to learn. Gérard deliberately made me room with Steve Staunton for the remainder of that season. He knew I would learn about being a proper pro from being around 'Stan'. We called him Stan because he looked like Stan Laurel.

Everyone at Anfield assisted me. Even Incey. I had some one-on-one chats with him, and got to know him. My perspective on him changed. I started to really like him. The memory of being terrified by him as a YTS disappeared, replaced with a feeling that he was all right. What had really altered was his view of me. After a few games, particularly the Celta Vigo match at Anfield, Incey realized I wasn't just a light-weight from the Academy. I could handle life among the heavyweights. Conversations with Incey really lifted me. Imagine it. Me talking to Paul Ince! One of my England heroes!

The season seemed like one long celebration for me. Liverpool were not enjoying the best of fortunes but I was loving just being part of the drama, good or bad. I was living the dream, playing against boyhood idols like Paul Gascoigne. I first bumped into Gazza when Middlesbrough visited Anfield in February

1999. More accurately, he bumped into me. There were thirty-six seconds on the clock and Gazza elbowed me. A full-whack right elbow straight in my left eye-socket. Off the ball. Bang. No reason at all. A gift from Gazza, my hero! Thanks, mate. I'd love to know the reason from Gazza. Maybe he heard I was doing all right, that people were talking about me as future England material, and he wanted to put me in my place. Maybe that elbow was a welcome to the big time. Bang. Clobber. My eye was throbbing. Boom, boom. I hadn't even touched the ball. It was a bit harsh.

'Right,' I shouted over at Gazza, 'is that how you want it?'

The next time he had the ball, I went in hard and fast like a steaming bull. I wanted to send him flying. No chance. I never got near him. He just turned sharply, like a matador, and swept the ball away, leaving me tackling thin air. Chasing Gazza was like trying to catch a ghost. Back I went again, this time winning the ball. Now it was Gazza after me. A game broke out within the game. Gazza closed me down dead quick, and I tried to slip the ball through his legs.

What the hell was I playing at? Trying to nutmeg one of the most skilful midfielders ever to play for England? I must be mad. I was so fired up by the challenge of taking on Gazza. 'Behave!' Gazza said. 'What are you up to?' Gazza stared at me and then added: 'You little runt!' Gazza was loving it. He knew he had wound me up.

After the game, Gazza strolled over, ruffled my hair and put his arm around me. 'You are a really good player,' he said. 'Keep going.' Unbelievable. I was still no-one at the time, third choice, a young kid fresh from the Academy. And there was Gazza going out of his way to congratulate me! Deep down, I think Gazza was happy with the way I reacted to his elbow. I never complained. I never hid. I just went looking for him. Unfortunately, I couldn't get near him.

I wore my black eye from Gazza like a medal won in battle. It meant the world to me to encounter him, however painfully. I wanted another memento, his shirt, but I was that intimidated. I was terrified of asking him. It must sound strange being in awe of someone you have just spent ninety minutes trying to smash to pieces, but that was the way I was with

Gazza. I grew up on his brilliance. I read his book. I bought his England shirt. His video, *Gascoigne's Glory*, was my prized possession. I must have watched it a million times. I used to watch that tape thinking, 'Oh my life, what a player.' It was a wonder the tape never wore out. Gazza at Italia 90. Gazza taking on the world. Skill, determination, cheeky smile. The whole package, the real deal. Gazza summed up everything I worshipped about football. He was the David Beckham of his day. I looked up to him so much.

When we collided at Anfield, I knew his career was on the downward slope. Of course, it was sad to see someone once so special on the decline. But just think about the career. Remember the good things about Gazza, the turns away from his marker, the dribbles and the fantastic goals. That free-kick in the FA Cup semi-final at Wembley in 1991 was like a rocket. His control and finish against Scotland at Euro 96. Gazza was a genius. Everyone said he was a wayward genius. I never used to believe the bad things I read about Gazza because I loved him so much. Black eyes apart, he was so good to me. I was fortunate enough to have some conversations with him when he was at Everton, living nearby, and he was top-class. On the pitch, he was always at it, slyly digging me in the ribs or trying to intimidate me. Off the pitch, Gazza was such a nice fella. He filled me with confidence. He praised bits of my game, and always asked me how things were going. I thought, 'Let me talk about you! I want to hear about Italia 90, Lazio, Spurs, everything!' When I was younger, Gazza's was the only autograph I craved. You see, Gazza lived the life I wanted: fame, fortune and England.

# 6
# England Calling

England obsessed me from my earliest days. Running around Ironside in my Gazza shirt, weaving past Huyton lads and sticking the ball between two dust-bins, I imagined it was the winning goal in the World Cup final. I pictured all the England fans leaping up, punching the air and screaming my name. 'Gerrard, Gerrard!' I saw myself mobbed by my England team-mates, celebrating the goal that brought the World Cup home. Pulling on the white shirt. Looking down and seeing the Three Lions crest over your heart. Walking out into a packed stadium, knowing the eyes of the country are on you. The adrenalin, the noise, the sweat, the glory. All of it. I wanted it big-style.

Countless obstacles were strewn across my path to senior international recognition. I had to fight my way to the top. First up, Lilleshall ignored me at U-15 level. England realized their mistake when I tore into the National School at Melwood. The season after that, when the England get-togethers started, I was straight in. I was soon involved with England U-16s, coming off the bench in a 4–0 rout of Denmark on 3 February 1996. That was me finally going, on the road to the England first team.

I will never forget my first U-16 start, seventeen days after that thrashing of Denmark. The stage was Lilleshall. The opposition was the Republic of Ireland. Midfield quickly became a battle zone against the Irish. I was up against Stephen McPhail, who was streets ahead of me. This was during my teenage years when I started growing fast. I needed to because I was really too small to compete in such daunting mid-fields. Apart from scoring England's first, I was awful. McPhail was a class apart. At least we won 2–1, with Phil Jevons netting the second. My first England start was a winning one. I was up and running.

I watched Euro 96 at home on the Bluebell Estate, cheering on Gazza, Alan Shearer and Teddy Sheringham. Wembley looked and sounded fantastic, packed with people waving banners and singing 'Football's Coming Home'. England treated the fans to some fabulous football, particularly in the 4–1 defeat of Holland. I so wanted to be there. I had just turned sixteen and I was desperate to reach the top.

I carried on up through the England age-groups, growing physically and developing technically. Come France 98, I sat transfixed in front of the TV at Ironside as my mate Michael took on the world. Go on, Michael! What a sight that was. A tireless trainer and relentlessly ambitious, Michael deserved his shot at World Cup glory. There had been a lot of speculation that Glenn Hoddle, the then England manager, might take Michael to France. His name was all over the press and on the telly. I was really buzzing for Michael to go. He was on the fringe of a few squads, then he scored against Morocco in Casablanca in one of the warm-up games. Suddenly, everyone talked about him starting. I so wanted him to be picked. Not only because he was a mate, but also because of what it meant for me. I played with Michael for so many years. If he was in with the England big boys, I must have a chance.

Those match nights were magical, extra special when Michael started, against Colombia and, famously, Argentina. I grabbed a bite of dinner and jumped on the sofa in front of the telly. I couldn't wait for kick-off, I was that excited. The Argentina game in St-Etienne was awesome. When Michael picked the ball up and began accelerating towards Carlos Roa's goal, pandemonium broke out in our front room. 'Trouble!' I shouted. 'If Michael gets you one-on-one with space behind you, you're history,' added Dad, almost as a warning to the Argentina defenders. Jose Chamot and Roberto Ayala had no chance. Too slow, too late. Michael was off and past them, racing into the history books and the hearts of a nation. I leapt up and down, screaming my head off, hugging Dad and Paul. I almost went hoarse shouting Michael's name. Yes! Get in! Brilliant, Michael!

I fell back in my seat and just tried to imagine how Michael's world was going to change. I looked across at Dad, who still had this massive smile on his face. He liked and respected Michael. Everyone did. 'What has Michael just done there?' I exclaimed. The camera focused on Michael, but he was concentrating on the game, as if he hadn't just struck one of the greatest goals in the history of football. 'That's him finished!' I laughed. 'That's his life changed. It's over for him now. He won't be able to do nothing. Imagine what it will be like when he comes back. It will take him days to get out of the airport there will be so many press and fans there.' I was so happy for my mate.

Michael's success made me believe even more I could make it. My own journey towards the England shirt I craved was assisted by Howard Wilkinson. During his time as technical director of the Football Association, Wilkinson looked after the U-18s and the U-21s and picked me regularly for both. He had a certain reputation. I knew that. Wilkinson was often slated for some of his management skills. True, he was a bit long-winded in team-talks. We wondered occasionally what the hell he was going on about. He often sounded like a school teacher addressing very young children. Howard also called team meetings when he didn't really need them. I don't care. People can snipe at Wilkinson if they want, but he was good to me and knew his football. I liked Wilkinson because he liked me. He always spoke well of me, always included me in his squads, always suggested things to improve my game. He even made me captain of England U-18s – a massive honour. All my family were so proud. We will always thank Howard for that. When I heard he got the U-21 job, I had half an idea that sooner or later the call would come for me to step up.

Throughout 1999 I was steadily making a name for myself in Liverpool's first team. One day in the late summer, a letter arrived from the FA. Finally calming my shaking hands, I ripped open the envelope. Inside were instructions to report for U-21 duty against Luxembourg on 3 September. Another rung up the ladder! Wilkinson must really have rated me because he started me in midfield. I repaid his faith by scoring after twelve minutes. We won 5–0, and there was a real buzz about the team.

Every English player knew the new season ended with Euro 2000. Every ambitious young player wanted to force himself into the thoughts of Kevin Keegan, the England manager. Whenever Keegan took his seat in the directors' box of a Premiership ground, all the English players on the pitch were aware of his presence, and determined to parade their abilities. I certainly felt under scrutiny. When Liverpool beat Coventry City 2–0 a week before Christmas, Keegan was there, watching me. When the U-21s then saw off Denmark, Keegan was there again, appraising me. I knew that. Howard marked my card. 'Do well and Kevin may call you up,' he told me. I never stopped running against Denmark.

I impressed for Liverpool in 1999/2000, scoring against Sheffield Wednesday and filling in all over the place. Right-back, left-back, right midfield, central midfield – no problem. Every challenge made me a better player. When Liverpool beat Leeds United 3–1 on 5 February, I bust my lungs stifling Harry Kewell, a real tricky winger. A week later I set up Titi Camara's winner at Highbury – a huge result for Liverpool. Arsenal are a class side, and Freddie Ljungberg almost scored. He rounded our keeper, Sander Westerveld, but I managed to get a tackle in to stop him. Victory came at a cost for me: I damaged my groin and had to walk off for some ice treatment.

About a week after that, Dad called. He could

barely speak he was so excited. 'Get on to Steve Heighway and Gérard Houllier quick,' he said. 'They have something to tell you.'

What the hell was going on? I rang Steve immediately. He had big news. 'Kevin Keegan wants you to go down to England to train with the squad before the game with Argentina,' Steve said. I couldn't believe my ears. Training with England? Gérard confirmed the news. England wanted me! 'Now, Steven, you have not been named in the squad, but you will be working with them,' warned Gérard. This was my chance. England! I was going to have a right go in training and convince Keegan to pick me for the friendly against Argentina on 23 February. Wembley. Full house. Argentina. Brilliant! Michael made his name against them, so why not me? Officially in the squad or not, I wasn't going down to England's base at Bisham Abbey just to train. I meant business.

The FA contacted Liverpool and offered to chauffeur me down to the team hotel at Burnham Beeches, a few miles from Bisham. But Dad lent me his Honda and I made my own way south because I was that nervous. At one point I thought there was something wrong with the car. I almost got out to check the noise until I realized it was me rattling. Getting so close to something I wanted so much filled me with self-doubt. Was I good enough? Let's turn round. Get back to Liverpool. Steve Heighway can call Keegan. Apologize. Gerrard's too nervous. Not ready. That would save me the embarrassment of looking an idiot in training. But I kept going. I had to conquer my insecurity, kill the panic attack. Go on. Drive through the gates of Burnham Beeches. Park the Honda. Don't hit the smart cars. Into reception. Up to your room.

I sat on the edge of the bed, knowing I had to report downstairs to Kevin in the dining room. The players were all eating. What do I do? I couldn't face the thought of walking into a room crammed full of my heroes. Alan Shearer, Tony Adams, David Beckham – world-famous names. How could this newcomer at Liverpool stroll calmly into the middle of the England dining room and coolly sit down next to Beckham? I had another panic attack. I phoned Jamie Redknapp, who was downstairs with the squad. 'Jamie,' I pleaded, 'I'm upstairs scared witless. Come and get me, please.' Jamie was brilliant. He quietly left the dining hall and sprinted to my room. 'Come on,' Jamie said. 'Keegan wouldn't have called you here unless he really rated you. Let's go.' The other Liverpool lads also came out, so we were all able to walk in together. Without the support of Jamie, Robbie, Macca and Michael, I would have spun on my heels and raced back north, back home, where I felt safe. With my club-mates by my side, I found the strength to enter the dining-room of Burnham Beeches.

Stepping through that doorway was still one of the most intimidating things I have ever done. Looking around the room, I caught my breath. Top players were everywhere; it was an autograph-hunter's paradise. 'What am I doing here?' I thought. 'Get me back to my room!' Somehow, I negotiated my way to the staff table.

Kevin Keegan looked up and smiled. 'Hi, Steven, welcome to England,' he said. He shook my hand, then stood up.

He was only going to address the whole room.

'Lads, stop eating and talking for a second,'

Keegan said. A host of household names looked up. Keegan pointed at me. 'This is Steven Gerrard. The kid will be training with us. He's a player. Don't be going easy with him because he certainly won't be going easy with you. He is going to be with you full-time very shortly.'

I squirmed from one foot to the other, my face as red as a Liverpool shirt. Shut up now, Kevin. Let them carry on eating. Forget about me. I'm nothing compared to all these superstars. They know of me, but these are heroes who have played in World Cups and had hundreds of career games. And Kevin Keegan was talking to them about me! I thought, 'What is going on here?' I felt every England player staring at me.

Thankfully, Keegan did stop. I retreated to a table with familiar Liverpool faces and sat down to a fantastic meal, but I couldn't eat. No chance. My stomach had space only for butterflies. Just the thought of food stirred a nausea inside. All I wanted in that England meal-room was an escape route. At least I was surrounded by club-mates. I heard and read about these cliques with England, how the tables were split up along club lines. Being in that meal-room confirmed it was true: tribal rivalry ruled.

The Liverpool boys took me round to all the other tables and introduced me to the rest of the squad. To David Seaman. 'David, this is Stevie.' To Sol Campbell. 'Sol, this is Stevie.' I was in a daze, shaking hands with some of the greatest footballers ever to represent England. I was unbelievably nervous. I have sweated less in games. The last table I visited belonged to Manchester United. Phil Neville, David Beckham, Andy Cole and Paul Scholes looked up and smiled at me. What the hell was going on? Shock-waves ripped through me. These people were supposed to be my enemy. I'm Liverpool. They're United. We don't smile at each other. We snarl. Growing up in Huyton, I was taught to loathe Manchester United, their fans, players, manager, kit-man, mascot, megastore workers – everyone associated with Old Trafford. But almost twenty years of being conditioned to hate Man U went up in smoke that day at Burnham Beeches. There I was, shaking hands with Beckham and Scholes, thinking, 'But they hate me and I hate them.' But they didn't hate me. They were brilliant at putting the new boy at ease. The United lads couldn't have been more welcoming. In fact, they were so nice I began to wonder about all this long-standing hatred.

Before coming down to Burnham, I talked to my mate Boggo about what it would be like seeing the United players. 'I am convinced in training the United lads will have a pop,' I told Boggo. 'They'll wind me up. Kick me. I'd love it to go off. United don't like Scousers, so they might kick me. I'll be on my toes.' I was ready to kick all of them. Scholes, Beckham, the lot. That misconception also disappeared in a flurry of handshakes and smiles.

Whether United or whoever, all Keegan's players greeted me really kindly. They treated me as if I were actually in the England squad and was in contention for the Argentina friendly. They couldn't do enough for me. After that first meal, I returned to my room at Burnham and flicked the telly on to kill some time before bed. After ten minutes, there was a knock at the door. Arsenal's huge centre-half Martin Keown stood there. 'I'm rooming next door,' said Martin. 'I know it's difficult with all the times for meals and trainings and meetings. People are always late. If you get stuck for the right time, just phone me. I know you are with the Liverpool lads, but I am next door. Just give me a knock if you're bored.' How good was that? Martin had won Premiership titles, he'd been to big tournaments, yet he was kind enough to help a new boy. I got to know Martin dead well straight away. What a top fella. Honest to God, Martin is probably one of the funniest men I have ever met.

I wasn't the only new boy at Bisham that week. Jonathan Woodgate, the young centre-half, had been doing really well at Leeds United so Keegan brought him down as well. Woody was the same as me on the bus going to Bisham, dead nervous, quiet and intimidated. Neither of us could believe we were on the England coach, heading off to practice with all our heroes. Keegan was so good to us on the way to Bisham. He stood up again and sang our praises to the players. Keegan talked about me again. 'Just wait till you see this little fella play!' The Liverpool players shouted back: 'We are with him every day!' When we arrived at Bisham, Keegan treated me and Woody like we were the best two players in the squad. How unreal was this? I was on the England training field, keeping a ball up in the air with Beckham and Shearer, and the media were out in force, filming us. I had a sneaky look to check where the cameras were to let the lads back home see me! Get on that telly! We then went into possession straight away, and that's when Keown began to put it about. I thought there would be some fireworks between the Liverpool and United lads, but it was physical all round. No chance of anyone taking it easy with a big match like Argentina coming up. People were getting right stuck in.

The possession was lightning quick, far quicker than at Liverpool. I never got anywhere near anyone. The session was too fast for me. 'Keep the ball, keep on your toes,' I kept telling myself. 'Concentrate.' It was tough, though. The skill and speed levels were nothing I had experienced before.

Even though I felt out of my depth, I was loving it. I wanted afternoon sessions, anything to get back out on the training ground. The next day, the training was even more incredible. I couldn't believe some of the things I saw at Bisham that day when we did some crossing and finishing. Shearer in the finishing – my life! Every one, top corner, keeper no chance. Bang, take that. All around, the quality was frightening. This was the first time I had seen Beckham cross a ball close to. When it was my turn to run in to finish one of Beckham's crosses, it was a goal before I touched it. He was that accurate. Beckham puts his crosses in just the right place; it is in fact harder to miss. We had a game after the crossing and finishing, and Beckham was again sensational. After only a couple of hours' training with England it was obvious who the top players were.

Back at Burnham after our first session, I counted down the hours and minutes until we returned to Bisham. I was so wired into training that I stupidly ignored a few little niggles in my back. On the bus going back to Burnham, I felt it stiffen a touch. If I had been at Liverpool, I would have mentioned it to the physios. But I was that scared to go to England's physios and tell them, 'Look, my back's sore.' The main England physio, Gary Lewin, is a top guy, but I just couldn't admit my problem, and there was no way I would have told Keegan. 'Forget it,' I said to myself. 'I'll just take a painkiller when I get back to the room.' I took two. Before the second practice, I gulped down another one.

I survived that second session, but the pain deepened. I called Dad.

'What shall I do?' I asked him.

'Just make them aware of it,' he replied.

'Dad, I can't, because they might send me home.'

I sat in my room, in tears of frustration. I had to make a decision. Eventually, I went in to see Lewin. He called Kevin down to the medical room and explained the situation. 'Listen, Steven,' said Keegan. 'We have got to be careful with you because of Liverpool. If we let you continue, it gets worse, and you miss games, we would get into trouble with Liverpool. Let the physio and doctor have a look, miss the session, and we'll see how you are.' Keegan then went off and phoned Gérard Houllier.

'Get him back here,' said Gérard.

Keegan came to my room and broke the news. My England dream was on hold. 'Listen, I am under strict orders to get you back to Anfield,' Keegan said. 'But you have done well. Keep doing what you are doing. I will be watching you. Hopefully, next time when you come back it will be as a proper squad member.'

When Keegan left the room, I collapsed in tears.

A sense of devastation overwhelmed me. I returned to Anfield with a sore back and a heavy heart and they immediately sent me off for a scan. My back really troubled me from then on. Now, if I feel something in training, I go straight off. I don't take risks.

The problem having eased temporarily, I launched myself back into games. England still occupied my thoughts: the door remained open to Euro 2000. The biggest U-21 international that season was the Euro play-off against Yugoslavia on 29 March, in Barcelona. This was serious stuff, with qualification for the European U-21 Championship at stake. England had to win. The papers were full of talk about the tie. Everyone speculated over who would be in Wilkinson's party, as if it were the senior squad. Keegan announced he would be watching the Barcelona game closely for any likely young lads to take to the big show in Holland and Belgium that summer. Some incentive.

Good as gold, Wilkinson picked me in the squad. When the list of names came through the post, I thought, 'This is a proper U-21 squad.' Players like Rio Ferdinand and Jamie Carragher had racked up loads of Premiership games. The squad was packed with names who wouldn't have looked out of place in Keegan's full squad. All of us youngsters who flew out to Spain felt this was a ninety-minute audition for Euro 2000. After settling into our Barcelona hotel, we engaged in a final training session that was sharp and full-on. Everyone was up for this. And the quality of the players there was frightening. Sitting down for dinner that night at a table with Lee Hendrie, Kieron Dyer, Frank Lampard and Ferdinand, I was too scared to talk. These lads were serious players. I felt an apprentice in comparison. My experience of top-level football ran to a few first-team outings for Liverpool and a handful of U-21 matches. I knew my place.

The mood mellowed a bit as the trip went on. My nerves began to disappear. I became increasingly involved in the banter, while guarding against appearing cocky. In my heart, I still didn't feel I belonged with England. I knew I had done well against Luxembourg and scored, and I'd played in U-21 wins against Poland and Denmark, but a play-off against Yugoslavia was a proper game. Everyone was talking about it. I never expected to start. So I was shocked when Wilkinson told us the team after dinner. My name was among the eleven chosen ones.

As the meeting broke up, Howard sat me down for a quick chat, basically to mark my card. 'Tomorrow is a very important game for you,' he told me. 'The top people are going to be studying you. This is the game to perform in. Kevin Keegan is particularly looking to see how you do. He's watched you before. There's a possible place up for grabs in the Euro 2000 squad. Go get it, Steven.'

Music to my ears! A ticket to Belgium and Holland!

I walked back to my room, lay on the bed and tried to get my head around the size of the challenge hurtling towards me. My mobile rang. It was Dad. As usual, he called to wish me good luck and to remind me to seize my chance.

'I'm starting tomorrow, Dad,' I told him.

'Well, Steven, this really is the game you've got to deliver in.'

It sounded like a warning. The stakes were that high. Sky's cameras would be rolling live. Keegan would be taking notes and looking for names. Could

I handle the pressure? But then I remembered a saying Dad loved to tell me: 'Big players come into their own in big games.' And I wanted the big time.

I smiled to myself. I couldn't wait to get to the stadium.

I almost ran there the moment morning dawned. The game was held next door to Camp Nou, at Barcelona's reserve-team ground. Wilkinson fielded a strong team, lining up 3–5–2 in front of Richard Wright in goal.

Glancing around the dressing-room, I was thrilled by the wall-to-wall talent. Defenders of the quality of Carra and Rio were slipping their shin-pads on, ready for battle. Juggling a ball in one corner was Kieron Dyer, buzzing with energy; he was an amazing performer in training out there. Midfield comprised me, Lampard and Lee Hendrie. We all knew how good Lampard was. Everyone had seen him shine for West Ham. And Hendrie was probably the best young midfielder around at the time. In training, he was the busiest, the cleverest, a good kid as well. Up front, we had Andy Campbell and Emile Heskey. We won 3–0, and the game went brilliantly for me. Dad told me later that on Sky, Ray Wilkins said I played really well, which was a great compliment coming from a former England midfielder. The press lads all gave me decent write-ups, too. My career started moving quicker after that game.

Keegan watched me more and more. One day, in the middle of May, I was walking through Liverpool city centre with Dad when my mobile went. 'Private Number' came up on the screen. I pressed the green answer button.

'Steven? It's Kevin Keegan,' came a voice.

I didn't believe him. 'Yeah,' I replied, 'good one, whatever. Go on then.'

I was convinced it was mates stitching me up. Probably Boggo. But the bloke on the line kept talking, and I got a bit worried. If it's not Keegan, they have got his accent in the bag, absolutely spot-on. How do I play this?

'I am calling you up for the game against Ukraine,' the voice said.

It was possible. I had been playing well for Liverpool, and I remembered the last words Kevin said to me: 'It won't be long before you are in the full squad.' So I decided to go with the flow – act normal; don't let on any suspicions – even if I eventually had the mickey taken out of me. Dad looked at me, wondering what the hell was going on. I walked away. If it was a wind-up, I didn't want him witnessing my embarrassment.

Two minutes into the conversation I was sure it was Keegan. It couldn't be a hoax. This bloke knew too much stuff about the squad and about the FA staff who organize the travel. It had to be Kevin. But even when the caller signed off with a cheery 'see you at Bisham', I still wasn't 100 per cent certain. Fortunately, a couple of hours later someone from Melwood phoned to say they had an FA fax confirming I was in the squad. Until then, I had been waiting for a mate to ring, laughing. 'Ha, ha, it was a wind-up!' The next day, I got a text off the England team administrator, Michelle Farrer, giving me details about meeting up. Keegan then announced the squad officially. That phone call had been a call-up, not a wind-up.

Stories stating I would start against Ukraine on 31 May kept appearing in the newspapers. 'Don't believe none of that,' Dad urged. 'Just keep doing what you are doing in training. Until you're told, keep playing for a starting place.' On the Monday, two days before the game, Keegan pulled me during training at Bisham. We were doing some shape work, tactical pattern-of-play stuff. 'Come Wednesday, don't do that, do this,' said Keegan, indicating a position he wanted me to keep. His words stopped me in my tracks. Had Keegan just dropped a big hint there that I might be involved? I pretended I never heard it. Me? Starting for England? The possibility still seemed unreal.

I phoned Dad the moment I got back to my room at Burnham. 'I might be playing some part, Dad, for England!' I said. 'The gaffer talked me through a move he wanted me to do on Wednesday!'

Dad got a bit buzzing, but then played it down. 'Take no notice of it. Keegan might just have slipped up, or not meant it.'

So I got on with training the next day, giving my all.

Distractions blew into Burnham on the Tuesday. It was my twentieth birthday, and I certainly got given the special treatment by the England lads. The day started off nicely. Burnham's chef did a cake. I got up and blew the candles out as all the lads shouted 'Speech, speech!' I went red and sat back down sharpish. It was all really friendly. Afterwards, we all went off to Bisham. With England, you leave your doors open. We have the hotel to ourselves, so no problem. No-one would break in. So I just wandered out of my room and didn't think twice about locking the door. When I came back from training, I almost died. My room had been trashed good and proper. It looked as if a hundred kids had enjoyed a wild birthday party in there. Toothpaste was everywhere, over the mirror, my bed, the table. 'Happy birthday' was smeared in toothpaste on the wall.

I've always suspected the mischievous hand of Robbie Fowler behind my trashed room, but I got a much better present from someone else to make sure my twentieth birthday was certainly memorable. After training, Keegan tapped me on the shoulder and said, 'Are you looking forward to tomorrow night?'

'Yeah, I can't wait.'

He then looked me in the eye and said, 'You're starting.'

I almost fainted! These were the words I had dreamed of hearing. Starting! For England!

'Thanks, boss, I won't let you down.'

Keegan went off to announce the news to the media. They immediately demanded to see me in the big press tent outside Burnham. Interest was massive in the England new boy. I couldn't escape. I was terrified. I nearly had to put a nappy on to do that interview.

The FA's press officer, Adrian Bevington, told me not to worry as we headed towards the battery of cameras, microphones and notebooks. Don't worry? A bit late! 'They'll go easy on you,' said Adrian. It was like being led to the wolves and told to relax because they had already eaten once today. I couldn't believe how many journalists were waiting for me. More than a hundred, I guess, although I didn't really want to look up and count properly. I sat down and tried to handle the questions as best I could.

I managed finally to slip out but immediately ran into another ambush, this time by photographers. They swarmed around me, clicking away. Eventually, Bevington imposed some order and me and Keegan posed for a picture with an England cap. My first cap.

I couldn't wait for the game to start. All the fussing about and official stuff in the build-up to an international wound me up. I was relieved to get back from the media village. I had only been out of my room for ten minutes but I had ten missed calls and a load of text messages. The word was out. I was starting. Sorting out tickets for family and friends was a nightmare. So many people wanted to come to Wembley. It broke me up having to tell a few I couldn't get them tickets. 'Hopefully, there will be another time,' I said, crossing my fingers. I didn't want to go over the top, promising there would be another game.

Ukraine's visit was a night match, so the lads killed time before kick-off sleeping in their rooms at Burnham. That shocked me. How could players calmly kip hours before going into battle for England? I sat in my room, rattling, on the phone, trying to pass the time away. Eventually we were on the coach to Wembley, people shouting messages of good luck and sticking their thumbs up as we passed. This was just a friendly. Just imagine the atmosphere for a full-on

World Cup tie. Kick-off was more than two hours away, but the fans were flooding into Wembley, tens of thousands of them. Groups of blokes. Fathers and sons. All chanting 'England!' Young boys, eyes shining in anticipation, had their faces painted with the flag of St George. Their exhilaration intensified my own excitement. It was only Ukraine, only a friendly, but the sense of expectation was incredible. England have always mattered to me, and as I looked through the coach window at all the fans, I began to realize how much the England team meant to the nation. These people loved England with a passion. I resolved then to never, ever let them down.

Nothing could have prepared me for the atmosphere when I crossed the threshold into the home dressing-room at Wembley. Of course, I had experienced the Liverpool dressing-room where determination hung in the air, an emotion so real you could almost stretch out a hand and touch it. But with England I couldn't believe the atmosphere. The mood stepped up big-time over Anfield. What a special place! Some of Keegan's players, like Sol Campbell, sat there quietly, undergoing familiar pre-match routines that have served them so well for so long. Others, like Robbie and Macca, were chatting and laughing, behaving as if it were a normal game at Liverpool. For a while it was pretty restrained, just a few words from Keegan and his assistants Derek Fazackerley and Arthur Cox. But as kick-off approached, the players talked louder and louder, the mood rising to fever pitch. Battle-cries began. Each player was made to feel that nothing else in his life would ever matter as much as this. Club affiliations and expectations were irrelevant. Shout after shout. This is England. Our country. Millions watching. Don't let them down. Don't miss a tackle. Don't give the ball away. Every eye is on us. Make sure you deliver.

The noise was unbelievable. In the middle of the dressing-room stood Alan Shearer and Tony Adams, whipping up the storm. Changing-rooms are always loud, but Adams and Shearer cranked the volume up to a different level. Shearer was getting everyone going, standing there like a warrior preparing for combat, screaming at his fellow soldiers. Adams was going around the room bawling at players individually. I was so hyped up I almost couldn't tie my laces. Let me at Ukraine. Where are they? Bring it on.

Ukraine must have heard us. The racket coming out of the England dressing-room was so loud it could have been heard in Kiev, let alone down the corridor. Even Gareth Southgate, such a calm, cultured individual by day, stirred up the players, sending the decibel level rocketing higher. My admiration for senior pros like Southgate, Adams and Shearer doubled that day. I knew they were great players, but this showed me why they ascended to the pinnacle of their trade.

The referee, Lubos Michel, rang the bell to call us to the tunnel. Walking up the Wembley tunnel was special. I saw the light at the end, heard the crowd going crazy, and was almost knocked over by the wall of noise as I emerged onto the pitch. Wembley is the best place I have ever played at. It's the history that makes it unique. I know they've rebuilt the stadium now and demolished landmarks like the Twin Towers, but it will always be Wembley, the Venue of Legends. I have watched so many finals from there on television, and attended many games there. For a lad from Huyton, Wembley was like the promised land. To play at Wembley for Liverpool or England, that is huge. Looking around at the stadium and all the fans, I was just in awe as I lined up for the national anthem. Standing shoulder to shoulder with England team-mates for the first time, I felt so proud singing 'God Save the Queen'. But there was serious work to do.

The moment Michel blew the whistle for the first time, I immediately learned that international football was a real step up from the Premiership. I sat in mid-field with Macca and Scholesy pushing on in a 3–5–2. And, boy, was I busy. Technically, the Ukrainians were a lot better than us. Their strikers, Andrei Shevchenko and Sergei Rebrov, were different class, at the time one of the most potent partnerships in the world. When we watched the tapes before the game, Keegan picked them out as Ukraine's dangermen. They kept dropping off Southgate, Adams and Campbell so I had to pick them up. Shevchenko and Rebrov were very good, always keeping the ball, particularly Shevchenko. When I got near them, I was dead wary. They had touches and skills that could make a fool of anyone rushing in. But I did all right, and grew in confidence. It felt fantastic, charging around Wembley, spraying passes to world stars like Beckham and tackling class operators like Shevchenko. My spirits lifted even higher when we took the lead through Robbie, and then Tony added another.

With nine minutes remaining and victory secured, Keegan replaced me with Kieron Dyer. As I walked off, I glanced back and memorized the image of Shevchenko standing there. I had shared a pitch with the great Shevchenko! It was a dream. Mad. Afterwards, a soggy pile of Ukraine shirts were delivered to our dressing-room. I picked out the one belonging to the fella who used to play right-back for Arsenal, Oleg Luzhny. I gave it to my dad. I sent my shirt to the Ukrainians and kept another. I wanted a personal souvenir of my England debut. It's upstairs at home, on display in a special room.

After the game, I was quickly on the phone, ringing friends and family. I just wanted to talk about the incredible scenes in the dressing-room beforehand. So many positive emotions raced through my mind as I walked out of Wembley that May night. Elation at a

2–0 win. Pride that my parents were watching and listening as the England fans clapped me off. A sense of relief as well. For this was by far the hardest game I had ever experienced.

The match flashed by in a blur. Mentally and physically I was shattered. But deeply happy. I knew I had been in a battle where wits and stamina were tested by the very best. And I survived. I knew Keegan was impressed. Euro 2000 beckoned.

# 7
## Love and Hate in Spa

Homesickness ruined Euro 2000 for me. Uncertainty crept into my mind shortly after we left home, and it grew during a stop-over in Malta, where England played a warm-up match on 3 June. Valletta seemed a beautiful place with lovely weather, but I was not in the mood to take in the scenery. An Achilles problem had flared up, ruling me out of the game and casting doubt over my fitness for the start of Euro 2000. At the time I didn't realize my moodiness was actually homesickness; I thought it was frustration over the Achilles. When I was eventually able to resume training, I brightened up a bit.

I checked into the England hotel near Spa in Belgium eager to get stuck into practice. I was excited at arriving for such a big tournament, no question about that, yet still I couldn't shake off this depression. What the hell was wrong with me? I was living every man's dream, competing against the best players in Europe for a fabulous prize. So many huge names were out there: Thierry Henry, Alessandro del Piero, all of the continent's big guns. Euro 2000 seemed the perfect stage for me to perform on, yet I wanted to fly home to 10 Ironside Road, Huyton, where I felt secure. This tournament was the first occasion I had been away from my family for any amount of time. Holidays and football trips had separated me from my family before, but only for a week. Seven days cut off from my family I could handle; Euro 2000 was different. Five weeks away sounded to me like a prison sentence.

My stomach was a mess. I desperately wanted to get back to Mum, Dad and Paul. To familiar surroundings. Friends. Neighbours. Relatives. I longed for all that again. Watching Mum get the tea. Talking to Dad and Paul. I hated being away. At home, I felt safe. I sat in a chair in my room in Spa, stared out of the window at that dark forest and wanted to scream for help.

At first, I couldn't bring myself to tell Mum and Dad when I rang home every evening. Embarrassment stopped me. 'Oh yeah, everything's fine, it's brilliant out here,' I would say. And it should have been. I was a professional footballer earning good money and privileged enough to represent my country. I was surrounded by good guys in the squad, players I could share a laugh and a joke with, friends like Michael Owen whom I had known for more than ten years. Kevin Keegan was always brilliant with me. Kevin had taken a gamble in picking a young, untried midfielder for Euro 2000. I was lucky. Everyone back in England would have jumped at the chance to swap places. Homesick? Grow up. Get a grip. But I just couldn't shake the feeling.

One night, I confessed all to Mum. 'I don't want to be here,' I told her. 'I just want to be home with you. I get feelings in my stomach. I can't sleep. I want to be home.'

Mum and Dad were obviously concerned. They care so deeply for me and Paul. But they didn't want me to do anything rash and ruin all I had worked for. Dad came on the line. 'Steven, you are missing nothing here,' he said. 'If you come back for a day or two, you would want to go to Spa. Enjoy it.'

'I am enjoying it, Dad. I'm loving it. I want to be here, but I also want to come home. I don't know how long for, but I want to come home.'

'Do you want to mention it to the manager?' Dad asked.

'No,' I replied firmly. How could I? After one cap, I could hardly go knocking at Kevin's door, saying, 'Listen, boss, I'm homesick.' He might bounce me out for good. Euro 2000 had not even officially started, so I was worried Kevin would replace me with a stand-by player. Persevering was the only answer, and focusing on the tournament.

Homesickness is a part of me that will never go away. I still feel homesick at times. I endured a bad couple of days at Euro 2004 in Portugal. I'm prone to the blues when I travel. I am a home person. Fact. If I wasn't a footballer I wouldn't go away from home for two months. I hate being on my own. Hate it.

It's strange, I know. At tournaments, two emotions run through me: happiness and sadness. Even with the shadow of homesickness at Euro 2000,

I was still buzzing. Friends called, told me how lucky I was, how made up they were to see me selected for England. For all my gloom, I was still delighted to be in Spa. I was experiencing a world most people aspired to.

Before we left England, the sense of excitement gripping the country was inescapable. Flags fluttered outside houses and in the back of vans. England stickers appeared everywhere. Newspapers were bursting with page after page of build-up coverage. I was desperate to be part of it. When Keegan named his final squad shortly after the Ukraine game on 31 May, I was blown apart to be included. I thought I had missed too many games. No chance, surely? Yet there was Keegan, reading out my name among real stars such as Alan Shearer, David Beckham, Tony Adams and Paul Scholes. After only eighty-one minutes on the pitch for England, I was off to the European Championship in Holland and Belgium!

For all my problems, Spa was good. Kevin and the FA made sure we had plenty to occupy ourselves with back at the hotel: there were pool and table tennis tables, an arcade packed with computer games, pitch and putt, eighteen-hole golf, the works. We lacked for nothing. No expense was spared by the FA. Along with all the entertainment laid on by the FA, the players organized race nights, Macca and Robbie strutting about as if they were at Aintree. A card school also formed, sharpish. Kevin joined in with the players at the back of the bus. Press criticism of Kevin for being involved in the card school was ridiculous. His approachability was good management, not a sign of weakness. He opened up to the players, and they opened up back. I prefer a manager to be sociable rather than stand-offish; a cold, distant coach would have intimidated me. Kevin was straight and honest and always open. He acted like a father figure to me during Euro 2000.

Despite my inhibitions, Kevin's upbeat personality meant everyone mixed around the camp, and I was slowly drawn into the England family. It wasn't cliquey at all. I would be walking down the corridor and Gary Neville would pull me in for a game of pool – Liverpool v. United, but with cues, and smiles. I spoke to all the players during the tournament. Initially, I was wary of Dennis Wise, but during the

**The Future is Red** I'm staying with Liverpool.

*Above*: **Digging for victory** Here I am, aged two and a half, playing with my brother Paul, five.

*Left*: **First team bib** me at six months

*Below*: **Blond ambition** I loved being in Paul's company.

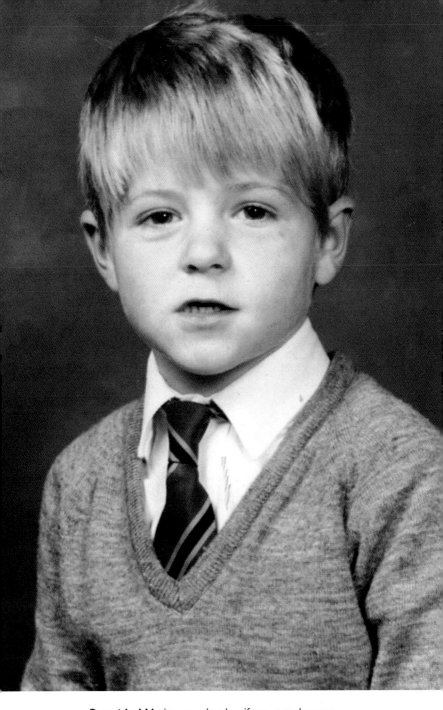

**Smart lad** Me in my school uniform, aged seven.

**That winning feeling** When the older lads were winning Dave Shannon (*left*) and Hughie McAuley (*right*) let me and Michael Owen soak up the atmosphere.

*Opposite page from the top*:
**In the middle of it** Dave Shannon (*back left*) was there from the beginning, I'm right at the centre of the middle row. Frank Skelly from the Academy is on the far right.

**On the ball** training at Melwood was a dream come true.

**Raising the bar** Dave Shannon made me want to be the best.

**Surrounded by class** Steve Heighway (*on the left*) with Michael Owen, Dave Shannon (*with me in the middle*) and Hughie McAuley (*on the right*) took care of the Melwood lads.

**Young dreams** Me and Michael Owen, looking good in our England Under-15 blazers.

**My Two Loves, Family and Liverpool**
Lilly-Ella meets the Anfield crowd in 2004.

*Above*: **Three lionesses** Alex Curran has changed my world, settling me down and giving me two beautiful daughters.

**Home fixture** my mum loves looking after my girls.

**Helping Hand** Gérard Houllier was my manager, mentor and father figure at Liverpool.

**Team-mates And Soul-mates** Jamie Carragher and I share a passion for lifting Liverpool to great heights.

Above: The Treble, Step One Beating Birmingham City's Stan Lazaridis to win the Worthington Cup in 2001.

Above: The Treble, Step Two Me, Danny Murphy and Robbie Fowler celebrate the FA Cup final win over Arsenal.

Left: The Treble, Step Three Shooting to fulfil, I batter Alaves' defence in the UEFA Cup final.

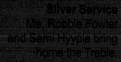

Silver Service
Me, Robbie Fowler and Sami Hyypia bring home the Treble.

I'LL NEVER WALK ALONE

tournament he too opened up with everyone and was good company. No-one, however famous, was off-hand with a newcomer like me.

I was still scared stiff of Shearer. If I came down from my room and England's celebrated captain was at the dinner table, I would avoid sitting by him. I was that intimidated. During my YTS days, all the talk was of 'Shearer, Shearer, Shearer' and 'Fowler, Fowler, Fowler'. Luckily for me, I worked with Robbie at Liverpool so I knew him; I gradually shed my fear in his company. Shearer was different. He was an idol to me when I arrived at Spa. No-one possessed his aura. When he marched into a room, everyone stopped what they were doing and looked. He just has this phenomenal presence. During Euro 2000, I discovered what a terrific bloke he is, as well as a magnificent centre-forward. No airs or graces. No big 'I Am'. A typical Geordie, so welcoming and friendly. He kept telling me to sit down for a chat. Eventually I plucked up enough courage to join the great man. 'Are you all right?' he enquired. 'Are you enjoying the trip? How's Liverpool?' Shearer's public image is of some-one hugely competitive on the pitch but quiet off it.

On TV, he comes across as a serious person. Meeting him properly surprised me. Shearer was fantastic with me, telling jokes, talking about everything, trying to make me feel at home. Top man.

Hanging out with Shearer, playing pool with Gary Neville, listening to the craic at the card schools – it seemed a perfect way to relax. Spa should have been paradise, but as I said, it felt like hell at times. As well as the homesickness, I just couldn't shake off a feeling of insecurity at being surrounded by superstars. I didn't feel comfortable knocking on the door of a household name who had won titles and cups and saying, 'Do you fancy a game of table tennis?' I waited to be asked.

Thankfully, Aston Villa's Gareth Barry had made the trip too. Each player had his own room, but mine had a shared living-room. None of the other players wanted it so Kevin allocated it to me and Gareth as the new boys. Our bedrooms opened out into this living-room, and it worked out well. Gareth became a really good mate of mine at Euro 2000, and has been ever since. We just clicked. Like me, Gareth was shy and frightened by the big names in the England squad.

He too comes across really quiet, but from rooming with him I know his banter is good. I found him excellent company. We played pool and table tennis, and went down to meals together. It was like we were married! Everyone knows what a terrific player Gareth is. I remember him doing some crosses from the left in training and even the senior England players were saying to each other, 'That Gareth Barry is class.' Keegan always checked on the two of us, making sure we were part of the party.

Kevin's assistant, Arthur Cox, was also different class with me. So were three of the other guys Kevin called into the camp, Nigel Spackman, Peter Beardsley and Kenny Swain. These three were good football men who understood how newcomers like me and Gareth could be prey to nerves. Without Nigel, Peter and Kenny, my homesickness would have been far worse. They weren't really part of the coaching staff, so I could open up to them, almost as if they were friends. When we were in the swimming pool or the Jacuzzi, or playing table tennis, I would confess that I was struggling to settle in. Nigel, Peter and Kenny became my confidants; their support was both immense and genuine. 'Chin up,' Nigel would say. 'How you doing?' Peter would chip in. 'Fancy some pool?' Kenny might add. They were like three brothers protecting me. As well as encouragement, these respected former pros pointed out things in my game I needed to improve. Even in our short time together in Spa, Nigel, Peter and Kenny made me a better person and a better player. I'm for ever grateful to them.

They helped me to push the homesickness to the back of my mind. I wanted to give myself a chance of looking forward to the games. I was desperate to force my way into England's starting eleven, so I really got stuck into training at Spa.

Even though I was making my mark in Spa, and coming out of my shell a tiny bit more every day, I knew I had no chance of starting England's first game, against Portugal in Eindhoven on Monday, 12 June. Paul Ince was the man of steel in our midfield. He had a calf problem for the game against the Ukraine, but now he was fit, and he was well established in the side. Whenever he pulled on the Three Lions, Incey was brilliant, shifting up a gear from his Liverpool form.

He was my hero. Incey had the job I craved with Liverpool and England: tackle, kill, pass. My ambitions were obvious to him, but he was still as good as gold with me around the England camp. Even when he moaned at me, I felt he was helping me. Anyway, Incey knew he was top dog. Keegan might have rated me, but he wasn't stupid. He was never going to put an untested kid in against the likes of Luis Figo, Rui Costa and João Pinto ahead of an experienced international like Incey. No chance.

I was on the pitch before kick-off, warming up with the rest of the England squad. The stadium was packed out, but I caught a glimpse of Dad in the crowd. The FA had set up a scheme whereby friends and families could fly in and out; the cost was deducted from our match fees, and it was worth every penny to have Dad's reassuring presence in Eindhoven. Sneaking a look around to check if Keegan or any of the other coaches was looking, I sprinted over dead quick and shook his hand. 'Good luck,' he said, in case I came on. I knew I wouldn't.

I sat on the bench and watched the game. When Scholesy and Macca put England 2–0 up within twenty minutes, I was buzzing. England were up and running, playing like they owned the tournament.

Then it all turned sour, like a runner leading a race suddenly encountering quicksand. England began to sink. Suddenly, we couldn't cope with Portugal's clever passing. Figo was outstanding. What a player! What a leader! The Portuguese refused to give up. They simply would not be led that last step to their execution. So they went for us, turning the tables. I couldn't believe my eyes. It didn't make sense. We had the game sewn up. We had the players. Shearer, Owen, Beckham. The belief was there, but it just went. The confidence drained away as if someone had pulled the plug. Even the great Tony Adams, the rock on which England teams had been built for so long, made a mistake. England's jugular was exposed, and Portugal went for it. Figo and João Pinto made it 2–2 by the break and we knew the second half promised only more torture. The fire had gone out of Keegan's players. On the hour, Nuno Gomes got the winner, and Portugal's celebrations sounded like a nail being driven into a coffin. Nightmare.

Devastated, the players crept back to the dressing-room. Keegan had a little go. 'You cannot give away the lead, you cannot make defending errors,' he said. 'But the tournament's not over. We can get back into it.' Kevin couldn't say too much. No-one could. Everyone was shellshocked. I sat in the corner, telling myself how glad I was that I hadn't played. That game was a bit too big for me. When a team like Portugal turn on the power, it's like being run over by a juggernaut. The old doubts came racing back: could I cut it at this level? Good players, stars I had watched and admired week in, week out in the Premiership, were sitting there almost motionless. This wasn't a dressing-room, this was a morgue.

Slowly, life began to pump through those shattered bodies again. Some began to move towards the showers, as if to wash away the trauma. Keegan's coaches started to go round, Cox and Fazackerley having quiet words with each player individually. It was not a time for lectures or long speeches, just a few words about what the player had done right or wrong. Gary Lewin, the physio, tended to strains and bruises. Nothing, though, could heal the wounds Portugal had just inflicted.

Becoming invisible seemed the most diplomatic

move. I shrank into the corner. I hated intruding on private grief, although it was my pain as well: I was desperate for England to do well at Euro 2000. Nerves were so exposed that I didn't talk to anyone. I didn't even offer consoling words to my Liverpool friends, for fear of getting my head bitten off. Up until then, I had just played a few games. Football, to me, was fun. If I lost, yeah it was bad, but I got on with it. But this England embarrassment was serious. Defeat is sport's version of death.

It was time to leave. We filed out to the coach, resembling a line of captured prisoners as we walked, heads down, to the bus. As we hit the road to Spa, Keegan sat down briefly with me and Gareth Barry. 'I hope you are learning from all this,' he said. 'Watch the opposition. Learn. You will both be involved in this tournament somewhere down the line.' 'Yeah,' I thought, 'as if.' I was convinced I was just there to make the numbers up. Still, I would have loved just one minute on the pitch to say I had played in a major tournament for England. The next game was against Germany, the enemy. I prayed Keegan would give me a chance.

The feeling about England's game with Germany on 17 June in Charleroi was simple: do or die. Our loss to Portugal meant the lads were up for the match even more. All around the hotel, groups of players met and talked about our date with destiny. The pressure was on big-time. Everyone knew what was riding on this: our place in Euro 2000, our reputations even. The whole country would be thrown into depression if we lost to Germany. All the players understood this was a fixture like no other, almost a derby match.

I never thought Keegan would risk me in Charleroi. The stakes were too high, surely? A must-win game against opponents like Germany was no place for a kid. Keegan put me on the bench again. Before kick-off, I bumped into my Liverpool team-mate Didi Hamann, and we had a chat. He was starting for Germany but still had time for a word of encouragement for me.

I settled back to watch the match. Even while I was doing my warm-ups in the first half and during the break, I never thought I would feature. Eight minutes after the break, Shearer scored. Game on!

The Euro 2000 dream was back on. England were back in business. But could we hold on? Germany would not go down without a fight. Keegan whispered something to Derek Fazackerley, who turned and shouted at me: 'Go and get warmed up. Really warmed up.' This was it. None of the other sub midfielders had been ordered down the touchline. I had to be coming on.

I warmed up like a madman, getting every sinew and muscle ready. Then the moment came for Keegan to let me loose. Michael Owen's number went up – a brave move by the manager. Michael can make a goal out of nothing, but Keegan wanted to sit on the 1–0 lead. I stood on the touchline, flicking up a boot behind me to let the linesman check my studs. Butterflies danced in my stomach. I had played for Keegan only once, in a friendly. What was he putting me on for in a competitive match as crucial as this? 'I don't need this,' I was thinking. Sensing my unease, Kevin put his arm round me and said, 'Just do what you do for Liverpool. Be disciplined. Keep the ball for us. Break up Germany's attacks, because they are starting to come on to us a bit.' Kevin paused then.

His next comment will stay with me for ever: 'Steven, enjoy it as well.'

Enjoy it? I was about to step into a storm for my competitive debut against the team England loathed most, and Kevin was telling me to treat it like a stroll in the park! Unbelievable. But that was fantastic man-management by Kevin. To tell a nervous kid to enjoy himself in such a serious situation was inspired.

The Germans had a good team, class from back to front. Oliver Kahn – one of the best keepers in the history of football. Defenders of real quality in Markus Babbel, Jens Nowotny and Christian Ziege. Legends like Lothar Matthaus. Big target-man in Carsten Jancker. Tricky playmakers like Mehmet Scholl. 'Get tight to Scholl,' Kevin had told me. 'Stop Scholl.' I knew all about the Bayern Munich man. I hadn't been expecting to play, but I'd still watched the tapes to learn who Germany's dangermen were. Sitting in the team meeting, I'd day-dreamed about how much I would love to test myself against Scholl. Now was the time to put theory into practice. I immediately put a big tackle in on him. He was class, so I tackled him again. And again. No doubt about it, this was an exceptional German side that would not go quietly.

Certainly not with Didi in their midst. I knew Didi too well to believe Germany would surrender tamely. That's not Didi's way. He gives everything, and then some more, drawing from a well of resilience few other pros have. I have always watched Didi, picking up little tips to improve me and I was gutted when he left Liverpool in 2006. My admiration for him as a man grew during my twenty-nine minutes in opposition to him in Charleroi. After my first few passes, Didi ran past and said, 'Keep doing what you are doing.' Unbelievable. I was stunned. We were sworn enemies until the referee's final whistle, representing rival countries in a vital game with half the world tuned in. Yet here he was, helping me. Incredible. Germany themselves had so much riding on the game. They had drawn their first match, with Romania, and were trailing here. Yet even in the heat of battle, Didi was prepared to think about me, a young club-mate struggling not to sink in unfamiliar international waters. Didi could see in my face that I was sweating, nervous and panicky.

When the ball next went out of play, I turned to him.

'I am bricking myself here, mate,' I said. 'I'm terrified.'

Didi looked at me. 'Relax, Stevie,' he said. 'Just do what you do normally.'

Didi's kindness to an opponent that evening showed he was a real mate. As long as I live, I will never forget our exchange of words in Charleroi.

I still wanted to thrash his team though. No amount of generosity of spirit from Didi could dull my desire to run Germany out of town. A couple of minutes after my chat with Didi, he went past me with the ball. He was making a dangerous break. I had to bring him down. I chased after Didi and hit him with a full-whack tackle. Bang. Take that. Down you go. Don't try to go past me. Didi shouted something in German, and I didn't need to understand his words to realize he was not happy.

I treasure the shirt he gave me at the final whistle. It's upstairs, and when I look at it all the memories of that night in Charleroi come flooding back. The nerves, the tackle, the three points. 'All the best in your next game,' said Didi, before heading off to the demoralized German dressing-room. Typical Didi. Even then, in what must have been a time of real heartache, he was prepared to think about someone else. My life took a turn for the better the day I met Didi Hamann.

As Didi disappeared, I was engulfed by people. Well done. Brilliant. Congratulations. Well played. Kevin was in tears, hugging me. England's changing-room was buzzing, players and staff happy. Me? I was on cloud nine. Keegan stood in the middle of the room and said, 'We've got a chance of qualifying now, boys!' I shook hands with all the lads and congratulated them. But it hadn't yet sunk in; it was as if I hadn't played. Me, a hero for England? Impossible. Only when I left the room and had had time to gather my thoughts did I start to appreciate that it really had been me out there, flying into tackles, helping to get England back on track at Euro 2000. It really was me playing a part in England's famous victory.

As I walked back to the bus, I wanted to share my joy with my family, so I called Dad. He didn't go over the top in his praise – that's not Dad's way – but I could tell from the tone of his voice that he was really happy for me. It was Father's Day, and Dad said, 'That performance was a tremendous present, Steven.' Just to detect that pride in my dad's voice meant the world.

Back at the hotel, the dining-room felt different. The gloom was gone, dispersed by Shearer's goal. That night, I actually looked forward to coming down from my room. I knew everyone would be happy. After the Portugal loss five days earlier it had been a case of in for your meal sharp, back to your room sharp. Gareth Barry was made up for me. 'Brilliant, Stevie, well done,' he said as we unwound in our sitting-room. Tiredness soon overcame me, and I said goodnight to Gareth.

The moment I shut the door for the night and lay down in bed, I was besieged with all my old nerves. The homesickness kicked in again, bringing me down from my Charleroi high. I almost packed my bags and ran for cover. It was so strange. I should have been on top of the world after the Germany game; instead, I felt like I was staring into a black hole of depression. I just wanted to be at home. I missed Ironside.

First thing next morning, I rang home. Just

hearing my parents' voices calmed me down. I asked them to read out the headlines in the English papers (we never got the papers straight away at Spa; they were often a day late). 'Full Steve Ahead: an England Star is Born' declared one. 'Move Over Ince, Gerrard is the New Guv'nor' said another. That cheered me up! When I finally got hold of the papers myself I almost ripped them to pieces, such was my haste in turning the pages. Some of the things I read, about me being 'England's future', I felt I shouldn't be reading. 'Ignore those,' Dad urged me. 'Don't believe it. Just focus on doing the same again.' Good advice, as always with Dad. But I was drawn to those papers. It was fascinating reading about myself. 'Don't take any notice of the hype,' said Gérard Houllier when I spoke to him later that day. Steve Heighway said the same. Foot on the ball; don't get carried away. Keegan did, though. 'Steven Gerrard gave a cameo of what England's future will be,' said the manager. Didi also spoke well of me in the press. 'Stevie will be England captain one day,' he said. 'I wish Germany had a few players like him.' Top fella.

We had three days to prepare for our final Group

A game, against Romania, who were fighting for their lives with only a point to their name. Again, we were really up for the match. Training was unbelievable, with a real bite to it. I was flying. All the papers were full of my name. Everyone, it seemed, was talking about me. As I walked out to training, Michael was alongside me. We were chatting about everything and nothing, just joshing around. My old mate then turned serious. 'You played really well against Germany,' he said. 'You have to be pushing for a place against Romania.'

A situation vacant sign did hang in central midfield. Scholesy was too good to drop, but one position was still up for grabs. Wisey could slot in there, but Kevin tended to use him out wide. Incey's position was the vulnerable one, according to the papers, who said he looked tired in the first two games. But I wasn't plotting on nicking Ince's job, I just wanted to impress as much as possible in training and let Kevin make the decision.

I went to work as if my life depended on it. The day before the Romania game, I couldn't wait to get stuck into my last chance to convince Kevin. Such was my desperate enthusiasm that I charged into a nightmare of my own making. Off the bus, top speed on to the pitch, couldn't hold back, let's get cracking, and then I felt it go. My calf. Pulled. No question. Didn't warm up properly.

Desperation coloured my subsequent actions. Because of what a few players and papers had said, I thought I had a chance of starting, so I didn't tell anyone about the calf. Not the physios, and definitely not Kevin. I trained on, running hard to disguise the problem. It hurt, but I knew missing Romania would cause me more pain. I didn't realize how badly I had pulled it.

The high of Germany suddenly seemed a world away. I dropped into a depression, sent tumbling there by a simple failure to warm up. How stupid was that? I cursed myself under my breath as I continued to train. 'Come on, let's get back to the room, see if we can find an escape from this nightmare,' I told myself. My heart pumped fast, my mind working overtime with thoughts. Uncertainty about whether or not I was in Keegan's plans still reigned. He gave no clues in training; we did no shape work that signalled who might start in midfield. Kevin was obviously going to announce the eleven in that night's meeting. I had to get my calf right.

Back in the privacy of my room, I hobbled around. This felt like something more than a bit of tightness. This was serious. 'I can't play, but I am going to play,' I told myself. Somehow. I've just got to.

I left my room early as dinner-time loomed so that no-one would see me walk in slightly stiffly. The other lads soon bounded in and sat down, chattering about Romania. Some of them believed Keegan would start me against Romania. They'd been talking to journalists they knew. 'You're playing tomorrow,' Robbie said to me. A weak smile came to my lips.

After dinner, I snuck down to the physio room to see if Gary Lewin could have a look at it, maybe weave some magic. I opened the door and walked straight into Alan Shearer and Tony Adams, who were enjoying some banter with Gary. Spinning 180 degrees, I sped back out, terrified at the thought of revealing my injury to Gary in front of England's two senior players.

Back up in my room, I reconsidered my options.

In times of trouble, my first instinct is to call home. Dad answered the phone.

'Dad, I can't believe it,' I said. 'I've done my calf. Badly. In training.' I was stuttering. Disappointment prevented me from speaking properly. Tears formed in my eyes. 'Dad, I really think Keegan is going to pick me against Romania. We've got a meeting in an hour and I'm sure I'm in the team. But my calf's a mess. It's really tight. There's no way I can play.'

As I was talking, there was a knock on the door. 'Come back later!' I shouted. Flipping cleaners. They were so busy, in our rooms all the time. You'd hardly put a cup down and they'd come flying through the door like the SAS to tidy up. Another knock. Can't they leave me alone? They had only just left the room ten minutes earlier.

'Hold on, Dad, I have to get rid of the cleaners,' I said.

I went over to the door, opened it, and standing there was the England manager.

'Boss! Come in, come in.' I picked up the phone again. 'Dad, the manager's here, I'll phone you back.' Dad tried to say something, but I buttoned him. My mind was on Keegan, the calf, and the game with Romania.

'How are you, Steven?' Keegan began.

'I'm all right, boss, fine.'

'Sit down, Steven.'

So we sat at this little table, a smiling England manager on one side and a heartbroken kid with a wrecked calf on the other.

Keegan looked directly at me. 'You're starting tomorrow,' he said.

No! No! Don't tell me that! I felt trapped in a horror story that kept getting worse. It was unreal. Keegan had just knocked on my door to tell me I was starting a European Championship game for my country, and I was seconds away from limping down the corridor, tapping on his door and confessing all. I had to come clean. Keegan had always been so good with me. I couldn't mislead him now; it would be unfair on him and the team.

'Thanks, boss,' I said, 'but I have something to tell you.'

A confused look spread over Keegan's face. 'What is it?'

I paused, searching for the courage to get the words out. Speaking to Keegan was a new experience. I was shy, relieved in the past just to listen.

'Come on, Steven, what is it?'

Finally, I found the strength. 'Boss,' I began, 'listen, I'm sorry. I have something to tell you, something I have been hiding from you. I've done my calf.'

The world stopped spinning for a moment. A silence took hold for what felt like an eternity.

'What?' he said, his voice crackling with disbelief. 'Why haven't you mentioned it?'

'Boss, I just wanted to play so badly. I went down to the team room before but the physio wasn't there.' Gary had been there, of course. I was lying, hiding behind any excuse so that the England manager wouldn't think so badly of me.

'Have you pulled it or is it just tight?' Keegan asked.

'There is no way I can possibly play tomorrow,' I replied. 'I did it early in training, but played on because I .wanted desperately to be involved tomorrow. I didn't mention it to the physios in case they ruled me out or told you. It wasn't until I got back to the room that I realized how bad it was. I'm struggling to walk properly. It's getting worse.'

A big lump formed in my throat. How I'd got the words out I will never know.

Keegan took hold of me and said, 'Thanks for telling me. I appreciate it.' He knew how gutted I was.

'I'm sorry, boss,' I said again.

'Don't you be worrying,' he said. 'Your future is sorted. Get it right for the game after. Forget about it. I will take the blame. I will tell Gary you told me but that we were going to see how it was.'

And Kevin did take the whole blame. If I had been older and more experienced, Kevin would probably have hammered me. He could have hung me out to dry with the physios and in public, but he didn't. Keegan cared for his players, and to me his sympathy meant everything.

He led me, this distraught kid, down to the physio room where Gary Lewin examined my calf. 'No chance,' he announced, and that was it. Officially ruled out.

Word spread fast in the camp. Everyone was brilliant, consoling me, telling me they would go out and beat Romania so I could play again later in the tournament.

Keegan cared, even when I was of no use to him. He put me on the bench, stripped, as if I were available to come on, covering up my injury from the media so I didn't get stick. He knew the papers would give me all that old rubbish about being a young crock. Kevin did me a huge favour that day. Although the press were informed that something was wrong with my calf, they thought it was only a twinge, and that Kevin was being wary by starting with me on the bench.

I sat there in despair, wishing I was playing against Romania. What a mad game it was, swinging one way and then the other. England lost 3–2, to a penalty in the final minute after Phil Neville brought down Viorel Moldovan. The dressing-room was bad afterwards, with players going crazy, screaming and shouting as the bitterest of post-mortems was conducted. A look of anger took up residence on the faces of Ince, Adams and Martin Keown. They sat there spitting out venom over an abrupt end to Euro 2000. Nothing got thrown. Players raged at the situation, not at each other. A few people sought to console Phil Neville, but no-one blamed him. Other players just sat there, towels over their heads, unable to speak. Keegan was distraught. Everyone was. As a squad we knew we had failed. People had expected England to have a right good go after promising displays at Euro 96 and France 98. We had let the fans down – a crime, given their fantastic support. Being on the first flight home from Euro 2000 was a disaster.

Grim inquests soon began. Keegan got some unbelievable criticism thrown at him. I knew Michael was unhappy with Keegan. Michael loathes being substituted, as he was in all three games. He feels it is an insult, and that's the right reaction. When I'm taken off, I feel almost physically ill. What I didn't know during Euro 2000 was that Michael wasn't enjoying Kevin's training sessions. He was also critical of Keegan's organization. It got personal between Michael and Kevin, and their relationship broke down.

Keown also laid into Keegan, slamming him as 'tactically naive'. Everyone made a big fuss about his comments, ignoring the fact that players not in the starting eleven always have an axe to grind with the manager. But during Euro 2000, tension was written all over people's faces as the manager read out the team. Nerves raged around the room. Everyone wanted to be in that eleven. It felt like the worst failure not to be picked. This is England. We are ambitious individuals not used to being overlooked, so feathers are bound to get ruffled.

Kevin got stick because he was not so good at looking after those like Martin who were not in the team. I felt differently towards the England manager. I flew back from Holland and Belgium thinking that he was different class as a man and a manager. Keegan treated me as if I were Pele. He made me feel like I was the best player in the world. He made me feel so important. He gave me my debut and stood by me in my darkest hour. My respect for Kevin Keegan will never die.

# 8
# Make Mine a Treble

My homesickness was cured the moment I set foot in Merseyside again, but a new problem awaited. Photographers lurked outside the house – a first for me. This was the England effect, the price to be paid for twenty-nine eye-catching minutes against the old enemy Germany. The media seized on me as the one scrap of hope from England's disappointing stay in Holland and Belgium.

I don't mind being recognized, but this was organized stalking. The morning after the Germany game, the intrusions began. Reporters knocked at relatives' doors and shoved microphones in their faces, demanding their take on 'Stevie G – England Hero'. What were these reporters after? Leave my family alone! My relatives reacted differently. 'No comment,' some said. 'We're really pleased for Steven,' replied others. Nothing satisfied these reporters. Like locusts, they spread across Merseyside hunting juicy morsels about me. They invaded Cardinal Heenan and St Mick's. On returning home, I found the papers full of my old teachers coming out left, right and centre and reminiscing about me. The press got hold of all sorts of pictures of me, past and present. Me at school. Me in the local team. The full paparazzi treatment was focused on me. Germany changed my life for ever. I became public property – a prospect that didn't exactly fill me with joy. Sharpish, I disappeared on holiday, got some sun, caught my breath and readied myself for the new season. The pressure was on, big-time. Could I repeat my Germany display? Everyone was watching me. Was I just a flash in the pan, a one-game wonder? I had to produce.

Just before that 2000/01 season kicked off, I learned Bryan Robson was chasing me. Middlesbrough were prepared to offer £5 million – a massive sum for someone as inexperienced as me. Liverpool were having none of it, and sent Robson packing in no uncertain terms. Leaving Liverpool was a million miles from my thoughts, but it was still flattering to hear an icon like Robson rated me. After the Euros, Robson was interviewed in the papers talking me up. When I read those articles, I wanted to cut them out and frame them. Bryan Robson, England legend, praising me! His approval meant the world. I looked at the pieces and thought if I could become a tenth of the player Robson had been, I'd die happy.

As a kid I once wore a Manchester United shirt with 'Robson' and his number 7 on the back. I detested United with a passion and loathed the idea of putting on one of their strips, but this was different. A mate of mine owned this Robson top, the old blue-and-white one with dashes on it. We were kicking about on Ironside and I asked him whether I could be Robson for a while. I slipped out of my Liverpool shirt, and put on the Robson one. It felt fantastic. I wore it for an hour, charging all over, flying into tackles, scoring brave goals, pretending I was Robson. Because the shirt had Robson's name on it, I forgot about the United bit. It didn't seem like treachery to Liverpool, more homage to an England god.

Unfortunately, Dad looked out the window and went ballistic. 'Get inside now!' he screamed. Scarcely through the door, I ran into a right good grilling. 'What the hell are you playing at, wearing a Manchester United shirt?' he asked.

'But Dad, it's Bryan Robson's shirt,' I explained.

Dad couldn't have cared less. 'You should know better,' he said.

It was a United strip, and Dad wasn't having any son of his dragging the Gerrard name through the Huyton gutter. What would the neighbours think? Honest to God, I thought I was going to have to move house! I was only a baby, but I was convinced Dad would kick me out for putting on that United shirt.

Apart from those trial matches when I tested Liverpool's loyalty, I never made the mistake of wearing United's colours again. My admiration for Robson never disappeared, though. I was buzzing that he believed in me. The new season couldn't start soon enough. Robson's interest meant I was steaming even more to get stuck in. This was going to be my year. Still, not even in my wildest dreams could I have envisaged what an extraordinary year it would be. One cup would have been good, two unbelievable, but the Treble? No chance. Surely not? We needed to rewrite all the odds and predictions to lift that Treble.

Liverpool had a good team that season. I knew that. Gérard Houllier assembled a quality outfit. The odd concern still nagged away at me, though. I wasn't completely convinced by our goalkeeper, Sander Westerveld. The Dutchman's kicking was excellent, and his shot-stopping and communication skills good, but he was prone to mistakes.

Sander was fortunate that he was protected by a brilliant defence. Our right-back was Markus Babbel, a smooth German whose name was rarely chanted at Anfield but who was highly regarded in the dressing-room. Gérard pulled a belter out of the bag with Babbel, who arrived from Bayern Munich on a free as a centre-half, but shone at full-back. Liverpool got one magnificent season out of Babbel. Sadly, the following year Markus contracted a weird illness called Guillain-Barré Syndrome that causes havoc with the nervous system. He was away from Melwood for months. 'Where's Markus?' everyone kept saying. 'We need him back.' He eventually returned from

Germany in a wheelchair. I was stunned. I couldn't believe this was the same person. Markus had been toned, clean-shaven, a good-looking guy glowing with health. Now, I found myself shaking hands with a ghost. He was grey, and much thinner. His weight dropped from almost thirteen stone to eleven stone. His muscle tone went, too. All I recognized was the familiar Babbel smile. One of the best players of our Treble season was suddenly in a wheelchair.

Markus recovered, but he was never the same all-action defender again, not like he had been during our march to the Treble in 2000/01. Markus was switched to right-back because Sami Hyypia proved a revelation in the middle. From the moment Sami arrived in 1999, he was brilliant. Sami was just what Liverpool craved: an aerial presence in defence. Liverpool had been slaughtered for years for not having someone commanding in the air. Any cross came in against Liverpool and we were in trouble. Whenever we played Man United, David Beckham notched up three or four assists from crosses or corners. Sorting out the defence became one of Gérard's urgent requirements.

I remember seeing Hyypia for the first time at Melwood. 'Who is this?' I whispered to the other guys. No-one had heard of Sami Hyypia. We thought he had been bought in case injury or suspension knackered our main centre-halves. The next thing I knew Sami was clearing balls a hundred yards, making fantastic tackles and passing the ball out well. Left or right foot, no problem. His only weakness was speed. Sami never boasted the pace of centre-halves like Rio Ferdinand or the Italian Alessandro Nesta. But it wasn't an issue. Sami's reading of the game was so good that during his first couple of years at Liverpool nobody got past him. He was truly world class for those two seasons.

Sami struck up an immediate understanding with Stéphane Henchoz, who came in from Blackburn Rovers. Stéphane was solid, never giving anything away, always there to make vital interceptions. He and Sami were like rocks at the back. Opposing attacks just crashed onto them and fell back, bruised physically and mentally. Sami's partnership with Stéphane won us the Treble. No doubt. They were the heartbeat of a magnificent defence, with

Babbel on the right and Jamie Carragher on the left.

I love Carra. So do managers. He'll play anywhere across the back, no problem. Carra's best at centre-half, but he never complained when Gérard shoved him in at left-back for the Treble season. A true pro, Carra just knuckled down. In training, he worked overtime developing his left foot. He got YT boys to ping balls at him on the left, time after time. He almost wore a hole in his left boot. Practice, dawn till dusk, turned Carra into a brilliant two-footed defender.

I have always admired Carra as a bloke, a footballer and a leader who has never needed an armband. He always behaved like a captain. In that Treble season, I often turned to Carra for advice. If I had the raging hump about something, and was steaming in to see Gérard, Carra would stop me, calm me down and sort me out. Television interviews don't give the right image of Carra. He's bright, as well as being a top lad.

When another wise head, Gary McAllister, joined Liverpool, I was not alone in the dressing-room in wondering what the hell Gérard was doing. He seemed an odd buy. OK, he was once a terrific midfielder for Leeds United and Scotland, but McAllister was now thirty-five, his best days surely behind him. His arrival was of particular concern to me. Would he limit my appearances? 'It's a bit of a strange signing,' I remarked to the lads when Gérard wasn't around. 'Isn't McAllister over the hill? I've seen him play for Coventry recently and, yeah, he's good, but why've we signed him?' No-one came up with an answer. The word from above was that McAllister had been brought in as cover. I rang my agent, Struan Marshall, who knew McAllister well. 'Stru, what's all this about?' I asked.

'Don't worry, Stevie,' replied Struan, 'Gary Mac will be brilliant for Liverpool, and for you as well. Listen to him. Learn from him.'

Meeting Gary Mac was an important moment in my career. As a midfielder and a man, he was special. He strolled into the dressing-room at Melwood and immediately went around all the players introducing himself. That was class. We knew who Gary bloody McAllister was, but that gesture showed his modesty. We liked that. He also had the medals, the caps and poise that trigger instant respect. It felt like football royalty breezing into Melwood. Should I bow? Gary was never destined for the ressies. No chance. Almost immediately, he was a fixture in the first team, directing operations like a general at a battle, turning the game Liverpool's way with his vision and touch. What a player.

And what a teacher.

During matches, if I lost possession, Macca would say, 'Keep the next one.' He was such a clever man in possession himself, and his opinion was valued by everyone. Macca was one of those players who could stop a session and suggest something and everyone listened, even the coaches. Just watching Gary in training improved me. He was a master-class on legs.

Gary combined the experience of his thirty-five years with the phenomenal engine of a twenty-five-year-old. He was as fit as anything, but then he always looked after himself. Gary Mac made twenty-one Premiership starts that 2000/01 season, starred in the three cup runs and became an instant legend at Liverpool. Gary's brilliance in the middle along with Didi Hamann meant I was often shifted out to right midfield. It annoyed me that if I ever had a bad game alongside Didi I was shifted out towards the flank. Gérard never gave me another game to put it right. Macca came flying in and I was left fighting with Danny Murphy and David Thompson for right mid-field. Danny, Thommo and I called it the 'graveyard shift'. 'Who's got the graveyard today?' we'd laugh with each other as Gérard read out the team. The graveyard was well named: anyone playing right mid-field for Liverpool that season was guaranteed to have their match killed off early. Whoever was on the Graveyard – me, Danny or Thommo – would start sweating after fifty minutes, knowing the man on the bench was about to signal the end. It became a running joke: 'Fifty minutes and you're dead.'

All three of us were handy players and we did get annoyed. Thommo was a good midfielder, full of energy, and he loved a tackle, but Danny was different class. Danny was my room-mate, almost my soul-mate. A schoolboy Red, Danny was the king of banter, really funny and sharp. We clicked immediately. For a couple of years we scrapped like dogs for the same place yet such intense rivalry never spoiled our friend-ship. We'd laugh, muck about, wind each other up.

Any problems I had in my private life, Danny gave me spot-on advice. I am still gutted to this day Danny is not at Liverpool. It kills me. Really does. He was a top, top player who was never properly appreciated by the management.

Liverpool were not short of talent in midfield. Patrik Berger suffered with injuries, a few really bad ones, which was tough on him and the team. When I did play with Patrik, he was the best left-footed striker of a ball I have seen. He could place the ball wherever he wanted – a breathtaking skill. As a bloke, Patrik was OK. He was from the Czech Republic, and he kept himself to himself. He was really cliquey with Vladimir Smicer, another Czech. Vladi was sub a lot, blowing hot and cold. When he flew in from the French club Lens for almost £4 million, he was sensational in training. His brilliant touch made things look so easy. But Melwood was one thing, Anfield another, and Vladi rarely transferred his training-ground form to match-day. The difference between what Vladi had and what he delivered disappointed me. The ability was there, but not the impact, although he was unlucky with injuries and Gérard rarely used him in his proper position.

We also had Nicky Barmby in midfield, who shone when he first signed for us from Everton in the summer of 2000.

Along with Barmby, Gary Mac, Didi and the rest, my job was to shift the ball forward to Michael, Robbie and Emile Heskey. Everyone knew about Michael's class, his deadly eye for goal. Same with Robbie. Emile was different. He had much to prove after leaving a smaller club, Leicester City, in March 2000 for as big a destination as Anfield. Emile was great to play with because he offered midfielders options. His speed meant I could ping the ball over the top for him to chase, but he also dropped short and held the ball up. I then bombed on and had a pop at goal. Perfect.

In January 2001, Liverpool's strike-force was strengthened further. From the moment I saw Jari Litmanen at Melwood, I was bewitched. This skilful Finn was different gravy in training, running the small-sided games with his touch and clever move-ment. Jari was like a chess grandmaster, always anticipating three or four moves ahead. He was certainly on my wavelength. Every pass I tried, he read. Few footballers worked that space between defence and midfield better. The very first time I drilled a ball in to Jari, I immediately understood this was a forward who'd spent his career alongside top players at Ajax and Barcelona. Jari knew how to receive a ball, how to turn an average pass into a good one. I sensed instinctively that he was a class act in his day. He was still useful, more than useful, but we were getting Jari as the curtain began to fall on a wonderful career. He never really had the legs for the Premiership, but he had the ability, cunning and awareness. In big games, Gérard liked playing compact, which didn't suit Jari. Someone schooled at Ajax and once resident at Camp Nou preferred a much more expansive game.

Litmanen arrived only after our run in the League Cup was well underway. The trophy was then known as the Worthington Cup, and I missed the first two rounds. But I returned for our fifth-round tie against Fulham on 13 December, which we won 3–0 in extra time. There was more London opposition in the semi-finals, Crystal Palace. Hoping for an upset, TV showed the first leg live. Liverpool were all over Palace. If this had been a boxing bout, the referee would have stopped it to prevent Palace suffering further. We pulverized them. Their goal led a charmed life. Michael was so unlucky. He could easily have got a hat-trick; 7–2 wouldn't have flattered Liverpool, honestly. Unbelievably, Palace won 2–1.

We were smarting at the injustice, desperate to get Palace back to Anfield to put them in their proper place. I wished the second leg had been the next night; waiting a fortnight for revenge felt far too long.

By the time it came around our players were certainly fired up. Poor Palace. We absolutely destroyed them. We were 3–0 up in twenty minutes, smashing them all over Anfield, and eventually won 5–0, and Liverpool were through to the final at the Millennium Stadium. Our opponents there were Birmingham, then living in the Football League, a rung below us, but still a decent, hard-working side who deserved our respect. Sensing a first trophy in six years, our fans poured excitedly into Cardiff on 25 February. Everyone wanted to be there. So did I, although I lacked sharpness because I'd been carrying an injury. Aware there might be a problem, Gérard pulled me on the eve of the final.

'Are you fit?' he asked.

'Yes,' I lied.

I wasn't. My sharpness wasn't there. I had a good run on goal early on, until their centre-half Michael Johnson clipped my ankles. Gérard took me off after seventy-eight minutes, putting on Gary Mac, with the game seemingly won.

Robbie's great goal in the first half vindicated Gérard's decision to start him ahead of Michael up front with Emile. The sight of Michael being relegated to the bench shocked all of us. 'I can pick only two out of three,' Gérard explained of his dilemma. He did, after all, have three England strikers.

At Cardiff, Houllier's plan worked until the ninetieth minute, when Birmingham equalized through Darren Purse's penalty. More spot-kicks decided the day.

The kicks were taken down at the Liverpool fans' end, which helped. Martin Grainger missed for Birmingham, Didi failed for us, so up stepped Jamie Carragher. He put the ball on the spot, turned round and started walking – and walking and walking. Carra's run-up was so long they should have put an athletics track there. It looked about a hundred metres! I didn't want to watch because I was worried a good friend would stick the ball in the stand. But I had to. With his socks down around his ankles, Carra's run-up and kick lacked the grace of a total footballer; it was more giraffe than gazelle. But up he came, like a runaway train, and smacked the ball in the top corner. Brilliant! Players and fans went crazy, particularly when Andy Johnson missed to give us the Cup. Carra, the penalty king! He's impossible now. He'll never let us forget it. When we have pens in training, Carra is unbelievable. 'Let me through,' he says. 'I have a 100 per cent record for Liverpool. I'm the best penalty-taker at the club.'

Carra was unstoppable that day. When the karaoke started at the party back in the hotel, we couldn't get him off. That's Carra. First on the karaoke mike. First on the dance-floor. I steered well clear of the karaoke. You'd never catch me on that, making a fool of myself. I can't dance, and I definitely can't sing. Anyway, I was just loving watching all the players and their relatives having fun. Liverpool won together and lost together. We celebrated together and commiserated together. The Liverpool way. Liverpool's family feel is essential to someone like me who works best in a strong, caring environment. No club in the country can rival Anfield's sense of community.

If the League Cup felt good, the FA Cup run was truly special. We started off against Rotherham in the third round at Anfield. We then got a pig of a draw, away to Leeds United, a class outfit at the time. Woodgate and Ferdinand at centre-half, Bowyer and Batty in midfield, Viduka and Keane up front. Some team! And Alan Smith came on for them. They ran us ragged. Leeds' fans were going crazy, screaming for a goal. Somehow Barmby and Emile struck in the last three minutes and Leeds were out, desperately unlucky.

I missed the fifth-round win over Manchester City but was back for the quarter-final on 11 March: Tranmere Rovers away. Across the Mersey, but still a derby. We knew Tranmere would be pumped up for our visit. No question. Tranmere live in the long shadow Liverpool cast over the region. Big brother was visiting, and this was a rare chance for Tranmere to give us a bloody nose. Short in miles, the journey still felt like a long trek into enemy territory. We knew what lay in wait at Prenton Park. We'd read the papers. We'd listened to Rovers manager John Aldridge talking about how his team would be right up for the challenge. We didn't expect anything less from Aldo or his players. Aldo is a top man, really honest, a Liverpool legend, and as passionate as they come. He was desperate to put one over on his old club. Aldo's no fool, though. He knew the gulf in class. Tranmere needed to drag us down to their level, and that meant only one thing: a kicking match.

Tranmere v. Liverpool was a scrap between neighbours, so Gérard threw all his home-grown players into the fight: me, Michael, Carra, Robbie, Danny and Wrighty. Us English lads understood what was at stake, the local pride as well as a ticket to the semis. Me, Michael and Carra had grown up aware of the amazing tradition of the FA Cup, its love of upsets. We were determined not to feel the underdog's bite.

Wound up by Aldo and their fans, Rovers came

flying at us. All that stuff in the papers about them launching everything at us was true. Tranmere didn't disappoint. Looking into the eyes of Aldo's players at kick-off, I saw the fire burning within each of them. Their existence depended on beating Liverpool. Brilliant. This was my kind of game. A good old English scrap on a poor pitch with only the strong-hearted surviving. And Gérard's decision to field English players paid off handsomely. Danny, Michael, me and Robbie all scored in a 4–2 victory.

The semi-final draw smiled on us: we could have pulled out Arsenal or Spurs, but instead got Wycombe Wanderers, a team two divisions below us. Without any press hype, Liverpool would have walked that game. But everyone built the semi up so much that suddenly Wycombe believed they could cause a shock. In Lawrie Sanchez, Wycombe had a manager who'd stunned Liverpool in the Cup before, with that header for Wimbledon in the 1988 final.

Like Aldo in the quarters, Sanchez had his team pumped up. It was raining cats and dogs at Villa Park, and we certainly made heavy weather of edging past Wycombe. They held us for seventy-eight minutes, but then Emile scored. Five minutes later, we won a free-kick in a terrific position, on the edge of Wycombe's box. Five of us gathered around the ball. Gary Mac took responsibility.

'I'm on it,' he said.

'OK,' I said, and stepped back, out of the way.

'All right, Macca,' said Robbie.

We all respected Macca's ability with a dead-ball, but Robbie had other ideas. He sneaked up and smacked the ball in the top corner. Bang!

'Flipping heck, Robbie!' Macca shouted.

'Get in!' laughed Robbie, and ran off.

Everyone thought Macca was chasing Robbie to congratulate him. He was actually trying to throttle him! Wycombe pulled one back, but it was too little, too late. Liverpool were in the FA Cup final. Class!

I couldn't wait to celebrate. I got home, went into town, and the atmosphere was quality. All the Liverpool fans were out in force, buzzing we were going back to the Millennium. Everyone around the world would be watching Liverpool's FA Cup final date with Arsenal – a real glamour pairing. As a kid, the FA Cup final had always mesmerized me. I always envied the players. Now it was me. Bring it on.

The build-up to the big day, 12 May, passed in a blur. Was I actually going to the final, or just locked in a childhood dream? I had prayed for this moment. The Cup final suits, the banter and interviews, the sense of expectation around the club and the city. Everyone flying. All the trivia on the telly, the speculation about line-ups, and cameras around the hotel. Non-stop rolling news, focusing on us, the finalists. The attention was unbelievable. It was like no other game ever mattered as much as this one.

This huge anticipation meant I never slept a wink on the Friday night. As I walked out of the Millennium tunnel, into the heat of the day and the fever of our fans, I thought of past finals. I followed the footsteps of so many men who made footballing history. All the clichés of the Cup flashed through my mind. Enjoy the day, seize the moment, and all that. Cup folklore also demands that a team needs a touch of luck to win, and our 2–1 victory over Arsenal certainly proved that. Arsenal smashed us all over Cardiff for eighty-three minutes. They deserved to win. No dispute. They had the ball while we chased mocking shadows. It was a good Arsenal side, with defenders like Tony Adams and Ashley Cole, and attackers like Thierry Henry and Robert Pirès. Patrick Vieira was immense in central midfield. We've faced each other many times, but never has Vieira played better than on that day. He was magnificent, winning the ball, running midfield, setting up attacks – head and shoulders above anyone. The final was hardly a classic, it just drifted by like a lazy stream, but Patrick moved to a different, faster rhythm. He took the game by the scruff of the neck and dominated. I wanted his shirt. Badly.

When Freddie Ljungberg scored I thought that was it. Game over. Dream dead. Shake Vieira's hand and go home. Loser. Try again. Arsenal were too good for us. How they were leading only by Ljungberg's goal, I don't know.

Everyone expected Arsenal to chew us to pieces and spit us out. They outplayed us, no question, but they never broke us. Liverpool had a spirit that wouldn't crack. When Freddie's goal went in, Arsenal got all cocky and thought they had won. But we are Liverpool. We don't throw in the towel. Never. Our fans wouldn't let us. I wouldn't let us. Suddenly, with seven minutes left, a ball fell in the Arsenal box and I thought I had a chance. I swung my foot back and then brought it down and in. No contact. The ball had gone. Michael had pounced in front of me. Half-volley, full impact, past David Seaman, 1–1. I couldn't believe we were level with Arsenal.

Hold on. Keep it tight. Steady. Arsenal will hit back. Extra time seemed our aim. Then, with the stadium clock showing eighty-eight minutes, Michael did the impossible. He has this fantastic knack of scoring spectacular goals at vital moments. The ball was put between Martin Keown and Lee Dixon, and Michael was in like a flash. Nine times out of ten when Michael runs through with the ball on his right foot it ends with a goal. On his left foot, Michael still had a lot of work to do, but what a finish! Bang. Take that, Arsenal. Lightning had struck twice. Seaman was beaten, and so were Arsenal. The life ebbed from them. What a turnaround. Still to this day the Liverpool lads joke about that 2001 FA Cup final being Arsenal versus Owen. I don't dispute we had luck on our side that day, but we also had Michael.

The final whistle sounded so sweet. I walked across to the Arsenal players, who lay scattered about like victims of a motorway pile-up. Vieira was my target. I found him, and we hugged. Two sportsmen who had hammered away at each other parted, a mutual respect deepened. But some Arsenal people were graceless in defeat. I wasn't interested in Arsenal's bitter reaction. I just wanted my Vieira shirt, my winner's medal, and to get back to the hotel to celebrate. I left Arsenal to their sour grapes and went off for some beer.

Typically, Gérard urged moderation, reminding us that the season was not over. Just four days away was the UEFA Cup final. 'Only two beers,' he ordered. We tried briefly to keep to the limit, honestly. Tried and failed. Two beers was insufficient to honour the FA Cup. I had a few more than a couple. All the players had a good drink. We were so happy. We weren't thinking about the UEFA Cup, we were thinking about the FA Cup, which was now heading to Anfield. I looked around at all the other players and sensed the deep satisfaction flowing through them. They had fantasized about this moment all their lives. So we drank, and we toasted Michael. Tomorrow could wait. Tomorrow, we'd get rid of the hangovers and get ready for the UEFA Cup. But that precious night, we sat and drank and joked and revelled in our achievement. For me, that was the highlight of Liverpool's Treble season. Nothing rivals the FA Cup.

Being French, Gérard felt differently. He was more turned on by the UEFA Cup than the FA Cup. Liverpool's dressing-room was split between the English lads excited most by the FA Cup and the foreigners more interested in the UEFA Cup. I smiled at Gérard's pleas after Cardiff. 'Live like monks,' he urged me, Carra and the rest. 'I know you've won the FA Cup, but the UEFA Cup means so much.' Gérard was obsessed with the trophy. He told us how much it weighed, and all about its history, but the UEFA Cup never raided my dreams like the FA Cup.

Europe was still a wonderful experience that season, though. The early rounds of the UEFA Cup saw Liverpool progress past Rapid Bucharest and Slovan Liberec, booking a third-round tie with Olympiakos. When we turned up in Athens towards the end of November, it was dead hostile: 50,000 loons, flares going off, and flags everywhere. The Greek fans were far away from the pitch, but they have a good arm on them. Their missiles still covered the distance. Great atmospheres like that really get me going, and I scored a glancing header off a Gary Mac corner.

Injury ruled me out of facing Roma in the fourth round, which was frustrating. I fancied playing against Francesco Totti, who's my kind of player – a real gladiator. Fortunately, Totti was also injured so I didn't miss out on a duel I craved. But I wasn't missed and beating the likes of Gabriel Batistuta and Cafu 2–0 in the Olympic Stadium gave the boys the confidence to believe the UEFA Cup could be lifted.

Next up were Porto, a really defensive side with a touch of skill. We got the clean sheet we wanted at the Stadio Das Antas in early March, because we knew Portuguese sides don't really travel. They were duly finished off at Anfield a week later.

Not even a rabid Evertonian could accuse Liverpool of taking the easy route to the UEFA Cup – the semi-finals brought mighty Barcelona. For many players, Camp Nou is the greatest stage on earth. I was buzzing to play there. Training there on the eve of the first leg, I couldn't concentrate. No chance. I was a tourist, looking round in admiration at this magnificent building. Carra and I kept smiling at each other. Having a kick-about at Camp Nou felt a long way from playing footy on Ironside. The next night, I wasn't really bothered about the result. Just let me on the Camp Nou pitch, let me hear those 90,000 mad fans. I just wanted to enjoy the occasion, and not think about winning or losing.

Barcelona were brilliant. Pepe Reina kept goal with the assurance he now shows for Liverpool. In attack, Rivaldo and Patrick Kluivert toyed with us. Barcelona never really had a front-man; those two just moved wide and deep, letting midfielders like Luis Enrique and Marc Overmars through. My job was in the middle, and rarely have I been so exhausted mentally and physically by opponents' unbelievable movement. Barcelona gave us a lesson in pass and move, qualities supposed to be Liverpool's hallmark. The possession stats must have been seventy–thirty in Barcelona's favour. On the few occasions we managed to get out of our half, I heard the shout from our bench: 'Great!' Nicking a 0–0 was a fabulous achievement. I immediately ran to Kluivert to swap shirts. I occasionally look at that shirt and remember that footballing lesson in Catalonia.

Tactically, we delivered a smart performance at Camp Nou and came away with a goalless draw, so I couldn't understand the criticism assailing us. 'Cautious Liverpool' was one of the kinder headlines. The press, particularly in Spain, labelled Liverpool as 'boring'. That got under a lot of people's skin at Anfield. It never worried me because I was building a medal collection in that 2000/01 season. One, two – count them. If Gérard had made us more adventurous that season, my haul would have been smaller. We were strong defensively and then hit teams on the counter-attack – bang, bang, you're dead. It suited the players we had. At Anfield in the second leg we reached our first European final in sixteen years with a Gary Mac pen and then another unbelievable defensive display in the second half. Job done.

Boredom was certainly not a word used to describe the final in Dortmund, Germany, on 16 May.

The atmosphere was special, because we were FA Cup winners. We didn't have the cigars out, but we certainly landed in Germany with our chests out. No matter what happened against our opponents, Alaves, Liverpool's season was a success. I was so relaxed, I slept like a baby every night in the run-up to Dortmund. I awoke on the morning of the final to discover our wonderful fans were everywhere in Dortmund, painting the town red. The journey from the hotel to the stadium was bedlam. Massive numbers of Liverpool supporters lined the streets, cheering us on, causing traffic chaos. Just parking the bus took half an hour. The fans wouldn't let us in. They had not seen us since Cardiff, and were determined to salute that victory. As security tried to force a way through, I looked out of the bus window and saw all the T-shirts: 'FA Cup winners 01' and 'Treble 2001'. Everyone believed the Treble was now inevitable, but no-one anticipated such an extraordinary match against Alaves, the surprise Spanish package. Finals don't come much more entertaining.

Because we had won the League Cup and the FA Cup, there was no pressure on us, and we just went out and enjoyed ourselves; if we had lost to Arsenal, we would have been a lot more cautious, sitting deep, stifling Alaves and playing on the counter-attack. Within four minutes, Gary Mac lifted over a ball and Markus Babbel put us ahead – a brave header, because he received an elbow for his troubles. Gary Mac's set-pieces were vital for Liverpool that season, and they were no flukes. Small details determine big games, and Gary Mac's constant practice, day in, day out, meant he had corners, free-kicks and penalties off to a T. He was in such good form that Gérard gave me the right flank against Alaves. Thanks a lot. Gérard took the easy option. Rather than take on a respected old pro like Gary Mac, he sent a youngster out on the grave-yard shift. Complaining was pointless. Gérard wouldn't listen, and moaning is not my style. Besides, I soon scored. I owe Michael a lot because his ball through was spot-on, inviting me to try my luck. Head down, smash it, 2–0. Alaves were no fools. They fought all the way. Ivan Alonso came on, pulled one back, but then Gary Mac slotted in a penalty: 3–1.

Coming into the dressing-room at half-time, we thought we'd won. Liverpool's fans were shouting about the Treble. Some players whispered it. The staff even mentioned that if we kept doing what we were doing, the Treble was ours. I was not alone in that Liverpool dressing-room in thinking that the Treble was done. Alaves never showed anything in the first half to worry us. That's why we returned to the fray far too casual. Alaves punished us, Javi Moreno netting twice. Unbelievable. Gérard sent Robbie on, and within seven minutes he had put Liverpool back in front with a fantastic shot. That seemed to be it. Alaves' resilience finally appeared broken. But we had one weakness. Sander suffered some dodgy moments during the season, and he messed up again here, missing a cross which Jordi Cruyff dumped into our net. It was 4–4, and extra-time. It had to be Jordi, ex-Manchester United.

Gérard switched me to right-back for the additional period, where I immediately began worrying about penalties. 'If Gérard asks, I'll take one,' I told myself. To refuse would be to let the team down. I'd never let Liverpool down. I was still thinking about penalties when Macca put that free-kick in and Delfi Geli headed an own-goal. Gérard had spoken about golden goals, but I'm not a good listener in meetings. I didn't realize the game was over and we'd won. I was waiting for the re-start. 'That's it!' I eventually shouted, and I started leaping about in celebration. What a weird way to decide a final, and how harsh that it was an own-goal. At least it finished in open play and not with penalties.

So that was it. The Treble was completed, and the singing began. All the fans were chanting 'Houllier, Houllier'. Liverpool supporters will always respect Gérard, because when he arrived at Anfield he promised trophies, and he delivered. He never got the main one, the Premiership, but to collect three cups in one season was phenomenal. But, once again, he would not let us celebrate properly. We had a match at Charlton Athletic three days later laden with significance. The Treble was good, but to beat Charlton to qualify for the Champions League was more important financially for Liverpool.

Throughout the season, we had worked hard to stay in contention for third place and had even won at Old Trafford for the first time in ten years. The memory of this match on 17 December 2000 will never leave me. The press built up the game as a clash between me and Roy Keane. 'Are you scared?' people asked me. No chance. I couldn't wait. I felt I might lose a fight with Keane, but I wouldn't lose many tackles. At the time, Keane possessed all the qualities that make a top midfielder. Obviously, I hated watching Manchester United, but I loved watching Keane. I wanted his aura, his ability to be everywhere on the pitch, tackling hard and passing well.

Over breakfast on the morning of the match, I flicked through the papers which all had page after page on the game. Ferguson even spoke about me. The biggest, and probably only, compliment someone from Manchester United ever paid me came from the United manager in the papers that day. I couldn't believe my eyes as I read his view of me. 'Gerrard's physically and technically precocious, a good engine, remarkable energy, reads the game and passes quickly,' said Fergie. 'I would hate to think Liverpool have someone as good as Roy Keane.' I knew how much Keane meant to the United fans, and to Ferguson. For Ferguson to compare me with his captain was some accolade. Still, his admiration was no secret to me. The United lads told me at an England get-together. After reading Ferguson's comments, I just wanted to go and prove him right, to let him know Liverpool did have a Roy Keane of their own.

Visiting Old Trafford is like negotiating an assault course as it rains vitriol. That 2000 trip was no different. Driving behind enemy lines triggered the usual stick. Liverpool's coach was belted, the United fans jumping up at the windows, their faces contorted by sheer hatred. Bang. A window splintered and a brick nearly bounced off my head. Here we go again. I ran for the gate leading to the dressing-rooms.

Of course I knew what Liverpool–Manchester United games were all about from my YTS days. I have never known hatred like United's. Everton fans have grown to despise me because I score against them so regularly, and because I keep saying I love beating Everton. They loathe me when I play against them, but I think they respect me as a player. At Old Trafford, it's different. Everyone there just hates me because I'm Liverpool. That winter's day in 2000 was no different. I almost couldn't hear the first whistle because of the booing.

For ten minutes, United gave an exhibition of possession. All of Fergie's players, not just Keane, kept the ball well. I had played against decent sides and players before, but United were on a different level. I didn't get a kick for ages.

But we held firm, and when Danny scored the free-kick to settle the game it was just an amazing moment. We had only a few thousand fans there at Old Trafford, but it was like winning a cup final. Playing against Keane felt like a ninety-minute lesson which improved me. He shook hands, said 'well done', and that was it. I was too intimidated to ask for his shirt. I would like one of Keane's Ireland shirts, but I would never take a Man United top home. United shirts are banned in my house.

That victory kept us on course for the Champions League, but qualification rested on that final game at Charlton, and we won it 4–0. We won all our final games that amazing Treble season.

On the back of my contribution to the Treble, Liverpool sought me out over a contract extension. Struan rang to say that Rick Parry, Liverpool's chief executive, had been constantly on the phone.

Liverpool sounded desperate. So we got the deal done and dusted sharpish. Maybe Liverpool were worried that someone would come in for me. Rick agreed to the four years and put me on really, really good money – £50,000 a week. Players who rise through the ranks rarely get top wages, but Liverpool were different class with me. It was a massive jump up financially, and Liverpool certainly made sure I knew that.

I was buzzing. The money was great, but my life had been comfortable before the new deal. For someone like me, a kid from Huyton, I was doing well. I had my own apartment. I sorted out Mum and Dad for a few quid. But money wasn't an issue. What really delighted me was the fact that Liverpool were anxious for me to stay. Brilliant. My love affair with Liverpool was continuing.

# 9
# Tackling a Problem

Playing abroad doesn't appeal to me for one dead simple reason: I love the blood and thunder of English football too much. Our league and cup competitions have an intensity and honesty that cannot be found anywhere else in the world. The physical nature of the Premiership suits my style. Tackle and be tackled. Get up and get on with it, mate. Don't roll around pretending you're hurt. I can't stand that. Switching from the Premiership to the Champions League is like speaking a different language. Over time, I've learned to adapt in Europe. Whenever I step onto a continental pitch, I'm very careful because opponents exaggerate the force of even harmless challenges. I hate that. Take the physical out of football and the game will be destroyed as a spectacle. For me, nothing beats a wet pitch, sliding into tackles, and going for the ball – brilliant. Nothing stirs me more than hearing passionate fans screaming 'Get stuck in!' That's me. I was put on this earth to steam into tackles. When I finally bow out of the game I love so much, I want to be remembered as hard but fair.

For most professionals, tackling is a technique. For me, it's an adrenalin rush. It's a chance to beat an opponent one-on-one, win the ball and then launch an attack. The sight of the other team with the ball makes me sick. If it's Everton, Man United, Arsenal, Chelsea, or whoever, I have to claim it back. It's my ball, and I'm going for it. Tackling is a collision which sorts out the cowards from the brave. I never hold back in a tackle. I can't. I put my heart and soul into it, as well as my body.

Down the years, that approach has sometimes got me into trouble. Even back in my YTS and reserve days at Liverpool, I was desperate to make my mark and occasionally did so literally. I'd see someone with the ball and that was it. Bang. I flew in, got the ball and left him in a heap. My boots were not guided by malice as they crashed in. He had the ball; I wanted it – end of story. Liverpool's coaches always warned me against it.

Eventually, Steve Heighway called Dad in. 'What's up with Steven?' Heighway asked. 'Has he got a problem at home? He comes in so angry. He wants to kill people in training.' Steve looked at Dad, waiting to make sure the seriousness of the situation was sinking in. 'We don't want to take away Steven's aggression, because that's one of his strengths,' Steve continued, 'but he's going through tackles wanting to really do damage. Please have a word with him. He'll either break someone's leg or injure himself.' Dad pulled me at home. 'You must calm down,' he said. I couldn't.

At sixteen, I saw a sports psychologist about the tackling. Bill Beswick is well respected in the game. Howard Wilkinson introduced me to Bill when I represented England U-18s. 'This guy is brilliant,' Howard said. 'Listen to him.' Bill talked to me about my tackling. 'Imagine a set of traffic lights,' Bill said. The idea was to know when to go for the ball, and when to stop. Bill advised me on how to approach games. 'Fire in your belly but ice in your head' was one of his favourite sayings. 'It will work perfectly with you, Steven, because we don't want to take aggression out of your game but we do want you on the pitch. That's where everyone wants you.' Bill even came to Melwood to chat to the Liverpool lads. My confidence was boosted by Bill. I would never consult him personally now, but at the time he helped me. But even with all this good guidance, from Bill, Steve, Ronnie and my dad, I still crunched into tackles as a youth-team player. Even when I made Liverpool's first XI I was a liability at times. Growing up as a player sometimes proved painful. A feeling of shame fills me when I recall the moments that scarred the early stages of my career.

The first came on 27 September 1999 at Anfield. We were up against the enemy, Everton. I was aching to play. In the team meeting, Gérard Houllier read out the eleven starters: 'Sander; Veggard, Sami, Carra, Stan; Vladi, Didi, Jamie, Patrik; Michael and Robbie.' Not me. Gutted. Big lump in the throat. I deserved to start but got bombed. Why? My head was a mess. I sat on the bench in a huge sulk, seething at the injustice.

On the pitch, it was all soon kicking off. Franny

Jeffers and Sander Westerveld tangled and got sent off. I wanted to be in there, sorting Everton out, showing everyone I should have started. 'If you get on,' I said to myself, 'just belt one of them. Belt a Bluenose. Let Gérard know he is not dropping me for another derby. Ever.' I was a red card waiting to happen the moment Gérard sent me on. My fuse was short and burning fast. Bang. I went in high and late on Kevin Campbell. No mercy, no excuses: straight red. I escaped the pitch as quickly as possible.

As the red mist cleared, I realized how much I'd messed up. Liverpool's players would be fuming. We were only 1–0 down, still with a chance of getting back into the derby. But then I nailed Campbell, and the lads faced mission impossible. I'd let them down badly. I expected stick off the players, off everyone.

When I switched my phone on, the first text was from Dad. He got straight to the point: 'What are you doing, you idiot?' I knew exactly what he meant. A crazy tackle and a three-game ban was not the best way to convince people I could be trusted with a place in Liverpool's starting XI.

When I arrived at Melwood the next day, I was

ordered to Gérard's office. The boss laid into me. 'Your head wasn't right from the moment I told you that you weren't playing,' he said. 'We could see you were sulking. You have got to sulk for ten seconds and then forget about it.' Gérard banged on and on. 'Think about the team, not yourself, Steven. Stop doing tackles like that because we need you on the pitch. We brought you on to change the game and you let us down.'

I'd heard enough. My natural defiant streak kicked in. 'I was expecting to play,' I answered back. 'You just dropped me in the derby. I was desperate to play.'

As I was about to add that Liverpool wouldn't have been 1–0 down if he had started me, I saw the look on Phil Thompson's face. Thommo was standing behind Gérard, glaring like a madman and ready to pounce if I dared have a pop back. That was Thommo to a T. 'Take it,' I thought. Arguing the toss was pointless. I knew I was out of order.

Fast forward a year, to 1 October 2000, and Liverpool were getting soundly whipped by Chelsea at Stamford Bridge. I'd just had enough. I hate losing.

Frustration squeezed all sense out of my mind and I went for Dennis Wise, belting him. Dennis grabbed me by the neck, and we were pushing and shoving, scuffling away. As fights go it was handbag stuff, and I thought people would quickly forget about it. Fat chance. A couple of days later, England met up at Burnham Beeches to prepare for a vital World Cup qualifier against Germany, the last international at Wembley before the bulldozers rolled in. Wisey was in the squad. So was I. Robbie Fowler and Steve McManaman dropped by my new place in Whiston to pick me up. The three of us all drove down to Burnham together and they were merciless all the way.

'Wisey won't be happy with you,' laughed Macca, winding me up.

'He's a tough cookie, him,' Robbie chipped in.

'If he wants some,' I replied, 'I'll give it to him.'

'Be on your toes, Stevie,' Robbie warned me as we drove into Burnham. 'Wisey's waiting for you.'

My heart pumped madly as I walked into the hotel, braced for an ambush by the little Chelsea man. I was ready. If he wanted another war, I wouldn't disappoint. He could have another scrap, big-style. But

Wisey wasn't in reception. 'Maybe he's waiting for you in the meal-room,' Robbie said helpfully. Slightly nervously, I entered the meal-room. Wisey was there, big grin on his face. He walked across. My fists clenched. Wisey's right hand came out sharpish, stretching towards me. But he only wanted to shake my hand. ''Ow are yer?' he said, and rubbed my head. And that was it. No war, nothing. Top man.

Liverpool against Leeds United is another lively old fixture. And on 13 April 2001, at Anfield, it was a top-of-the-table clash. I was up for it and was soon piling into tackles. I picked up a caution early on, for clipping Alan Smith. Nothing nasty. Hardly a yellow. Just doing my job, chasing the ball. Soon I was closing down David Batty, going in cleanly to win the ball. Batty stitched me up big-time. He dived. I never touched him. My heart fell as the referee reached for his notebook again. That was me off, for two nothing tackles. Ridiculous.

The next time I remember my blood really heating up was on 8 September 2001 during a match with Aston Villa, again at Anfield. We were struggling. I equalized just after half-time, but the match was turning into a nightmare. George Boateng was running midfield, out-muscling me time and again. Frustration took over. Suddenly there was Boateng in front of me, in my sights, and I just launched myself. It was a coward's tackle. I admit that now. I lunged with both feet and caught him with one, my studs thudding in high up on his leg. He went down and just lay there. No wonder. It was a filthy challenge, one I deeply regret to this day. It was unforgivable, and I knew it. The ref knew it too, because he waved the red card. And my team-mates certainly knew it. 'Out of order,' Gary McAllister told me. Other lads slated me as well. 'Sorry,' I replied. What else could I say? Gérard marched in and harangued me, which was fair enough. I felt terrible, miserable. My head was close to exploding. Dad called, and his words echoed Gary Mac's: 'You were out of order.'

Home should have offered some sanctuary, but sleep was impossible. I lay in bed, thinking, 'I could have broken Boateng's leg.' Fortunately, George was a strong, tough type. In the morning, the papers were brutal towards me – understandably so. The picture of me diving in was shocking. My agent Struan Marshall called. 'You must change your tackling or you are going to be remembered for it,' he said. 'Rather than being remembered as a good player. Still be aggressive, but just time your tackles better. Don't get frustrated.' Struan's words hit home hard. He was right. I loathed the thought of being remembered for hurting other players.

'Can you get me Boateng's number?' I asked Struan.

'Give me a couple of minutes,' Struan replied, and rang off.

I was just about to give Gareth Barry, the one Villa player I knew well, a call when Struan rang back with Boateng's mobile number. As I punched in the digits, I thought, 'I never, ever want to be in this situation again.'

Boateng answered.

'George, it's Steven Gerrard. I'm phoning to apologize. It was a bad tackle.'

I paused, expecting him to have a rant back.

'Listen,' he said. 'You are a very good player. Just get that out of your game and you'll be all right. I'm OK. But you're lucky you never hurt me. I accept your apology.'

Relieved, I said goodbye and pressed the end-call button. Thank God that was over.

I was banned for three games. No complaints. The banishment should really have been longer. Gary Mac was so concerned about my tackling that he spoke to Struan, and then confronted me. 'Calm yourself down,' Gary said. 'You are going into tackles wanting to kill people. You are going to end up doing yourself in. Take it from me, I've had some bad injuries. Tackling is not just about throwing everything into it, there's an art to it. Learn when to tackle, how to tackle, how hard.' Gary Mac's advice on tackling made sense, but altering something so ingrained would take time.

The Community Shield is supposedly an exhibition match to kick the season off, and it certainly did kick off in August 2002. Meetings between Liverpool and Arsenal are always hugely competitive. Patrick Vieira and I have had some bruising run-ins, and this was definitely one of them. Wanting to stamp my authority on the game early on, I deliberately hit him with a hard tackle after five minutes. Vieira made the most of it, writhing around and whingeing. 'Shut up, and be a man,' I thought. I got booked. So what? Liverpool needed to show they were not scared of Arsenal and all their big names.

There was more mayhem on 22 December 2002 in the derby at Anfield. Avoiding controversy against Everton has never been easy for me. Being nice to the neighbours is not in my nature. Derbies agitate something in my blood. In this game, I challenged for a loose ball with Everton's full-back, Gary Naysmith. I thought he was going to do me, so I got my retaliation in first. I'm not proud of my reaction as Naysmith came in. I left the ground with both feet and lunged for the ball. In mid-air, I knew it would hurt Naysmith, but there was no stopping. I had to land somewhere. I hurtled into his legs, opening a gash and splashing blood on his white shorts.

Pandemonium erupted. Out of the corner of my eye, I saw this rampaging ox charging at me. It was Wayne Rooney. At full tilt, he shoved me and then grabbed me round the neck. He almost took my head off. So this is the famous Wayne Rooney. Everton's wonder-kid needed little introduction. I watched him in the FA Youth Cup and knew all about his talent. He was brilliant against us that day in 2002, a whirlwind in blue. As well as bundling into me, Rooney smashed into our keeper, Chris Kirkland, and then hit the bar. What a class act! Even in the warm-up, Everton's fans sang 'Rooney's going to get you'. How right they were! Me and Wazza laugh now over our scuffle. 'I'd have done the same to you, Wazza,' I tell him. Sorting out whoever topped my team-mate is the way I am. Wayne too. We share an aggressive streak. It's part of life in Huyton and Croxteth. And Rooney had every right to wade in. The kid was just defending Naysmith. Fair dos.

Some of Everton's senior players tried to get me sent off. Fortunately, their efforts to persuade Graham Poll to give me my marching orders failed at Anfield. Poll was looking the other way when I went into Naysmith. The ref knew something bad had gone on, but he couldn't punish me for something he hadn't seen. Straight away, I tried to explain to Poll: 'Listen, I caught him, but I didn't mean to hurt him.'

Things calmed down a bit, the game finished 0–0, and I immediately went to apologize to Naysmith. In the corridor near the dressing-rooms, I spotted David

Moyes, Everton's manager, being interviewed by Sky. After he finished, I approached him.

'I'm sorry,' I said. 'I know the tackle looks bad, but I didn't mean to do him. Is Gary about for me to apologize?'

David said, 'I will send your apologies on to him.'

I don't think Moyes wanted me going in Everton's dressing-room. I might not have got out again.

Poll saw the tackle again on television and high-lighted the incident in his report. The FA summoned me to a disciplinary hearing at the Reebok, Bolton Wanderers' stadium. I felt fairly confident. Naysmith was going to nail me, so I'd had to tackle that way. It was defensive. During the hearing, the suits from the FA said they understood. 'In mid-air, you wanted to pull out but couldn't.' Exactly. 'But we have to think of the other player and your previous tackles.' They recalled my tackle on Boateng, and gave me a three-game ban for the Naysmith incident.

Graeme Le Saux was the next player to feel the full force of my frustration. On 11 May 2003 we were battling Chelsea at Stamford Bridge for the final Champions League position. So much was at stake.

People bang on about the dosh for the club, but it's more than money. For players, the Champions League is the only place to be. It's where the big teams and big players live. So everyone was flying into tackles that afternoon. Chelsea were too good for us. My pre-match fears were coming true. Our record at the Bridge was never the best, and Chelsea had some class players: Frank Lampard and Eidur Gudjohnsen started, and Gianfranco Zola came on. Sami Hyypia scored with a header early on, but Marcel Desailly equalized, and then Jesper Gronkjaer bent one in. Half an hour gone and we trailed 2–1. The Chelsea fans were crowing about them heading for the Champions League while we were destined for the UEFA Cup. Liverpool had spent all season slaving to get in the Champions League. Now the dream was dying.

With a minute remaining, I couldn't stand it any more. Anger swept through my brain, breaking all the restraint mechanisms. Chelsea's full-back was nearest to me, and he received a good old-fashioned clatter-ing. Some people thought it was something personal against Le Saux. It wasn't. Graeme's a likeable bloke who was always fine with me when we crossed paths with England. He was just the closest when I flipped. Bang. Second yellow, straight off, season over.

I sat in the dressing-room, livid about the way the season ended. Gérard was outside, talking me up. 'If we had ten more like Steven Gerrard, we would be in the Champions League,' the gaffer said. Nice sentiments, but nothing could console me. Missing out on the Champions League was a disaster. The atmosphere, quality, excitement and interest levels of the UEFA Cup are far below those of the Champions League, which is closer to playing for England. No wonder I lost my cool at the Bridge.

Come 3 August, we found ourselves playing Galatasaray at the Amsterdam ArenA. There was no chance of this being a gentle pre-season work-out. Tensions between England and Turkey were running high at club and international level. A few months earlier, in a Euro 2004 qualifier, England had beaten Turkey at Sunderland's Stadium of Light, and it was a real battle. In two months' time, England were heading to Istanbul, so everything was being built up, every little fire stoked into an inferno. In Amsterdam,

Galatasaray targeted Liverpool's English players. I was on the bench, watching the Turks laying into Michael and Emile. I was steaming to get on, because there was so much going off out there. 'Put me on, put me on!' I kept telling Gérard.

With half an hour left, the boss relented. Harry Kewell got hooked, and I stormed on, looking for trouble. It was like a scene from a Wild West film. A fight raged between the two sides, and I needed to make up for lost time. Galatasaray's players were putting in nasty little tackles, pulling shirts and spitting at us. Hakan Sukur was right in the middle of it. All the Galatasaray players were. Suddenly an elbow jabbed into my face. My eye watered up, my lip thickened, my anger intensified. I went looking for Sukur and Hakan Unsal. I hit Unsal with a tackle, and the Dutch ref, René Temmink, booked me. Now the Turks were really after me. Another elbow. Bang. I was taking so many blows to the head, I felt like a bloody boxer. Chaos reigned. Neil Mellor, our young striker, was goaded badly. He tackled Gabriel Tamas, a nothing challenge, but Temmink sent him off. Shocker. Now I was really on the warpath, chasing around, kicking anything that moved. Temmink gave a silly free-kick against me, for a foul on Unsal, and all the Turks immediately surrounded us, trying to wind me up. I tried to walk away. Sukur pinched me. It was the old Turkish game of provocation, and I fell for a classic stitch-up. Wound up by the Turks, I was maddened by Temmink's decision, convinced he had been conned by them. I swore at him.

'What?' he said. 'Come here.'

Bang, second yellow, red, off. The Turks were all smug, knowing their cheating had paid off and they were cruising to a 2–1 win.

'You know that counts for the season?' said Gérard. It suddenly dawned on me: this red card could affect me in the UEFA Cup. Joe Corrigan, Liverpool's goalkeeping coach, also had a go at me. So did Thommo. I was fuming with myself, and with Temmink. Gérard went to see the ref and had a quiet word – a plea, really. The gaffer then returned with a quiet smile on his face. 'I talked to the ref, and Temmink said, "I am not putting it in my report."' Result! Fair play to Temmink!

Temmink's mercy still didn't erase the bad

memory of being dismissed. Red cards are humiliating. No indignity matches the despair of sitting in an empty dressing-room, listening to the shouts of the crowd outside and knowing your team-mates are struggling without you. Letting the lads down is a cardinal sin in football. I've played in teams when somebody has been sent off and it's pure graft, extra running, with little chance of getting anything from the match. I had to change, because I was becoming a liability to Liverpool. It was around this time that I really started responding to the advice of people like Struan and Gary Mac. I altered my tackling technique, going in with one foot, not two. The red mist still lingers, especially in derbies. After a silly booking for kicking the ball away against Everton in the 2005–06 season, I got another yellow for a late tackle on Kevin Kilbane and was sent off, so I've not eradicated the problem yet. I still love the thud of a good tackle.

Captaincy has matured me. Since the bad days of the Boateng and Naysmith tackles, my disciplinary record has improved radically. It is my responsibility to look after the younger players, to represent Liverpool the right way. Showing respect to referees is vital.

And as captain, I have to view refs in a different light. It's handy to build a decent relationship with a ref, to get him on Liverpool's side. A tight decision in the ninetieth minute may go my way if I've spent all game being friendly to the ref. He's only human. An official like Poll or Clattenburg is likely to be more sympathetic if I work with them than if I am in their face like a cheeky Scouser, as I was years ago. I used to think refs were steaming to book me, but since getting the Liverpool armband I've realized they have a tough job. So I try to help. Players should help them more. Sometimes, when Liverpool are doing badly, I blame it all privately on the refs. Then I think clearly and realize that, given what is at stake in modern matches, English refs do a good job.

But the best ref I've played under was Pierluigi Collina. Bar none. Foreign refs are far fussier than their cousins in the Premiership – apart from Collina. The Italian was pure class, demanding and getting instant respect. Boy did he scare me. 'Gerrard!' he'd shout if I crossed the line into what he considered unacceptable, and he'd wave that long, bony finger at me in admonishment. Collina's bulging eyes were terrifying. Answering back was one step from suicide. I did once, and Collina gave me a glare that screamed, 'Don't mess with me!' I miss him. It's a shame for all football that Collina has retired. He would have been a star in the Premiership, because he does let a good tackle go. And I love a good tackle.

# 10
# Three Lions

My world turned upside down on Saturday, 7 October 2000, and I wasn't even playing. Kevin Keegan quit after England's 1–0 World Cup qualifying defeat to Germany at Wembley, a decision that really distressed me. I felt terrible for Kevin. He's a proud man who loves England intensely, the country and the team, and no-one hurt more at losing to Germany. I let him down, I suppose. I ached to face Germany until an old enemy of mine, the hated groin injury, hacked me down.

If I can walk, I always report for England duty, whatever the state of my injury. So I showed up.

'How's the groin?' Kevin asked as I arrived at the hotel.

'Not too bad, boss,' I replied, although it wasn't the best.

Little mentions were made in the media that I might start. Incey was out, so I had a chance of the holding role. Me against Didi again – bring it on. Please let the groin get better.

On the Friday, I stepped gingerly out for training and headed off for some work with the physio, Gary Lewin. Kevin jogged over. 'Steven, you're in the team tomorrow. How is it?'

'Not brilliant,' I finally admitted.

'Try it a bit more, and if it's no good, then fair enough,' said Kevin, and nipped back to work with the team.

With Gary watching, I tried twisting and turning, but the groin wouldn't respond. No chance. I was out.

Wembley's stands were a depressing place to be that afternoon. Gareth Southgate stood in for me, a centre-half in midfield, a decision Kevin copped a lot of flak for. I sat there, helpless and frustrated, watching a rubbish game in nasty weather. Of course, Didi went and scored the bloody winner, the last goal at the old Wembley.

As Germany celebrated and England fans howled their anger, I shot down to the dressing-room to see the boys. Consoling words were useless; I just wanted to show solidarity. As I reached the dressing-room area, there was a buzz along the corridor. Groups of people, some telly and some FA, were whispering to each other. 'He's walked out,' I heard someone say. Who's walked out? Must be one of the players, upset with the result. I hurried on, and entered the dressing-room. All around sat shell-shocked players, my friends. They were all down, silent, devastated. Normally Kevin would be going around, lifting spirits.

'Where's Kevin?' I asked.

'He's speaking to the press,' someone mumbled.

Then Keegan walked back in, his eyes dulled with pain. He didn't hang about. 'My time's up,' he said. 'It's time for somebody else to have a go.'

Keegan had resigned! I looked around, embarrassed, not knowing what to say. Tony Adams tried to talk Kevin round, pleading hard with him. 'Don't do it now. Wait. Kevin, slow down, don't do it.' Too late, Tony. Kevin's mind was made up. 'Thanks for everything you have done, lads,' he said. 'You are a great set of players. I'm proud to have worked with you. But that's it, lads. I'm off.' Kevin had told the FA, informed the press, and he was now off out the door. Amazingly, he stopped on the way and looked at me.

'How are you, Steven?' he asked.

What could I say? Kevin had just quit as manager of England but he was still concerned for me. 'I'm all right, boss,' I muttered.

'What did you think of the game, Steven?' he added.

What a time for chit-chat! I was gobsmacked. Words failed me. Kevin smiled and disappeared, out of Wembley and out of my life. I kicked myself. Say something. Shout after him. He capped you. He believed in you. Too late – he'd gone.

Selfishly, I was hacked off. England lost a manager and I lost a mentor. Keegan rated me. The moment I was fit I was straight into Keegan's England, first choice in the middle, no question. Now I must start again. Impress the new man. Best behaviour. Every day I flicked through the papers to see who was being linked with the job. I prayed the FA would choose an Englishman. They would know me, appreciate my strengths. I wasn't against foreigners, of course. If they have a top CV they are good enough to manage England. But I had reservations. Would an overseas coach like me? Would he even know me? Would he prefer the experienced players to fresh names? If only Kevin had stayed. Many people in the press, pundits and ex-players, were screaming that England shouldn't have a foreign coach. 'Maybe they are right,' I thought.

My nerves tightened when the FA appointed a Swede. But all my fears disappeared the moment Sven-Goran Eriksson picked me in his first squad for the friendly against Spain at Villa Park on 28 February 2001. In interviews, Eriksson spoke well of me, so maybe he'd be all right. On reporting for England, I was quite looking forward to meeting the man. Injury again ruled me out, but I drove down to the Midlands to have the problem checked over by Gary Lewin.

As I climbed back in the car to head north, I got a call from Michelle, the team administrator. 'Steven, don't go home yet,' she said. 'The manager and Tord Grip want to see you over at training.'

Here goes. Important moment. Good impression. I drove over to training and found Sven and Tord, his number two.

'I have seen quite a bit of you,' Sven said, after shaking my hand. 'I rate you. Tord has been coming to Liverpool's games and watching you. We are desperate to get you fit. If you need any help, we can advise you. We are going to keep close contact with Liverpool's medical people. I've spoken to Gérard Houllier and Kevin Keegan and they rave about you. Get yourself fit, Steven, and you are in the team.'

Eriksson hadn't even seen me train with England yet! I certainly didn't know Tord was scouting me. After all the disappointment of Keegan's departure, my world began to come good again. Although gutted about my injury, I left the camp with a smile on my face. 'Get yourself fit, Steven, and you are in the team.' Sven's last words made welcome companions on the M6 home. I had got off to the right start with my new England boss. Eriksson's warmth surprised me. He was really friendly. I didn't know much about him, apart from his winning Serie A with Lazio, which was a tidy achievement. But Eriksson valued me, and that was all that counted. As I headed back to Liverpool, I thought to myself that Eriksson would improve me.

Eriksson's impact was immediate. He restored confidence, got England's shape right and had us playing to our strengths: shifting the ball forward quickly to exploit Michael's pace. When we arrived in Munich for the return with Germany on 1 September 2001, we were ready. Revenge was in the air. England must batter Germany, get back on track for the World Cup, and pay them back for the misery of Wembley. Privately, some of us wanted to win it for Kevin, too. I certainly did. The game was massive, like a cup final and a big Champions League tie rolled into one.

There was no escaping the huge interest in the game. Whenever I switched on the TV, all the channels, German and English, seemed full of pictures from training or pundits discussing what might happen. The two nations talked of nothing else. Good. Pressure suits me. All our players were up for this.

The atmosphere in England's final team meeting was fantastic. I looked around at Becks, Scholesy, Michael and the rest and knew they were all as pumped up as me. Let's get at the Germans. Come on! We wanted to win. We had to win. Simple. Everybody was focused. Eriksson was so calm that we felt completely in control. On the bus to the Olympic Stadium, all the lads talked about how much the match meant, the volume rising higher and higher. In the dressing-room, most of the players were really vocal. Eriksson said a little bit, but the real noise came from the players. The language was dead lively. Come on! No club dressing-room could ever compare with this decibel level. Unbelievable. Deafening. At Liverpool, one or two of the lads shout and get everyone going; with England in Munich that night, the whole room went mental. Shouts everywhere. Come on, lads, this is it! Gary Neville screaming. Let's do it! Rio, Sol, both psyched up. Germany didn't know what was going to hit them. Ashley Cole talked away, not loud words, but constructive, giving off a quiet determination. Everyone knew he meant business out there. This was England v. Germany, a derby with pride and vital points at stake.

In the tunnel, the Germans were yelling stuff. They, too, desperately wanted to beat us. I saw Didi, a friend for life but an enemy tonight. We nodded at each other, but this was no time for pleasantries.

Anyway, Didi knew how much I respected him. He also knew how ready England were for Germany.

Not that anyone could tell from the first ten minutes. Germany were all over us. It was a miracle they led only through Carsten Jancker's goal. Sebastian Deisler had a great chance. Germany were good, full of belief. Jancker dominated the air. Ballack ran the game on the deck. Doubts filled me. Away from home, the odds looked stacked against us. The German crowd began crowing: 'Olé, olé!' Let's show them. Come on England! Big Dave made a magnificent save. Thank God – 2–0 and it would all have been over. Just believe. Trust in your team-mates. Trust Michael to give us hope. Michael always does.

When he equalized, the whole mood spun round. Now let's go and win this. Suddenly, Eriksson's tactics looked spot on. We played 4–4–2, deep and compact, hitting on the break because we had burning pace up front in Michael and Emile. In all our team meetings, Eriksson instructed us to smack diagonal passes behind Germany's wing-backs. Hit Emile. Get Michael behind them. Now deliver. We had the passers to release them. In midfield, Becks was on the right and Nicky Barmby on the left, both working overtime. In the middle, Scholesy played more defensive than normal. My job was to break everything up, smash the Germans before they got going.

England were now playing it around, getting on top. Just before half-time we got a corner. A goal now would go through Germany's nerves like a wrecking ball through an old wall. Their walk to the dressing-room at half-time would be a funeral march. Here goes. Beckham, eager as ever to keep things moving, sprinted over to the flag, placed the ball and swept it over. Panic filled German eyes. All speed and flight, Becks's corners are a nightmare to deal with for defenders. I wasn't in the box. In our set-piece practice the day before, Eriksson had me lurking on the edge of the area, looking to pick up the pieces and any nod-downs. I never got a touch in training. No clearances came my way. Nothing. I was a spectator. Match-day proved different. As 63,000 fans watched, Beckham's corner flew across, German heads straining to reach it. Rio was magnificent, timing his leap well. 'Set!' I screamed at Rio. 'Set!' I was perfectly placed. If Rio set me up, I knew I'd score. Nailed-on goal. Would Rio hear and see me? His awareness was brilliant. Jumping with other players, Rio somehow managed to see me. He met the ball superbly, heading it down to me. Great flick, perfect set. All yours, Stevie. Don't mess up.

As the ball came down, I knew there was no margin for error. People think it's a dead good position, hanging around on the edge of the box, waiting for a loose ball to ram back in. The risks are huge, though. If England got hit on the counter, it was so dangerous. Beware their pressure. Shoot quickly. Don't let the Germans nick it. Good touch and hit the target. Luckily enough, I caught an absolute worldie. The ball flew into the bottom left-hand corner. Take that, Kahn. He was nowhere.

Afterwards, everyone banged on about my accuracy, but I never intended to place it there. I just meant to hit the target with power. Bang. Get in! Not a bad time to score my first England goal! I couldn't believe it. I took off in celebration. Seeing the England fans in the corner, I sprinted towards them. Get close to them. Share the moment with them. I began to run out of pitch, so I dived full length, screaming with joy as I slid on the Munich turf. Dad was among the fans going crazy. I pointed towards them. 'That's for you, Dad,' I thought. 'You backed me all the way. You made this possible.' Emotion overcame me. All the hard work, the years of training and dreaming, had paid off.

Racing down the Munich tunnel at the break, 2–1 up, I knew what our dressing-room would be like. Buzzing. The lads were flying.

Eriksson was his usual self at half-time. Calm. Composed. His message was simple. 'You played really well for the last twenty-five minutes of the half,' he told us. 'Keep doing what you are doing. The next goal is important. If we get the next goal, we have won the game.' This was it. Let's finish the Germans off. No mercy.

Amazingly, the Germans had nothing left. Their hearts and legs had gone, drained like a boxer who had taken one too many punches. They were on the ropes, and we spent the second half battering them. With their wing-backs high and centre-halves slow, Michael's runs down the channels into all that lovely space on such a big pitch destroyed Germany. Becks and Scholesy kept picking him out, and his pace, touch and eye for goal did the rest. Michael was Michael in Munich: quiet, then bang, bang, bang. Three goals. Michael and England were unstoppable.

The atmosphere in the dressing-room afterwards was different gravy. Everyone was shouting, punching the air, shaking hands and laughing. Eriksson said little; he just sat there smiling, but he must have been bursting with pride inside. We all were. England sent out a message to the world that night. We are fearless. We don't give up. We have players like Michael Owen who can demolish any defence. After that victory and performance in Munich, we genuinely believed we could go anywhere, however inhospitable, and succeed.

England still faced a huge obstacle before qualifying for Korea and Japan. Greece came to Old Trafford a month later and we had to match Germany's result against Finland to keep top spot. A massive game, no doubt. The build-up to the match on Saturday, 6 October, was very intense.

Every time I got on the ball at Old Trafford, the

ball felt like a hand-grenade coming at me. I played really badly. Going into the last minute, England were 2–1 down and automatic qualification for the World Cup was going up in smoke.

I was shaken from my nightmare by a roar sweeping around Old Trafford. Becks and Teddy Sheringham were lining up a free-kick outside Greece's penalty area. Who would take it? Becks was captain, and he was confident of his ability with his free-kicks. 'It's mine,' he told Teddy. Becks's courage has never been in doubt, but this was a real pressure moment.

Old Trafford went quiet. I could feel my heart beating loudly. Becks didn't let us down. The ball flew in and Old Trafford went crazy. What a worldie goal from Captain Marvel! In fact, Becks was brilliant all afternoon. England didn't play well, but Becks was everywhere, dragging us to the World Cup almost single-handedly. When England desperately needed someone to take the game by the scruff of the neck, he stood up to be counted. He was man of the match by a million miles. Top man.

When the Dutch ref, Dick Jol, blew the final

whistle moments after Becks's wonder-strike, a sense of unbelievable relief rushed through me. Thanks to Becks, we were off to the World Cup. As I dreamed of what lay in store in Korea and Japan, I thought of all the great players who have graced World Cups. I thought of England in 1966, and how special it would be to bring the trophy home. I couldn't wait.

But a dark cloud swept across the sky. Injury. The curse of my growing years. My personal stalker. I hated it. Why me? Why would I be charging around, limbs pumping away like pistons, and then seize up? All that season my groin was troublesome, a persistent pain and worry. Getting on the pitch was still possible, but I needed to break the bad cycle of three matches on, one match off crocked. Liverpool's players sensed my frustration. And Didi recommended a guy called Dr Hans Müller-Wohlfahrt to sort me out. I talked the situation through with Gérard. He knew all about the famous Dr Wohlfahrt, who treated Michael's hamstrings. 'Go over, hear what he says, come back and then we'll decide,' the boss said.

Accompanied by the Liverpool physio Dave Galley and club doctor Mark Waller, I flew out to

Munich. Before long I was in a cold clinic being examined by Dr Wohlfahrt from head to toe.

'To sort your body out you need four operations,' he told me.

'One knee operation, one on the ankle, and two hernias.'

Forget the scalpel to the knee, groin and ankle, this was a knife to the heart. I looked anxiously at Doc Waller. He clearly wasn't convinced. 'We'll call you,' Doc Waller said, before we beat it sharpish back to the airport.

I flew back to Liverpool with my head all over the place. I felt a write-off. My body was giving up as my career was really starting.

Back at Melwood, Liverpool held a crisis meeting. Me, Gérard, the physios and Doc Waller searched for the right solution. 'There's no way you need four operations,' Doc Waller kept repeating. I trust Doc Waller with my life, but these German guys were specialists. The walls of Dr Wohlfahrt's clinic were covered with diplomas and degrees from the best medical schools. He came recommended by Didi. Michael swore by him. Jürgen Klinsmann and Boris

Becker used him. Dr Wohlfahrt was the business. But Doc Waller stood his ground. I had a choice: go with a foreign specialist's advice or trust in a Liverpool doctor's instincts. As usual, I stuck with Liverpool. I have worked with Doc Waller so long. He lives around the corner and tends my family. He has always had my interests at heart. Doc Waller would never put me through surgery unless it was the last resort. My faith in him is unshakeable. 'OK, let's do it your way,' I told him. He sent me to see other specialists. I got four more verdicts with different solutions. None of the four said I needed four operations; a couple said I needed at least two.

Gérard was still worried. Even if it was only two ops, Gérard didn't want me cut open unless it was absolutely vital. An op meant missing a long stretch of the season, and it's always risky. But was there any alternative? Gérard thought so. 'Go and see Philippe Boixel in Paris,' he said. 'He will make you more supple through stretching. That may help.'

So off I went again, passport in my hand, fear in my heart. I flew to Paris where I met Boixel, an impressive man who works with the French national team. He examined me and made me do all these com-plicated stretches. 'You don't need any operations,' Boixel said at last. 'Your groins just need strengthen-ing work. My mentality is don't fix it, work on it, and avoid surgery.' I placed my future in the strong hands of Boixel. 'Come and see me once a week at first, and then once a fortnight,' he said. He went to work first on my back, the root cause of all my troubles. 'Because of the shape of your back, it puts pressure on all your muscles,' said Boixel. 'Not just your groin, but ankles, knees and calves. That's why you're getting niggles.'

Maybe I didn't need surgery after all. An op would have been a nightmare, timing-wise. Liverpool needed me, and I would never let the club, the fans, the players or the management down. So between matches I kept nipping over to Paris, where Boixel sorted me out a lot by changing the shape of my back. My groins improved. Injuries were less frequent. Two games a week became manageable. Liverpool were pushing hard for the second automatic Champions League place, and I was right in the thick of it. We had to get that spot. Liverpool needed the money, and the

Champions League was the only stage for me. I strained and sweated hard to get the points.

Little did I realize that my body still wasn't right. The healing hands of Philippe Boixel could only help so far. The pressure built up. On the last day of the 2001/02 season, 11 May, we tore into Ipswich Town at Anfield, knowing victory would book our ticket to Europe's best arenas. I was right up for it. I sprinted on to the pitch, determined to smash down the last barrier to the Champions League. No holding back. Get stuck in. After thirty-three minutes, I stretched for a ball. Bang. My groin ripped. No, no! Not again! Not now! Back to square one. Back to the treatment table. Back home while the boys are at the World Cup.

Gérard called a meeting for the following morning at Melwood. When I arrived, everyone around the place was made up because Liverpool's 5–0 win had guaranteed us Champions League qualification. Next season would be good. Brilliant. But I couldn't think or talk I was so devastated. I wandered around Melwood like a zombie. Up the stairs to Gérard's room, sit down, listen to the gaffer and the doc. 'Steven, even if we patched you up and sent you off to

Japan, your groin could go again in the first game,' Gérard said. 'You probably wouldn't even be ready until the semis. I know it's not what you want to hear, but it's really best that you stay home and we get you ready for next season.'

The club-versus-country balance is always delicate. Liverpool respect England and understand how much the players love pulling on the Three Lions shirt. Representing England is such a boost to a player's career. But clubs are selfish. They pay our wages. I understand their fears. Gérard's priorities were straightforward: winning games for Liverpool, and qualifying for the Champions League. England was not Gérard's problem; getting me ready for next season was.

So the boss sent me to another groin surgeon. 'You do need two operations,' this specialist said, 'but not hernia ops as you've been told. You need a simple operation on both sides to release a muscle. You have a muscle either side that keeps getting tighter and tighter because of the position of your back. I can release them because you don't need them.'

And so my dreams of the 2002 World Cup ended

up on an operating table. The closest I got to Japan was Dubai. I was going mad hanging about at home, so I took my girlfriend Alex off on holiday. 'I've got to get away, Alex,' I told her. 'I can't be here with the whole country going crazy over England.' I was steaming to leave, to get on a beach and bury my frustration in the sand. I checked with Gérard. 'Steven, we'd rather you had the op now and got going with the rehab,' he said. I checked with the surgeon, who was spot on. He sensed how desperate I was for a break. 'You'll need a holiday this summer, so take one now and I'll operate on you when you get back,' he said.

As the players boarded their plane for Japan, Alex and I climbed on a flight to Dubai. Swimming in the sea felt good, but nothing could wash away my anger. I missed the World Cup so badly that I even walked up and down the beach in a pair of England shorts. Inevitably, I was drawn to watching the matches on television. Michael, Becks, Scholesy – they are my friends. I was desperate for them to do well, so I found a bar with a massive screen for the Argentina game.

A punter walked across. 'I wish you were out there, Stevie.'

'Thanks, mate, so do I.'

A few other fans came over, asking for autographs. They were good as gold. They knew how bad I was feeling. They gave me some space and left me to watch the pictures from Sapporo.

From the first whistle, I kicked every ball with Nicky Butt, Becks and Scholesy. In my head, I steamed into tackles on Diego Simeone and Juan Sebastian Verón. Take that! Come on, just win. We have to win. Penalty for England! Bar goes mental. Becks steps up. Just bury it. He does. Bar goes completely crazy. Suddenly, I'm not a frustrated injured player any more, I'm an England fan, shouting the place down, singing the songs, fist in the air. Here we go!

The next day, I scoured Dubai for the papers. Look at the pictures, read the match reports. Every word. One paper carried an interview with Pele where he said I was the best player not at the World Cup finals. Pele implied that England really missed me in midfield. Thanks, mate, but what about Butty? He had a stormer against Argentina.

My holiday over, I returned to reality. The surgeon's knife awaited. The operation complete, I limped around my apartment in Southport, catching the rest of the World Cup. A few friends called and asked me round to watch the Brazil quarter-final. I couldn't. England v. Brazil was too personal for me to share the experience with other people. All my mates would be sitting around, buzzing, when I would just be sunk in a depression over missing such a colossal occasion. World Cup quarter-finals against Ronaldinho and Ronaldo don't come along too often. I had to watch the game on my own. Doors locked. Phone off. Just me and my misery.

The game passed in a blur. Michael scoring. Brazil hitting back. Ronaldinho's goal. Seamo's tears. Heartache. Brazil looked fresher, better suited to the hot climate. At the final whistle, England's players slumped to the ground, drained and defeated. I sat there in silence, my heart breaking for them. They are not just England players to me, star names people see in papers and on the telly. They are good friends, and I was devastated for them. For all my frustration and jealousy, I would much rather have seen Michael and Becks with World Cup winner's medals around their necks than Ronaldinho and Ronaldo. I am selfish, I want to fill my upstairs room with medals, but there was no sense of private relief at watching England return home from Japan empty-handed. I was as distressed as them. Like Becks and Michael, my determination doubled to bring the World Cup home in 2006.

# 11
## Good Guys and Bad Buys

For all my frustration over missing the World Cup, my admiration for Gérard remained immense. He cared passionately about Liverpool. People forget he almost lost his life working for the club. I will never forget when he was almost taken from us.

The boss seemed fine and healthy as he gave us some last-minute advice on 13 October 2001, talking us through what we should expect from Leeds United, the visitors to Anfield that Saturday afternoon. We returned to the dressing-room at half-time 1–0 down, expecting Gérard to be waiting to have a go at us. Instead it was Thommo. 'Gérard's not well,' Thommo explained as we looked around for the boss. 'He's gone to hospital for a check-up.' The staff were outwardly very calm. Thommo didn't want to distract us from the task of turning the game around. Points were at stake. But we couldn't help but worry about our manager. We knew it must be serious for Gérard to be rushed off to hospital. We managed to focus enough on the game to equalize, through Danny Murphy, but everyone was down afterwards. Being without Gérard hit us hard. Imagine Manchester United coping without Sir Alex Ferguson. I drove home feeling worried. When I got in, I sent the boss a text: 'Hope you are all right'. No reply. My concern deepened. Gérard is usually sharp back on the text, or he calls. But nothing. Not a word.

At Melwood the next day, Doc Waller gathered all the players in the meeting room. 'Gérard has undergone emergency heart surgery,' he told us. 'It took eleven hours and it was a dissection of the aorta.' Such medical terms meant little to me, but the serious look on Doc Waller's face told me everything I needed to know about the manager's plight. 'He will be away for some time,' Doc Waller continued. 'He sends his regards and asks you to focus on the next games, not on him.'

Typical Gérard. Always thinking of Liverpool,

never himself. I feared his 24/7 commitment to leading Liverpool had damaged his health. Constant pressure takes a toll. Gérard would never have listened to any signs from his body to slow down. Now he had been at death's door, saved only by a surgeon's skill.

'Gérard will be back,' insisted Thommo, 'and until he does, I'll be taking over. We must stick together to make sure we are in a good position for when the boss gets back. He has all your interests at heart. He fights for you. We must show that fight for him.'

We flew out to Kiev later that day for a Champions League game, and the long trip was desperately gloomy. When we got to Dinamo's stadium, Thommo put a sign up on the dressing-room wall: 'Do It For the Boss'. We did. I poured all my concern for our missing manager into that tie, even scoring the winner in a 2–1 victory.

Gérard Houllier was a well-liked manager, a player's manager, and very human. He is one of life's good guys. So is Thommo. Like Gérard, everything Thommo did was for the good of Liverpool Football Club. He was a Scouser like me, and I respected him because he lifted the European Cup for Liverpool. He was always honest with me, always told me when I was not training or playing well enough. I liked him. Still do.

When Thommo was named caretaker during Gérard's illness, it felt strange, but no-one could question how much effort he put in. But we missed our leader. When Gérard eventually reappeared at Melwood five months later, in March 2002, while Thommo was preparing us for a big European game against Roma, we were all overjoyed, but I was shocked how pale he looked. He'd lost a lot of weight, and wasn't sharp at all. But he still knew how every game had gone, how each of us had done. Typical Gérard. Even while recuperating, he was obsessed with Liverpool. 'I want to be on the bench tomorrow – if the doctor lets me!' he told us. Well, that just made training even sharper. Everyone was flying to know the boss would be back watching us. The atmosphere at Anfield is always special on European nights, but that evening was unbelievable. Word spread fast that Gérard was in the ground. The Kop went crazy, chanting his name. The whole place was buzzing. We needed to win 2–0, and we knew we would. Our manager was back. All was well in the world.

Gérard's return kept us rolling on, riding high in the Premiership and in Europe. Just before our Champions League quarter-final at Bayer Leverkusen on 9 April, Gérard declared, 'Liverpool are ten games from greatness.' Everyone seized on the boss's comment, debating whether this Liverpool side really could win the Premiership and the Champions League.

But in sight of both finishing lines, we faltered: knocked out by Leverkusen in the last eight in Europe, runners-up in the Premiership. Arsenal deserved to win the league. They were a great team, better than Liverpool, but we got eighty points. Such a total would have won the Premiership in another season. After the Treble, and then coming second, I felt the title was only just around the corner. If Liverpool strengthened in the right areas for the 2002/03 season, the Premiership dream could become real.

Before the start of every season, Gérard handed around pieces of paper and told us to write down our ambitions for the year. I usually scribbled, 'Improve league position and try and win a cup.' In August 2002, I wrote, 'We'll win the title.' But then Gérard signed El-Hadji Diouf, Salif Diao and Bruno Cheyrou for nearly £18 million. Those three were meant to be the signings that took Liverpool to the next level, to the Premiership title and Champions League glory. That was the plan. But after a promising start, Liverpool slid downhill fast.

I respect Gérard immensely for what he did at Liverpool. He brought me six trophies, and I still keep in touch with him, but managers are judged on signings. The players Gérard bought in the summer of 2002 let him down. They were bad buys.

But we did win the Worthington Cup final win over Manchester United on 2 March 2003. At least that trip to Cardiff gave us some silverware for 2002/03. My shot hit Becks and deflected in over Fabien Barthez, United's keeper. No matter how lucky the goal was, it felt brilliant to score against the old enemy. Michael, as usual, also found the mark as Liverpool ran out 2–0 winners.

That was the high point of a season that descended into disappointment. Fifth was nowhere.

No Champions League for 2003/04 was a killer. Liverpool were in decline, and Gérard came under mounting pressure. I began thinking about my future. 'I'm worried, Stru,' I told my agent. 'Playing in the Champions League helps get me in the England squad. Sven always watches Champions League games. People look down on the UEFA Cup.' I knew I could survive one season out of the Champions League, but two would harm my career. Struan took a few phone calls from agents representing clubs in Europe, enquiring about the situation with my contract. Barcelona, Roma and Inter Milan were apparently interested. I was flattered to read pieces saying Real Madrid were chasing me, but I wasn't tempted. Liverpool's season had been disappointing, but I didn't want to leave the club I love.

# 12
## Darkness in Basle

The most depressing point in my relationship with Gérard Houllier came in the pretty Swiss town of Basle on 12 November 2002. Everyone in Liverpool's colours needed all their energy and focus for this massive Champions League tie, the most important game of the season, but my head wasn't right. For some time, I'd been a bit moody. Tension between me and Gérard built and built. When the boss took me off against Spurs at Anfield on 26 October, I snapped. Straight down the tunnel, no acknowledgement. Straight into the dressing-room, door slamming, boots flying, absolutely steaming. I hate being hooked, however rubbish I'm playing. But not in front of the Kop, where my mates are watching. When the fourth official holds up my number it feels like a judge passing a sentence. Game over. I have no control; I have to leave the pitch, and everyone stares. Not good enough today, Stevie lad. The humiliation kills me.

Storming past Gérard at Anfield annoyed him big-time. The boss immediately sent Doc Waller to come and get me. But I didn't budge, and stayed in the dressing-room, alone with my anger. Gérard went mental and fined me. Even an apology couldn't repair the damage. He put me on the bench against West Ham, and then subbed me at Middlesbrough. What a mess. As we flew out to Basle, Gérard wasn't in my good books, and I wasn't in his.

It was my fault. My form wasn't right. Bad problems off the pitch distracted me. I couldn't tell anyone at Liverpool because it was too personal. Mum and Dad were splitting up. There was trouble in the house, arguing, fighting. I love my parents so much it was desperate to watch them tearing each other apart. It was supposed to be perfect. I had bought a house in Whiston and the three of us lived there, with Paul, my brother, keeping Ironside. I was gutted Paul didn't come with us. Family means every-thing to me, all together, sitting around and laughing, under one roof. I wanted the magic of my Ironside childhood to last for ever. However crazy my life became with Liverpool and England, I wanted that protective wall of my family around me. But Paul decided to stay at Ironside. Still, there was Mum, Dad and me living together. Together. That's what mattered.

Family life at Whiston seemed great to start with. The better I did on the pitch, surely the better life should be at home? That's how I thought it would work. We had money, a nice house, each other. Mum and Dad weren't working, so it wasn't as if they were spending time apart. They were always close. What could go wrong?

Everything. People fall out of love with each other, I suppose. At first, I didn't know my parents were quarrelling. They kept it from me, didn't want to upset me, didn't want to disrupt my career. But they couldn't hide the tension for ever. I found myself getting dragged into their nightmare. When I came back in from Melwood or a match, I heard the arguments which they quickly tried to stop when they realized I was home. I tried to speak to them about it, tried to help, but they were too far down the road to breaking up. Even now, looking back, it still rips my heart apart. I just wanted everything to be perfect, for everyone to be together.

The turmoil at home destroyed my game. My form hit a brick wall. As I pulled my boots on and did up my laces, my thoughts were miles away. In training and matches, all I could think about was that two people I adored were going their separate ways. The split happened over a couple of months, and I couldn't handle it. It felt like a bereavement. Only one word can describe my life as winter approached: carnage.

I revealed my anguish to one person. In Basle, I shared a room with Danny Murphy, and I told him everything about Mum and Dad. Danny endured the same grief with his parents. He understood the pain I was going through, how it affected my football. Danny was superb. I would not have survived that Basle trip without him. 'Don't worry,' said Danny. 'You'll get through. Be strong. Just forget what's happening for a moment and go out and play.'

Amazingly, I started against Basle. After an argument with Gérard, I assumed I would be on the bench again. The boss played me in my favourite position, too, central midfield, but I was shocking. Not focused. Not involved. Every pass I made went to a Basle player or into the crowd. I wasn't running enough. I felt so detached, as if I was watching someone in a horror film. Liverpool needed a big performance from me. We had to beat Basle to reach the knockout stages of the Champions League. But my mind was else-where. I looked around St Jakobs Park and just wanted to be back in Whiston, trying to keep Mum and Dad together. With me off the pace, Basle grabbed a three-goal lead by half-time. And my night was about to get even worse.

In the dressing-room, I was scarcely through the door when Gérard shouted, 'Steven, shower.' That was it. Me off. All the lads felt embarrassed because I looked stupid. If a player has a nightmare, a manager can react in two ways at half-time: either give the player another five minutes so the subbing doesn't appear that bad, or humiliate the player by not allow-ing him out for the second half. Gérard should have allowed me five more minutes, just to give me a chance to make some impact. I deserved better treatment than being shown up in front of the team. Gérard had embarrassed me like that before, bringing me on and taking me off in the same game against Newcastle. That annoyed me no end. This was worse, far worse.

I stood there in the shower, listening to Gérard giving instructions for the second half. Liverpool pulled three goals back, through Danny, Vladi and Michael, which made me look even worse. Afterwards, when the staff came into the dressing-room, I just walked into the toilets and stayed there while they talked to the boys.

We stopped the night in Basle. The next morning I got word Gérard had had a pop at me. The boss told journalists, 'Once a player starts to believe everything that is written about him and thinks "I am king of the world", there is difficulty and danger.' Basically, Gérard questioned my commitment. At the airport, I sought out Joycey, who I knew would have been at the press conference with Gérard. Joycey would give it to me straight.

'You're not going to like the papers in the morning, Stevie,' he said.

The next morning, the stories were as brutal as I feared. Gérard accused me of reading too many headlines. I certainly read these ones he whipped up. I talked to two people I trust, Chris Bascombe of the *Echo* and Liverpool's press officer, Ian Cotton.

'Did Gérard say it the way it has been printed?' I asked them.

'Yes,' Basco and Cotton both replied.

I needed to know for sure. Sometimes a manager's words get twisted on the way from a press conference to a headline. Not in this case.

When he called me, Gérard claimed it was typical press overreaction. 'I had a go at you in the press, but they blew it out of proportion,' he said, but I knew the truth. Gérard meant every word. It wasn't malice. The boss just wanted to shake me out of my poor form. In Gérard's mind, he'd tried every angle, from one-on-one talks with me to the full firing squad, and nothing lifted my depression. Basle was the last resort, the shock tactics, and it hurt like hell.

Liverpool managers have always kept criticism in-house, saying things privately to players rather than in public. What Gérard did in Basle broke the code. At the very least he should have warned me what he was planning to tell the media, not throw an unexpected bomb at me in a crowded press conference. Managers must be careful what they say to the media. I felt badly let down. My phone was red-hot with calls from the team. Everyone was saying or texting how shocked they were by Gérard's action.

Robbie, Gary Mac and Jamie Redknapp gave me good support. So did Struan, my agent. My dad hit the roof when he picked up the papers.

'What is going on?' he asked me. 'I know why you're not playing well. It's not because you are a bad player, or have the wrong people around you. It's because of what is happening in our house between me and your mother. Doesn't Gérard understand that?'

I couldn't reply. It was too painful.

'Doesn't Gérard know?' Dad said again.

I shrugged my shoulders. 'I've not told him,' I replied eventually.

'It's our fault, and I am going to tell Gérard,' Dad said.

'No! Leave it!'

'Come on, Steven, either you tell him or I will.'

'I'm not.' I was really upset by this time. I felt trapped.

Dad was livid. 'Give me Gérard's number.'

'No.'

'Right, that's it. I'm going down the training ground to have it out with him.'

I couldn't stop Dad. He was out the house before I could react. I hoped he would calm down and have second thoughts as he drove there. No chance. Straight down to Melwood, straight up to Gérard's office, knock on the door, and in. Nothing was going to stop Dad saying his piece. He was raging. He explained everything to Gérard and Thommo. 'It's mine and Julie's fault that Steven's off his game,' he told them.

While Dad was in there, I got a call off Boggo. 'Stevie, your dad's in with Gérard.' I was gutted people knew my old fella was in the boss's office. My mobile went again. It was Gérard, asking me to come in for a meeting. I rushed over.

Dad was just sticking up for me, I know. When I got back to Whiston, I thanked him. He knew how unhappy I was. Dad knows me better than anyone. 'I haven't seen you smile for ages, Steven,' he said. 'You are not the happiest of people anyway! But I can tell.' Dad got everything out in the open, and from then on my form came back sharpish. I felt as if a huge stone weight had been lifted off my chest. I was grateful to everyone at Liverpool for keeping news of my parents' split quiet. No-one outside the club or house knew. Mum and Dad broke up, but it was not an aggressive fall-out in the end. They just sat down, talked, and went their separate ways.

Fortunately, Basle didn't harm my relationship with Gérard in the long run. Before we travelled up to Sunderland in December, the boss called me into his office. 'Sami is out for the game and I want you to be captain,' he said.

Captain of Liverpool!

Basle seemed a distant memory as I led Liverpool out at the Stadium of Light. We lost, but the feeling of having the armband on was special. 'One day, you will captain the club permanently,' said Gérard. 'Keep learning.' He mentioned the captaincy a couple of times that season, but I never really thought anything of it. During training one afternoon the following season, 2003/04, Gérard said, 'Come and see me afterwards.' I showered, changed, and ran upstairs to the boss's office. Thommo was sitting there next to Gérard.

'We've had meetings with the staff,' Gérard began, 'and have spoken to a few players. We feel as if we need to change the captaincy of the club. Sami has been a good captain, but we feel you are ready to take the captaincy on. We feel it would help the team.'

I was stunned. Everyone respected Sami. A big, vocal centre-half, Sami was a natural leader.

'How is it going to be with Sami?' I asked.

'Don't worry,' replied Gérard. 'I've spoken to Sami.'

When I left the office, I looked around for Sami, but he had gone home. Pity. I wanted to address the issue as quickly as possible.

I didn't sleep much that night. Feelings of pride mixed with concern over how Sami would react. Sami hadn't been playing that well, so maybe taking away the armband would allow him to focus on his own game, rather than the team. Still, it can't be nice to have such an honour taken away. I'd be devastated.

As I arrived at Melwood the next day, Sami pulled me.

'Stevie, can I have a word?'

'Yeah, of course, Sami.'

'Listen, I spoke to the manager and Phil yesterday and I want you to know there are no hard feelings. You deserve the captaincy. It was only a matter of time. Good luck. If you need any advice, I'm there for you.'

Some man, is Sami. That can't have been easy for him, but he handled it with real dignity. My admiration for him rose even higher. I wanted to be a captain like Sami, a good ambassador. Becks was my other role model. Until he stepped down after the World Cup in Germany, Becks proved an outstanding captain for England. Becks always led by example, always gave everything on the pitch, always gave sound advice off it. Becks was brilliant with the young lads, especially those new to the set-up and slightly in awe. When I became Liverpool captain, I watched Becks even more closely with England. Saw how he dealt with issues, how easily he handled the responsibility.

Sometimes I stop on the drive home from Melwood and just sit in the car and tell myself, 'I'm captain of Liverpool Football Club.' For a kid who grew up in Huyton, who stood on the Kop, being Liverpool captain is an unbelievable honour. I think of all the greats who have led out Liverpool, real leaders like Ron Yeats, Emlyn Hughes, Thommo, Graeme Souness, Alan Hansen. And now me. I can never thank Gérard Houllier enough. I owe Gérard so much. I'll always remember what Gérard did for my career.

# 13
# Stars and Strikes

I even captained England. It was only a friendly, a trip to Sweden on 31 March 2004, but it felt like the World Cup final as I led my country out in Gothenburg. This was a moment I had dreamed of since I wore the Bryan Robson shirt while kicking about on Ironside. We lost, to a goal from Sweden's clever striker Zlatan Ibrahimovic, but the armband and the memory will stay with me for ever.

Just before then, the press questioned how much we players love representing England – a disgraceful claim. The controversy stemmed from the build-up to our final Euro 2004 qualifier in Istanbul on 11 October 2003. Six days before this massive tie, I drove to Manchester airport with Emile and Carra for the flight down to London. We met the United lads at the gate and had a chat. Usual stuff, until Carra noticed Rio Ferdinand was missing. 'Where's Rio?' Carra asked. 'Is he not in the squad?' Scholesy, Butty and Gary Neville explained Rio had been left out on Football Association orders, because he missed a drugs test. Well, he hadn't deliberately missed it. He'd forgotten, left the training ground, and when he remembered, the testers had gone. Rio took a test later and passed. But the FA were livid and stopped Sven picking him. Carra, Emile and me were shocked.

The saga was only just beginning. When we arrived at Sopwell House, our base near St Albans, the place was in uproar. Quite a few of the England lads were steaming over the FA's treatment of Rio. We should have been focusing on training with Sven and getting prepared for Turkey, but all the boys could talk about was Rio. Carnage lay around the corner.

On the Tuesday we managed to train in the morning, and then Becks called a meeting. He spoke, and so did Gary Neville, very forcefully. More speeches. More debate. Then Becks and Gary organized a ballot over whether to support Rio, with the understanding that could mean not going to Istanbul. A strike! Just mention of the word makes me shudder. It would be a hugely controversial call, a decision that would live with us for the rest of our lives.

Fortunately, David James spoke out, calling for clear heads before we considered striking. 'We've got to think about the fans,' said Jamo. 'With all due respect to Rio, and I want him back in the squad as much as anyone, there are going to be more problems than we all think if we go on strike.' People say goal-keepers are mad, but Jamo always talked sense. I really admired him for what he did and said at Sopwell. Jamo made everyone realize the dangers of a strike, that it wasn't going to benefit any of us. Gary put forward one argument, and Jamo just looked at the situation from the point of view of a few others at the meeting, the ones like me who never said any-thing. After Jamo spoke, I felt better. The consequences of not going to Turkey were obvious. 'If we support Rio 100 per cent and don't go to Istanbul, we'll all have to take the flak,' said Jamo. Flipping heck, I thought, this is so serious. My heart beat fast.

We can't go on strike, but we must stick together. Send out a message to the FA: don't mess with us. The best sides are those where the players stand shoulder to shoulder, like soldiers in a war. We were all in it together, even those with reservations. Eventually, I decided to follow the experienced players like Becks and Gary. So did the rest of the squad. We all agreed the FA had to bring Rio back or face the consequences. Whatever the reservations of players like myself, we were united. One out, all out. Though I prayed we wouldn't have to go through with the strike. Gary and Becks knocked up a statement from the England squad which read: 'It is our opinion that the organization we represent has not only let down one of our team-mates but the whole of the England squad and its manager. We feel they have failed us badly. They have made the team weaker.' We gave the statement to the FA and sat back to see their reaction.

Becks quickly told Sven. He wanted the dispute settled sharpish, but he backed us all the way. On the Wednesday, as the controversy intensified, Sven told all the cameras at Sopwell that he was behind us.

Every England player really respected Sven for that. He could have ducked the issue, or sided with the FA because they pay his wages. Sven didn't. When the team needed the support of the manager most, Sven stuck up for us. It was a horrible day, though. Whenever I flicked Sky on in my room, people were criticizing us for talking about striking. We were getting unbelievable stick. I felt we'd made our point by publicly backing Rio and it was time to move on, to get back to football. I was not enjoying the caning. None of the players were. A sombre mood fell over Sopwell.

That evening, the players held another meeting. 'Right, we've made our point,' said Becks. 'We've shown the FA that they cannot mess about one of our players.' We all agreed we should now go to Istanbul.

As the plane hurtled across Europe, my mind finally turned to what sort of reception the Turks would lay on for us. Our home game, at Sunderland on 2 April 2003, had been quick, intense and nasty. The Turks were up to all their old tricks at the Stadium of Light, leaving the foot in, pulling shirts, the usual sly stunts, anything to break up our flow.

Even players who have spent time in the Premiership, like Tugay, an opponent I respect, tried to provoke us. But when Tugay and his mates arrived at Sunderland, they ran into Wayne Rooney. Turkey didn't know what hit them. Rooney was brilliant in that 2–0 victory, all muscle and touch.

In those few days up in the north-east of England, I realized exactly how special Rooney was. One day, in training at Slaley Hall, Rooney announced to the whole England squad the massive size of his talent. We were playing a practice match towards the end of training when Rooney picked up the ball, dribbled past a few players and chipped Jamo. Astonishing. Silence reigned for a split-second, as if everyone was trying to take in exactly what we had just seen. Then we all burst into applause, everyone, even established stars like Becks and Owen. We all glanced at each other, as if to say, 'This boy can play.' Only seventeen, and already heading for greatness. I knew Wazza was talented because I had seen the goals he scored for Everton, I'd watched him on the telly, and I'd read all the press coverage. But that day at Slaley Hall made me realize quite how brilliant he was. I needed to train alongside him, watch him close up, to appreciate the quality of his first touch. His self-belief too. Most players would be cautious during the build-up to their first start. Not Wazza. He charged into Slaley Hall, trying all sorts of skills. Nothing fazes Wazza. It's a Scouse trait. No wonder we hit it off immediately.

By the time we landed in Istanbul, Wazza and I were good mates. What I love about Rooney is, however big the occasion, he's relaxed. England's journey to Fenerbahce's home ground would have unsettled even the toughest customer. Not Rooney. Wazza just smiled out the window at all these Turks throwing bottles at us, screaming abuse. When Rooney was ready, he just ran out of the tunnel into this wall of noise and laughed. Is that your best? Try harder, shout louder, because I ain't bothered. That's Wazza. He went towards one goal and started banging balls around. Scholesy was the same. Out the tunnel, pinging balls around, no warm-up. I don't know how Scholesy and Rooney get away with it. If I had not done some stretching first, working on my hamstrings and calf, I'd have pulled every muscle in my legs. Not Rooney. How his hamstrings survived I don't know.

Before kick-off, Becks gathered us together and reminded us what would happen if we messed up. The fuss over the threatened strike would return with a vengeance. Doubled. Imagine the headlines, lads. We had to get that point. Qualify for the Euros, and we'd go from zeros to heroes in the fans' eyes again. All teams visiting Turkey need strong bonds between players, and the Rio controversy bolted all the players even closer. All that off-the-pitch unity now needed to be shown in the teeth of a Turkish hurricane.

The atmosphere in Istanbul was crazy. There were 42,000 Turks screaming blue murder at us. When I went near the crowd, to pick up the ball for a throw-in, Turkish fans drew fingers across their necks, making as if they wanted to slash our throats. Bring it on. When Becks missed a penalty, which was given after Tugay tripped me, no-one blamed him. He slipped. Penalty-taking is a lottery anyway, so no-one was going to dig Becks out. How many times has he got England out of trouble? Countless. We are a family at England, and we look after each other like brothers.

The goalless draw was enough to give us what

we'd gone to Turkey for: a place at Euro 2004 in Portugal the following summer. I fancied England's chances. Good squad, great spirit, and everyone up for it.

## 14
## Pleasure and Pain in Portugal

We landed in Lisbon among the favourites. Our team was settled, with Wayne now established alongside Michael, and the midfield situation sorted following two warm-up games at the City of Manchester Stadium. In the first, against Japan on 1 June, Sven shifted me out to the left of a diamond – a decision that disappointed me. I'll play anywhere for England, of course. No-one doubts my commitment to my country, but my strengths lie in central midfield. No question. Confronting the enemy head on, getting the ball, bombing on, finishing moves off – that's me. I envied Scholesy his position at the tip of the diamond against Japan, a real attacking role. I'd have caused chaos there.

Before kick-off, I was presented with a trophy for

England Player of the Year – a fantastic gesture from the supporters. I've had awards from journalists and players, but this honour was different: it came from England fans who spend their life, and their hard-earned cash, travelling around watching us. My heart swelled with pride. England Player of the Year! Sounded good. Time to show it was deserved.

Cutting in from the flank, I helped set up Michael's goal against Japan, but I hated life on the left. I love the centre-stage, not playing out on the fringe. Sven often used me in different positions, sometimes telling me only hours before a game or changing my role during a match. As a footballer and as a human being, I must feel settled before I can be happy and deliver. I crave the nod days before, so I can work on the role, eradicate mistakes in training, and talk the assignment through with Sven, the coaches and other players. Even good footballers find it difficult to adapt if told their role only twenty-four hours before a massive game. But whingeing is not my style. I never raised my unease in public after the Japan game. I just read with interest the debate raging on the sports pages over where I should play for

England. No debate, guys. I'm best in the middle. End of story. I do have the legs to play out there, but I'm not John Barnes, beating three and getting crosses in.

Fortunately, diamonds are not for ever. Four days later, Sven restored me to England's heart against Iceland. We thrashed them 6–1, and I was there to stay. Thank God. By then, Frank Lampard had edged out Butty, so England flew into Portugal with a midfield of me and Lamps in the centre, Scholesy on the left and Becks right. It looked good. 'This is my midfield for Portugal,' Sven told us. My sigh of relief was long and loud, although I felt sorry for Scholesy, who got the graveyard shift. I wanted Scholesy to shine on the left at Euro 2004 so Sven wouldn't banish me out there.

As we checked into our Lisbon base, the Solplay, everything appeared perfect. The hotel boasted all the five-star trimmings. The weather was magnificent, so in our spare time we gathered round the pool to relax, or nipped out for a knock of golf. Every camp needs a joker and we had David James, a bubbly character, brilliant at getting the spirit going. In the hours after training or between matches, Jamo always lightened the mood with his dry humour.

Gary Neville is more serious than Jamo, but is just as important to the squad. Always focused, always professional, Gary is the ideal team-mate with England. At Liverpool, Steve Finnan reaches towards Gary's level, but in terms of consistency over the years, Gary is the best right-back I've played with. Captain of Manchester United, Gary's a leader, a winner. Sitting around the Solplay, some had doubts whether we would do well at Euro 2004. Not Gary. 'We can win this,' he kept saying.

But, inside, we all knew it would be difficult. We weren't firing on all cylinders. Euro 2004 was do-able, but we needed to raise our game, individually and collectively. People had high expectations of me, particularly now I was back where I belonged, in central midfield. I was in the holding role, but at least I was central. Having a nation's eyes on me was not a problem. My club form had been good. But England faced a stiff start, against France, the champions, the team of Thierry Henry, Zinédine Zidane and Patrick Vieira – a familiar opponent from Premiership war zones.

Everyone made England underdogs for this opening Group B game at the Stadium of Light on 13 June. Everyone tipped France to thrash us. France's team-sheet was pinned up in our dressing-room. I looked at the names. 'Respect them, but don't fear them,' I thought. Zidane was class, but we had top players as well. 'I'm not having this,' I said out loud. 'Let's show everyone what we can do.' We had Michael. We had Wayne. Wayne! I looked across at him. Not a care in the world. Relaxed, confident, ready for any opposition, however good. He just banged a ball against the wall, first time, bang. Back it came. Bang. Back it went. Back and forth, almost hypnotically. Wayne was just messing about with the ball, as if he were going out for a Sunday League match. He stopped as Sven gave us some last-minute orders. When Sven finished, Wayne also had some instructions. 'Just give me the ball,' he told everyone. 'Give me the ball. I will do it. I want it.' Wayne wasn't being big-headed. He knows what he can do. Everything! We had a chance against France. Wayne would breeze through them.

The atmosphere in the dressing-room ripped into

life. Jamo, standing tall in the middle of the room, screamed encouragement. Becks, Gary Nev, Sol – all shouting. Sol is amazing. A great player for Spurs and Arsenal, he really comes to life at tournaments. The moment he stepped into the dressing-room before the French game, he became a different person. A leader, a warrior. So serene around the hotel, England's Colossus was fired up to face the French. His voice and presence filled the dressing-room. Shouts were now coming from all corners of the room. No-one was quiet. No-one was scared. This was it. France. Vieira. Come on! Door open, into the tunnel, out into the stadium.

Nothing prepared me for the sights and sounds that greeted me. The Stadium of Light held 62,487 that night, and they all seemed to be English. White flags waved everywhere. Even in the French corner, I saw hundreds of England supporters, faces painted with the Cross of St George, singing 'Three Lions', not giving a monkey's they were in the French section. Our supporters are truly fanatical. They launched into the national anthem so loudly the hairs stood to attention on the back of my neck.

Controlling my emotions was a struggle. Focus, focus. But the adrenalin was pumping, racing even quicker as I poured my heart into the anthem. Amazing moments. The singing and formalities completed, I sprinted into the middle. This was it. Into battle. Come on, Vieira.

England settled the quicker. All the predictions were being turned on their head. We passed the ball around well, even taking the lead. One of Lamps' main strengths is raiding into the box, getting goals. At Euro 2004 he got off to a flier with a fantastic header past Fabien Barthez. Pick that out. That goal was the making of Lamps, filling him with confidence.

France were caught out, sent reeling by the intensity of England's football. I got stuck into Vieira and Zidane. Frank raced forward. Rooney stretched France, pulling Lilian Thuram and Mikael Silvestre all over the Stadium of Light. France were totally un-prepared for this one-man tornado from Croxteth called Wayne Rooney. He battered them. Wayne never looks scared in matches, never hides from the ball. He could be back on the street in Merseyside. We all knew how special he was; that night at the Stadium of

**Shooting Star** I needed all my strength to break down Olympiakos's defence at Anfield and keep Liverpool on the road to Istanbul.

**Heading For A Comeback** I climb high to make it 3–1 and give us hope against AC Milan in Istanbul.

**Mission Impossible Accomplished** After an unbelievable final, I get my hands on the European Cup.

*Above*: **Letting Fly** I had just enough energy left to make it 3–3 in that amazing 2006 FA Cup final against West Ham in Cardiff.

**Romance Of The Cup** I have always loved the FA Cup and lifting it as captain was a schoolboy dream come true.

**Capped Crusader** I will always be grateful to Kevin Keegan for giving me my England debut in 2000.

*Right*: **National Service** Sven-Goran Eriksson did me a great honour by making me England captain against Sweden in 2004.

**Friends Re-united** Give me the ball with England and I will find Michael Owen, my old Liverpool team-mate.

**Power And The Glory** Not a bad way to open my England scoring – against Germany in the 5–1 win in Munich.

*Top*: **Left In No Dou...**
Not my strongest, bu...
found the target in th...
Trinidad & Tobago in...

*Middle*: **Happy Days...**
I've scored in Nurem...
Rooney is back in th...
injury, and all appear...
England in Germany...

*Bottom*: **In With A S...**
making it 2–1 to E...
five minutes left in...
I was convinced w...
Sweden but Henri...
equalized.

**Big Appeal** My passion for England to do well in the World Cup was immense.

**Spread The Word** I join in the celebrations of David Beckham's second-round winner against Ecuador in Stuttgart, helped by Ashley Cole, Michael Carrick, Rio Ferdinand and Wayne Rooney.

*Left*: **On The Move** Here I lead the charge against Ecuador in Stuttgart.

*Below*: **All For The Cause** I slide in to stop one of Cristiano Ronaldo's long runs in Gelsenkirchen.

*Below*: **All Played Out** I couldn't move from the centre-circle after the shoot-out in Gelsenkirchen, just sitting there shell-shocked.

Light was the moment the whole world realized England boasted an extraordinarily gifted teenager. A star was born in Lisbon. Since then, Wayne has become the key man for England. He's such a character and joker around the hotel. He is always up to something. I didn't know Gazza too well, but I heard all the stories about Gazza's antics lifting team spirit. Wazza is the same – always smiling, always happy. He'll wind anyone up. At the Solplay, all the players marvelled at his confidence for someone so young. Rooney knows he is the main man. He is brilliant between the opposition defence and midfield, always there, always looking for the quick ball to feet, a joy to link with. Wayne can run at players, beat them and set goals up. One of his many runs against France panicked Silvestre into giving away a penalty. Becks missed, but we still felt in control.

Sensibly, Sven sent Emile on for Wayne to see the match out and keep our new strike threat fresh for England's next game. Our fans were singing, celebrating, generally going wild. We were up and running at Euro 2004, three points surely in the bag. Surely? It still sickens me to record what then occurred at the

Stadium of Light. Emile fouled Claude Makelele, Zidane bent in the free-kick, and the life went out of us. Having led for so long, Zidane's goal was a crushing blow. Heads down. Play for time. Cling to the draw. Keep the point. No more mistakes. Almost there. In injury time, I received possession quite deep in our half and I knew instinctively what to do. Run the clock down, waste time, play it safe. Pass back to Jamo. Oops! Thierry Henry. The great French striker was lurking behind one of our central defenders, and if you are going to hide behind anyone, hide behind big Sol. Once I played the ball back and realized there was a Frenchman there, I prayed to God it was anyone but Thierry. He's lethal. I have passed accidentally to Henry since, at Highbury, and when he picks the ball up it can lead only to a goal. Jamo sprinted out, fouled Henry, and Zidane swept in the penalty. From 1–0 up to 2–1 down in the space of two minutes. Nightmare. My mistake made me feel so wretched I thought I would be physically sick. I could hardly look at the other England players, or our supporters, as I raced back to the dressing-room.

From down the corridor came the sound of

French celebrations. Their players were singing, trumpeting their victory. Sven made sure the door stayed open so we could hear them. 'Listen to them,' someone said. 'We'll prove them wrong.' French crowing spurred the squad on, making us doubly determined to recover from this setback.

As the other players got dressed, I stood in the shower, trying to wash away the frustration, the guilt. 'Be strong,' I told myself. 'Adversity will not kill you. Fight back.' I phoned Struan, and Dad. 'Keep your head up,' they said. I didn't switch my phone off, or hide from the fact that I messed up.

The next day's papers did not make pleasant reading. There was nothing for it but to make amends in England's next game, against Switzerland in Coimbra on 17 June.

Sven kept faith with the same players, apart from John Terry returning from injury in place of Ledley King.

Sven was good before the match. 'Just play like you did for eighty-nine minutes against France,' he said. 'Build on that.' Wayne certainly did. He was unstoppable, his confidence boosted by positive headlines about him after the French game. He charged out and destroyed the Swiss, scoring after twenty-three minutes. I was amazed how he kept sprinting about in the heat. I have never endured hotter conditions. At 48°C in the shade, breathing became difficult, let alone sprinting. After ten minutes I wondered whether I would survive. My head was pounding, heart racing and legs slowing. 'Keep the ball,' I shouted to the other players. We couldn't afford to give away cheap possession, or go chasing shadows. Every break in play, the staff threw us water-bottles. At half-time, there were ice-baths in the dressing-room. 'It will cool your muscles down,' said Gary Lewin, the physio. I stripped off and leapt in.

Refreshed, we tore into the Swiss after the break, Wayne adding another. Inevitably, tiredness began taking its toll, so Sven sent Owen Hargreaves on for Scholesy, and moved me to the left. With eight minutes left, we broke down the right, and I had enough legs to get into the box and finish the move off. Three goals, three points and a big win, particularly for me. I sweated my French mistake out of my system against Switzerland.

We were really firing by now, and Croatia stood no chance at the Stadium of Light on 21 June. Wazza, England's new super-hero, struck twice as we took them apart 4–2. Our French mess forgotten, we kept piling forward, committing too many bodies to attack at times. Sometimes it was just the four defenders and me left behind to deal with the Croatian counters. It was worrying. Against better finishers than Croatia, we would get caught out. Concern tempered our celebrations at qualifying for the quarter-finals. Three days to recover. Barely enough time to feel the life seep back into my legs. Exhaustion stalked me.

Portugal blocked the road to the semis: the hosts, the only team with bigger support than England, the team of Cristiano Ronaldo and Luis Figo. Ronaldo was all slick skill at speed, the king of step-overs, really loving his time in the limelight. He overdoes the tricks at times, but he's a nightmare to deal with because of the way he races through the gears. Figo was a different animal, slower, stealthier, but similarly capable of opening up any defence. I thought I knew everything about the great Figo – technique, pure class on the ball – but I didn't realize how strong he was.

When I tried to hound him around the Stadium of Light, I quickly learned he is physically strong, a hard man to dispossess. We knew we had to nail Figo and Ronaldo. If England stopped Portugal's creative forces, we had enough attacking threat of our own to hurt them. We had Rooney. We had Owen.

By the end of the Croatia match, me and a few others were trying to set up Michael, because he still hadn't scored, which was surprising. When Michael notched one, I knew he would net a dozen. When Michael is off and running with goals, his confidence soars; he would give us the goals to win the tournament. What impressed all the lads about Michael is that he was never down. Not Michael. Never. Even if he's suffering a bit of a drought, Michael always believes a goal is a second away, a corner away, a loose ball away. Less than three minutes after kick-off in the Portugal match, Michael scored. Brilliant. Great for him, and for us. That, surely, was the catalyst for England to go on and win the game. The last four beckoned. This was it, I felt; nothing could stop us now. A winner's medal glinted on the horizon.

Suddenly, bang, the wind was ripped from our sails. Chasing the ball with typical hunger, Wayne ended up with a broken metatarsal. As he limped away, I swore out loud. Losing Wayne was a massive blow. Portugal gained in confidence and possession. Ronaldo kept getting the ball. Ashley Cole kept tackling him or sending him down blind alleys. Lightning-quick wingers like Ronaldo can destroy full-backs. Not Ashley. He has every quality a world-class full-back needs. His touch is good, he's brilliant going forward, and he's really aggressive for his size. It was no surprise Ashley did so well at Euro 2004. He didn't give Ronaldo a yard. For me, this was the night when Ashley became the best left-back in the world.

Portugal tried other attacking avenues. I was tiring fast, chasing Figo and Deco around, putting out fires, sweat pouring from me. Cramp ram-raided my body. My muscles just locked, seized up. No more. No movement. Three games in quick succession caught up with me. My fitness wasn't tip-top, I'll admit now. Some massive blisters prevented me training fully. With nine minutes remaining of normal time, I hobbled off, replaced by Owen Hargreaves. Two minutes later, Helder Postiga headed an equalizer. Yet England still could have won it in normal time. Sol rose for a corner, and headed the ball in. 'Goal!' we all screamed on the bench, leaping up in celebration. Then Urs Meier, the Swiss ref, blew for a foul, apparently for JT on Portugal's keeper Ricardo.

I shouted at the TV boys who were nearby, 'Was it a goal?'

'Yes,' they replied. 'Nothing wrong with that.'

The ITV and BBC lads had the monitor. They could see JT hadn't impeded Ricardo. What was Meier thinking? I felt cheated. All the England players felt cheated. Poor Sol, who was also denied a similar goal at France 98. Poor England, too. Extra time beckoned. Rui Costa and Frank exchanged goals and it was off to penalties.

Watching from the bench, I felt confident. I looked at the two keepers, Jamo and Ricardo, and felt we had the edge. First up for us was Becks. Dead cert, I thought. This will fly in. No problem. In training, Becks is frighteningly accurate. He stepped up. Disaster. Becks slipped as he went in, the turf coming away as he planted down his left foot before he hit the ball with his right. Off-balance, he never made the right connection and missed. It is a risk Becks takes with his penalties. He goes in at an angle with his left foot so he can get full power and whip with his right. No blame could be attached to Becks. He just lost his footing. The Stadium of Light pitch was really greasy, and if the turf moves you are in serious trouble. No wonder they relaid the penalty spot after the game.

But we were still in it. Michael, Frank, JT and Hargreaves stuck their pens away, and Rui Costa obligingly missed his. When JT came back, he said, 'Lucky! I mishit it!' The tension intensified.

Sudden death arrived. Volunteers were needed. Ashley took responsibility, and stepped up to score. Postiga made it 5–5. The pressure was unbearable. Sven had asked Darius, 'Do you want a penalty?' Darius had declined. Fair enough. I could see he had no confidence in himself to take a penalty. Sven was looking round for anyone to take a kick. Anyone? Sol, Gary Neville and Phil Neville were available, but it needed a striker, someone who knew where the net was. It had to be Darius.

Poor kid. He was a bag of nerves, clearly dreading

the thought of walking up with the eyes of the world on him. He missed, and no wonder. Psychologically, he was a mess. Advantage Portugal. They, too, were running out of players, but no-one expected them to send Ricardo into action. A keeper! We couldn't believe it. Ricardo, carrying the expectations of all Portugal, turned, calmly ran in, and swept the ball past Jamo. Great pen.

My heart immediately went out to Darius. Shoot-outs always produce scapegoats, but we couldn't blame Darius for England going out of Euro 2004. 'It wasn't your fault, Darius,' I told him. 'We just didn't do enough in the ninety minutes or extra time.' None of the players pointed the finger at Darius.

England failed. We let the fans down. I let the fans down. They spent shed-loads travelling to Portugal, forking out fortunes to acquire match tickets, and they expected England to go further than the last eight. I'm sorry. We should have done better. The truth was that England were knackered at Euro 2004. 'If only we had got through,' I told Michael, 'we would have had a good rest before the semis.' Everyone was tired. A long, hard season took a terrible toll.

Some players had had enough. It didn't surprise me at all on the plane back when Scholesy announced he was retiring. Deep down, he knew he wouldn't get many more games in the middle because Frank did so well at Euro 2004. Scholesy is not a holding-role midfielder, so he couldn't compete with me. I sensed his rising frustration with England at Euro 2004. Scholesy wanted to be in the middle, getting on the ball, creating stuff, grabbing a game by the scruff of the neck. He was touching thirty, and wanted more time with his family. He'd done his England tours of duty and earned everyone's respect. Paul Scholes is one of the best players I have ever played with, blessed with a natural ability in abundance. I miss him.

And he wasn't the only one considering his future.

# 15
# Feeling Blue

The good times would roll with England again, but my career stalled at Liverpool. No question. I was running across quicksand. Striving to move forward, I found myself sinking deeper and deeper into mediocrity. A sense of depression blew into my life like a dark cloud that would not go away. Frustration bit deep. I hated constantly worrying over whether Liverpool would qualify for the Champions League, the playground of Barcelona and Real Madrid, AC Milan and Juventus. Names that inspire. Names Liverpool's history demand we mix with. Michael and I shared one fear: playing for a club that wasn't among Europe's elite. He and I both knew that Liverpool, the club we loved, was falling away from the top three of Arsenal, Manchester United and Chelsea.

The final Premiership table for the 2003/04 season showed Liverpool thirty points behind the champions, Arsenal. A massive margin. Doubts filled my waking hours. Did Liverpool have my ambition? Did we have the players to compete seriously for the Premiership and Champions League? Questions, questions. I certainly questioned my future at Anfield. Should I leave? Could I tear myself away from the club and city I love so passionately? Chelsea had ambition, resources, a bright new manager in José Mourinho, and they obviously wanted me. In the summer of 2004, temptation entered my life.

Another kick in the teeth was getting knocked out of the UEFA Cup by Marseille in the quarters on 25 March 2004. The UEFA Cup is nothing special compared to the Champions League, but it is still a trophy, still a winner's medal. Emile scored early on against the French, we controlled the game, but then Igor Biscan made a stupid mistake and got sent off. Marseille took over and we were out, thanks to Biscan. Liverpool could have won the UEFA Cup that year. We would have played Newcastle in the semis, Valencia in the final, and beaten them both. I was livid.

Liverpool were stagnating under Gérard. Everyone could see it, inside and outside Anfield. Shortly after the end of the season, Gérard was dismissed. I was devastated for him, but not surprised. Liverpool went backwards after the Treble. Fact. Gérard leaving was for everyone's benefit. After six years, he needed a different challenge, and Liverpool needed a new manager to freshen things up. I needed to play for a new manager.

The parting of the ways between Liverpool and Gérard made sense, but it was still painful to watch. I hurt bad. Gérard was a father figure to me, and that bond was now severed. A little part of me died when he left. He cared for me. Typical Gérard, when I called him to commiserate, he was more worried about me. 'Steven, you are at a fantastic club,' he said. 'You are going to be one of the best players in the world. Trust me. Just keep going, keep learning. And do not worry about me. I will be all right.' Gérard is a good, honest man, and I am so made up we have stayed in touch. He did so much for my career. My respect for him will always remain strong.

A couple of days after Gérard's departure, Rick

Parry, Liverpool's chief executive, called. 'Steven, can I have a chat with some of the senior players?'

'Yes, Rick, not a problem.'

'Get some of the lads over, and I'll be round.'

By then, I had moved to Blundellsands, so Rick came there. Most of the lads were busy, but I rustled up Carra, and we sat there and talked football with Rick. Usual stuff: ambitions, players we rated, teams on the rise. Suddenly Rick said, 'What are the players' feelings on another foreign manager coming in? Are there any problems with it?'

'No,' I replied. 'The majority of the players had a great relationship with Gérard. We won a Treble under him. If another foreign manager came in, took the club forward and brought success, then fine.'

Rick paused, looked at me, and said, 'What do you think of Rafa Benítez at Valencia?'

My eyes lit up. What a coach! I smiled at Rick. 'I'd go for Benítez.'

'Why do you rate him?' Rick asked.

'Tactically, Valencia are the most difficult side I have ever played against,' I said. 'They give you no space to play. Great organization. We just couldn't get the ball off them. We knew we couldn't beat them the moment we kicked off. Valencia were fitter than us, physically stronger, and very strong mentally.'

Could Benítez do that with Liverpool? Why not? What was to say Benítez couldn't give Man U, Chelsea and Arsenal a run for their money? Uncertainty still nagged away at me, though. Could one man really revive Liverpool? Would I remain stuck in a cycle of struggling to make the Champions League?

I flew into Portugal for the European Championship with a bag full of troubles. Anything to declare? Yeah, mate, a ton of doubts. If I was home-sick in Euro 2000, I was distracted at Euro 2004. My mind kept flicking back to events at Anfield. If I learned one thing in Portugal, it was to go into future tournaments focused solely on the job in hand. I admire players who carry on performing no matter the distractions in their life. I can't. My head must be clear. I never set Euro 2004 alight because I was thinking about Liverpool. After training or matches, I'd be on the phone home, wondering what was going to happen to Liverpool and me. Friends and family kept calling and telling me about the latest club I had been linked with in the papers. Chelsea, Real Madrid; Chelsea, Inter Milan; Chelsea, Barcelona; Chelsea, AC Milan; Chelsea again. It did my head in. 'Are you staying?' Dad asked. 'Are you going?' asked Paul.

A fire of speculation raged, and I ended up burnt. My football went to pieces. No-one was to blame for my poor performances at Euro 2004 except me. My fault. Mine alone. I was naive, inexperienced, incapable of handling all the rumours about my future while busting my lungs for England. I let down the players, the fans and Sven. On and off the field in Portugal, I was edgy. In the England hotel in the middle of a massive tournament was the worst time and place to learn top clubs were chasing me. Real Madrid definitely sniffed around. Arsenal, too. Both Milan clubs, and Barcelona. Fact. Everybody mentioned Chelsea because their owner, Roman Abramovich, is loaded. Many clubs were in the hunt, and all of them made their interest known through the papers, dropping little hints here and there. I couldn't pick up a paper without reading how much Real or Chelsea wanted me. When I should have been getting ready for kick-off, my thoughts drifted away into imagining what it would be like playing for Chelsea or Barcelona. Arsène Wenger, José Mourinho and Sir Alex Ferguson talked me up before the tournament, so I knew they fancied signing me. Fergie even did an amazing piece in the *Sunday Times* in which he called me the 'most influential player in England, bar none'.

If that comment wasn't enough to make me realize United were after me, an incident during Euro 2004 confirmed it. I was hanging around my room at England's Solplay Hotel in Lisbon, catching some football programme, when there was a knock at the door. I opened it, and one of Fergie's players stood there. He came in and said straight out, 'We'd love you to come to United.' That's how clubs' interest was expressed to me. The Arsenal, Man U and Chelsea players in the England squad kept coming up and saying, 'Are you coming to us?' I had no problem with that. It wasn't unfair of them to approach me. The boys respected me as a player and wanted me in their team. I've done it myself. I've said to Wayne Rooney, 'I'd love you to come and play for Liverpool every week.' That's just me showing my huge respect for Wayne. Come on, Wayne, come and play in my team. I love Wazza as a player. He'd be fantastic up front for Liverpool. Me on the ball in midfield, finding Wazza. Me running forward, Wazza finding me. Goal! I still dream of Wayne pulling on a proper red shirt. I'm not sure the Kop would be so keen, though!

That knock at the door made me realize all the top managers thought there was a race on for me. And that race couldn't wait until after Euro 2004 in those managers' minds. I was target number one, and it got messy. All the other players in the England squad thought I was leaving Liverpool; it was just a case of clarifying my destination. Of course, I was flattered. Big-time. It felt like I was back in the playground picking sides. But it shattered my focus on Euro 2004. Struan, as usual, tried to help. 'Right, Stevie, we are not going to talk about your future,' he said early in the tournament. 'Leave it for now. Anything in the papers, anything that anyone says, any approaches from the England lads, leave it until the tournament finishes.' Good plan, impossible to achieve. I could hardly tell close family to shut up whenever they mentioned a story in the papers to me. 'Barcelona are after you.' 'Chelsea definitely fancy you.' 'Hey, Stevie, Wenger's interested.' And always, 'What is going on?' My family love me, and they were concerned about me, about my happiness and my future.

No-one at Anfield called. I didn't really expect them to. Rick Parry's position was clear from what he was telling the papers: Liverpool wanted to keep their captain. Anyway, Rick was busy appointing Rafa Benítez as Gérard's successor. Rafa was unveiled on Tuesday, 16 June, and Liverpool's new manager flew out to Portugal on the Friday. He clearly wanted to talk to me, Michael and Carra.

I was fascinated to meet Liverpool's new leader. Me, Michael and Carra found a quiet room at the Solplay and sat down to chat with Rafa. Sven was OK about Rafa's visit. He understood that Rafa needed to talk to his new Liverpool players.

It was a strange meeting. Rafa kept asking for our opinions, but I sensed that whatever we said, it didn't matter. Rafa was his own man, not the type of manager to be swayed by others' views. He had his own methods, which worked wonders at Valencia, so why did he need advice? He was just judging us. At that time, Rafa's English wasn't too clever, so it was never going to be an in-depth chat. He had only just started learning the language, so the meeting was difficult for him. But he did make us understand his plans. 'I have been doing a lot of homework on Liverpool,' he said. 'I know a lot about the club. I am confident I can bring success to Liverpool. I will bring in my own training ideas, my own players. For Liverpool to go forward, I need all my best players. I want to keep all the good players. Anyone who doesn't want to play for Liverpool, or who I don't want, will leave.'

Rafa left the Solplay, and I returned to my room to think over my first meeting with my new boss. I was glad to meet him but my future remained unclear. The more I thought about it, the more I felt the meeting should not have taken place until after Euro 2004. Our Lisbon get-together was really a bad idea. Having met Rafa, I kept wondering what life would be like back at Melwood. More complications invaded my life, and I became even more distracted. One comment of Rafa's really chewed me up. 'Liverpool have not got loads of money,' he told me. 'There is money there for me to strengthen, but not massive amounts.' What the hell did that mean? Were Liverpool skint? Do they want to cash in on me? Are they going to bite on these offers? My head was battered.

Chelsea's pursuit quickened. The vibes I got off all the Chelsea lads at the Solplay was that Mourinho wanted me big-time. 'José really likes you,' they kept saying with a smile whenever I saw them. John Terry also told me, 'Claudio Ranieri wanted you before.' Now Mourinho had replaced Ranieri and their interest seemed even stronger. Chelsea definitely excited me. I cannot deny that. Mourinho is special, a top manager. Chelsea also boasted class players like Lamps and JT. They were going places. No question. The massive wages they were supposedly offering wasn't the issue for me. Silverware, not cash, sets my adrenalin going. Dazzled by the idea of trophies, I looked long and jealously at Chelsea. I envied Lamps going for the Premiership. I wanted a bit of that.

Chelsea's chief executive, Peter Kenyon, faxed Parry a bid for £20 million, adding that it was in everyone's interest to get the deal over with quickly. Mourinho said, 'I will wait for Stevie with open arms.' I didn't have a clue what was happening. Chelsea made their offer because they suspected Liverpool were short of cash. A new manager would need funds to bring in his players, so Chelsea hoped Liverpool would be tempted to sell me. Chelsea wanted to test Liverpool. Throughout Euro 2004, I was waiting for my phone to ring and to hear Struan say, 'Liverpool have accepted a bid for you.'

But that call didn't come. I spent a lot of time soul-searching and had countless talks with my family. My dad, a passionate Liverpool fan, said, 'Steven, you are not going anywhere. I don't want you to go.' Paul agreed. 'Stay,' said my brother. 'Benítez will sort it out.' Both Dad and Paul understood my frustration at finishing thirty points off the Premiership leaders, and off the pace in Europe, but I listened to them and to my heart and came to one conclusion: I couldn't leave Liverpool. My roots went too deep.

On 28 June, I rang Rick. 'I'm definitely staying,' I told him, 'but I need signs we are strengthening and improving.'

'We will be,' Rick promised.

# 16
# The Long Road to Istanbul

Rick was true to his word. Liverpool chased Xabi Alonso, who I knew was a decent player. Real Madrid were also pursuing Real Sociedad's playmaking midfielder, but he wanted to work with Benítez. Within twenty minutes of Xabi's first training session at Melwood, I thought to myself, 'Top signing. Pure class. Touch, vision, the creative works.' I looked forward to playing alongside him.

Another arrival was Djibril Cissé, from Auxerre, a signing put in motion by Gérard Houllier. I was still on my break, recovering after the Euros, when my phone shook to a text from Danny Murphy: 'You should have seen Cissé in training today. Unbelievable. Never seen anything like it. Frightening. He scored this spectacular overhead kick.' When I raced back into Melwood, the players were still banging on about the goal. Excitement was in the air, and I breathed it in deeply, big lungfuls of optimism. 'I'm up for this season,' I thought.

Liverpool gave Cissé the number 9 shirt, so as I was number 8 we sat next to each other in the dressing-room. I got to know him. The main thing about Cissé is that to do well, he needs encouragement. Now and then, a captain like me has to put his arm around players like Cissé to pick their confidence up, particularly when they are left out of the team. Cissé gets down a lot.

Our new Frenchman must have known he could never replace Michael. Before our Champions League qualifier at Graz in Austria on 10 August 2004, I noticed Michael was quiet, distracted. What was up with my mate? All the papers carried stories about Michael's future, but it was surely just the routine, page-filling speculation. No way would Liverpool sell Michael, one of our top players. No chance would they let him go. But the alarm bells began ringing when I noticed Benítez dragging Michael into a corner before the Graz game. They spoke, and the next thing

I know Michael is on the bench. That's it. He's definitely off. If Michael played, he would be ineligible for any other side in Europe that season. Benítez protected Michael's market value. The next moment, Real Madrid called and Michael was off to the Bernabéu. Bang, bang – just like that.

I was heartbroken. For me, Michael was the best striker in the history of Liverpool Football Club. Goals, work-rate, stamina, speed, intelligent movement and toughness – Michael possessed all the qualities that define the world's leading forwards. Now he was gone. I'd lost a fantastic team-mate, a striker whose runs I could pick out in my sleep. When Michael left Anfield, a part of me left with him. Michael is a friend, a man who always gives me honest advice, and I still miss him badly.

Another top team-mate and friend soon disappeared: Danny Murphy. A new manager had come in to Anfield and I was losing all my mates! I never blamed Liverpool or Benítez for Michael going. Real Madrid were too big a lure for Michael. But the next minute Danny was gone, sold to Charlton Athletic. Another blow to me. Danny and I shared a room on trips, so I took his departure really personally. I enjoyed chatting to Danny. He was one of the many reasons why life at Liverpool was so special. Now he was out the building. My good mate Michael was gone; my best mate Danny was gone.

Liverpool made a lot of money from selling Michael and Danny, so that would help Benítez bring in some talent. And my belief in Benítez was strong.

I still had Carra, Didi and John Arne Riise in my group. Didi is a top friend. Riise is another I get on really well with. Yet soon after arriving, Benítez set about breaking up the cliques. Our new Spanish leader called us together at Melwood and said, 'From now on, you must change your table every time you eat. Get to know people you don't know or you will be out. And when we travel, your room-mate will change every trip.' I saw where Benítez was coming from: having everyone eating at the same table and rotating rooms was good for team spirit. But life was difficult under Benítez at first. The atmosphere changed from Gérard's days.

Benítez was very different to Gérard – chalk and cheese. Gérard was really close to his players; at times, it felt like having a father overseeing training. He was a kind character, more of a man-manager than Benítez. Our new boss just focused on training, preparing us for games. Benítez is friendly, but I am not sure he is that interested in players as people. He rarely communicates with us on a personal basis. Fair enough, I've no problem with that. We're all professionals. Benítez's task is to win games, not popularity contests. All that matters to Benítez is football. To Benítez, I am Steven Gerrard, footballer and LFC employee, not Steven Gerrard, flesh and blood, thoughts and emotions. The boss is obsessed with football. Any conversation with Benítez is football, football, football. Matches, tactics, players. Not home. Not my family. This is not a criticism of him. However much I may prefer the human touch, I cannot question the success of Benítez's methods.

At Graz, Liverpool needed me to deliver. After my flirtation with Chelsea in the summer, I knew when I ran out against Graz that Liverpool's fans would be watching me like hawks, checking my body language closely. Is Stevie G committed? Is he still distracted by all the speculation that ruined his Euro 2004? Many questions needed answering in the Schwarzenegger Stadium that night. So I launched into an all-action performance to stress how much I wanted to wear that Liverpool shirt. I ripped into Graz, scoring mid-way through the first half. Rafa wanted me to get up and combine with the forwards and his plan was working: I bombed on, linked up with Cissé and caused real damage. With twenty-five minutes to go, Rafa signalled for me to push further up, playing just off Cissé. Never before had I done a striking job for Liverpool. Loved it. Brilliant. I netted another.

Liverpool lost the second leg 1–0 at Anfield, but so what? We were up and running, qualified for the Champions League group stage, back with the big boys again. Istanbul, the venue for the final, seemed a million miles away, though. The Turkish city was never in our thoughts in the autumn of 2004. Nor in our dreams. No-one thought it could be Liverpool's year. I was delighted to be involved, I watched the draw with a massive grin on my face. The Champions League is like an exclusive club, and Liverpool were members again. Bring it on. Group A pitted Liverpool against three decent sides, teams I respected. Monaco,

Olympiakos and Deportivo La Coruña. Liverpool stumbled through the group, managing only two victories and a draw in our first five games. No fluency. No real finishing edge. People continued to write us off.

Our final Group A tie against Olympiakos on 8 December was effectively a play-off. We needed to win 1–0, or by two clear goals. Inevitably, Anfield crackled with atmosphere at kick-off. Liverpool fans always believe. We couldn't afford any mistakes. If we conceded one we had to score three goals to go through.

Sure enough, Rivaldo scored, setting us a daunting mission. The Brazilian had not seemed a massive threat. He was in the twilight of a glittering career, going through the motions. This was not the Rivaldo whom I'd tried to mark when Barcelona beat us 3–1 at Anfield three years earlier. Rivaldo was frightening that night. Now, playing for Olympiakos, he wasn't on the ball so much. The Brazilian certainly should never have scored. His free-kick went over our wall and sailed into the middle of our goal. Our keeper, Chris Kirkland, came sprinting out and blamed the wall. Frustration got the better of me and I was cautioned for kicking out after the ball had gone. I'm out of the next game, I realized. Stupid yellow. Stupid goal.

That season in Europe, Liverpool encountered a few crisis points, and Olympiakos was certainly one of them. The fact that our problems came in the first half at least gave us the opportunity to regroup at the break, clear the air, fill our lungs, and let the boss organize the great escape. Benítez took control. He was calm. Straight away, the tactics board came out. He stood there, detailing the changes, making us more attacking. His half-time messages are always simple, always easily understood. 'No mistakes at the back,' Benítez stressed on this occasion. 'Let's have a go. We have forty-five minutes to stay in Europe. Go and show me how much you want to stay in Europe. Go and show the fans. Olympiakos are not the best side. Chances will come. If we don't make another mistake at the back, we can win.'

Benítez's substitutions changed the game. One of the gaffer's many strengths is that he genuinely has a magic touch with subs. 'Djimi off, Florent on,' he said.

Three at the back – brave! Pongolle's impact was immediate. Released by Kewell, Pongolle poached a close-ranger after two minutes and spent the rest of the match terrorizing the Greeks, stretching them and opening space for the rest of us.

Pongolle's goal changed the atmosphere. After Rivaldo scored, the mood went flat. Certain parts of Anfield had presumed that was that – game over. Pongolle's goal brought hope. The fans were right behind us, screaming as we chased every ball, every chance. People who have been around Anfield for many years described it as the best atmosphere since Liverpool beat St-Etienne in 1977. With the Kop at fever pitch, we laid siege to Olympiakos. Still we couldn't break through. With twelve minutes left, Benítez waved his wand again. He hooked Milan Baros, sent on Neil Mellor, and told us to bombard the Greeks. Like Pongolle, Mellor made his mark sharpish. He was buzzing around, full of confidence, determined to batter Olympiakos's defence. Within three minutes, he made it 2–1 with a typical goal, a loose ball lashed in from close range. No finesse, just raw power in the finish. Mellor doesn't do much in and around the box, but he scores goals. He's done it for the reserves for years. Two goals from two subs! When I look back on that amazing season in Europe, I never forget the contribution of Pongolle and Mellor that night against the Greeks. They grafted hard, making us play with a higher tempo. Olympiakos couldn't control us.

Anfield was going crazy. After Mellor's strike, we had nine minutes left to find the goal to keep us in Europe. Just one goal. One chance. One shot. As we raced towards the Kop, I kept glancing at the electronic clock. Time was running out. We tried everything but Olympiakos stood firm. The remaining minutes soon became seconds. Come on! Now or never. Liverpool's strongest characters came to the fore. Xabi slid into tackles, keeping the ball in play. Carra was immense, charging into midfield, doing Cruyff turns out wide, and, suddenly, chipping a cross in to Mellor. 'Set it, set it!' I screamed. Could he hear? Did he know I was perfectly placed? Please! Mellor heard, and he delivered, nodding down brilliantly towards me.

Twenty-two yards lay between me and glory.

Everything stopped around me, melting into a background blur. All that mattered was me and that ball. All my vision, all my concentration was focused on it as it dropped towards me. Keep the head still. Weight over the ball. Make good contact. Make the keeper work. Here goes. Bang! The ball flew away from my right foot and accelerated towards the goal. The Kop held its breath. A split-second of silence reigned, save for the sound of the net pulling at the stanchions. Bull's-eye! Goal! Everyone screamed it. Goal! We're through!

Pure joy swept through my body, sending me hurtling towards the Kop. I saw the fans, saw the expression of pure passion and love of Liverpool on their faces, and thought, 'Yeah, I'm with you, I'm one of you, I'm coming in.' I felt my team-mates breathing down my neck to catch me. I headed for the fans, launching myself into the arms of my people.

People always remind me of that goal. Millions saw it on TV. It was a good strike, one I am incredibly proud of for its execution and significance, but it is Andy Gray's commentary on Sky that really makes the goal. I've heard it since, and he goes crazy. 'Yes! You beauty!' Andy made the goal even more special. He summed up the emotion of the Olympiakos game brilliantly. And Liverpool deserved it. With Benítez's subs changing the match, we were awesome in the second half. Anything felt possible after that turnaround.

I looked around the dressing-room afterwards and saw the fire of ambition in my team-mates' eyes. It was a fantastic place to be. Smiles, handshakes, singing. With Benítez around, the dressing-room was never going to go completely mad, but we did celebrate.

Liverpool were now in the knockout stage, with no margin for error. UEFA's draw-makers threw us in against Bayer Leverkusen. Everybody outside Anfield considered the Germans slight favourites. Suspended and frustrated, I watched the first leg at Anfield. Liverpool survived a couple of scares early on but gradually took control. We were cruising to a 3–0 win when Jerzy made a mistake. He fumbled, Franca pounced, and suddenly Leverkusen grasped an away goal.

We just had to keep calm, and take our chances.

From the first whistle, we destroyed them, and we ran out comfortable 3–1 winners.

For the quarter-final draw, I nipped over to Mum's apartment. First out of UEFA's glass bowl was us and Juventus. I knew the Italians were a class outfit, certainly not one of the teams we wanted to face in the last eight.

UEFA could not have sent Liverpool down a more emotional route to the final, either. The Heysel disaster loomed large over the two legs. Inevitably. Liverpool had not met Juventus since thirty-nine supporters died at the 1985 European Cup final in Brussels. All the Heysel stuff started straight away on Sky Sports News. Everybody, it seemed, was talking about it. Liverpool never mentioned to the players how sensitive the match was. They didn't need to. Me and Carra knew all about Heysel. We also knew Liverpool fans would give the right reaction when Juventus visited on 5 April. On the night, the Kop held up a mosaic saying 'Memoria e Amicia' – 'In Memory and Friendship'. That was a nice touch. Michel Platini and Ian Rush paid a tribute towards the Juventus fans in the Anfield Road end. The behaviour of Liverpool's supporters really warmed my heart that night.

So much of the build-up was about Heysel, but the players concentrated on the here and now. We had to set the tone early, so I launched into Emerson, their hard-man midfielder. Take that. Juventus did not know what hit them. We were all over them, seizing a 2–0 lead through Sami and Luis García within twenty-five minutes. Scotty Carson pulled off a world-class save to keep out Alessandro Del Piero. As we went in at the break, I looked at the Juventus faces. They were in shock. They'd expected a gentle breeze blowing through Anfield, but instead found themselves in the thick of a hurricane. Our mood in the dressing-room was of quiet confidence mixed with respect for the Italians. Benítez warned us to be on our toes. 'Juventus will come back at you,' he said. Fabio Cannavaro pulled one back in the second half, and we knew it would be tough the following week over in Turin.

Except I wasn't going. Ruled out by a thigh strain, I got my mates round to the house in Crosby to have a few beers and watch the game on TV. But I couldn't stay in the room. Every time Juventus got in our half, I walked out and waited in the kitchen until the danger cleared. 'OK, Stevie, it's safe now,' would come the message from the TV room, and I'd return for a while. My nerves were being put through a shredder. I was so desperate for Liverpool to get through. When the shout of 'That's it, game over' came through, I dashed back in to see all the lads in Turin celebrating the goalless draw on the pitch. 'I'm not staying in,' I thought. Jeans on. Shirt ironed. Out to Southport. A few beers would be no problem; my damaged thigh was going to keep me out of next weekend's match anyway. As we sped into Southport, my thumbs were working like pistons over my phone, sending congratulation texts to Carra and the boys in Turin. They were awesome.

I couldn't wait to get in to work to see the lads. I shot into Melwood the next day, and they were all there, covered in smiles. Benítez, as usual, played the achievement down, but the boys were all proud of outsmarting the Italians. Too right.

Talk immediately turned to Chelsea. Everyone in England had a view on this all-English semi-final.

UEFA had set the pairings for the semis during the quarter-final draw, so the Chelsea semi was built up for weeks in advance. We lost interest in the Premiership. Our days and night-time dreams became filled with the thought of beating Frank Lampard, John Terry and José Mourinho and reaching the Champions League final. Liverpool had so much unfinished business with Chelsea. So many scores to settle. Chelsea had beaten us twice in the league and in the Carling Cup final back in February, when I scored an own-goal. A desire for revenge flowed through me, Carra and the boys. This was the big one.

The team were buzzing as we travelled down to London for the first leg at the end of April. 'It's good we're away first,' I told Carra. 'Let's go there, be compact, keep it tight, nick a draw, and do them at Anfield.' That season, Liverpool had a knack of getting the right away result. Worryingly, though, I arrived in London with a problem: an abscess in my mouth. Murder. The swelling intensified the night before the match. I could feel the pussy liquid inside waiting to erupt. Food was impossible. Just the thought of anything near the abscess made me almost faint.

Doc Waller gave me some pills but I couldn't sleep, and I went to see him again. He gave me stronger painkillers. 'Go and have your couple of hours' rest and see how you feel,' he said.

As usual, I followed the doc's advice, but it was no good. I was now in complete agony, my mouth ready to explode. The doc and I went to see Benítez, and he said, 'Find a dentist quick. Get it taken out.' Within the hour, I was lying back in a dentist's chair, my mouth full of tools and tubes. He drained the abscess, tidied up the mess, and sent me off to Stamford Bridge. I knocked back so many painkillers before kick-off I almost rattled every time I kicked the ball.

That first leg was cagey, but we felt the happier with a 0–0 draw. The only disappointment came when the referee, Alain Sars, booked Xabi for a challenge on Eidur Gudjohnsen, which ruled Xabi out of the Anfield return. What really angered us was that Gudjohnsen clearly conned Sars. He dived. No question about it.

Xabi was inconsolable, close to tears. He loves

playing and felt bitter resentment towards Gudjohnsen. We all did.

The temperature was stoked further by the papers. Any tiny comment was used to spark an inferno. In the papers, Benítez singled me out as the 'key' for Liverpool. Liverpool's manager heaped pressure on his captain. The boss thought he was helping me, giving me a boost by saying I was the 'key'. But I wished he had never mentioned me. I don't need motivating, especially not for a Champions League semi-final against Chelsea, of all teams. Anyone whose pulse isn't racing before such a meeting should retire. Benítez knew how ready I was. He told the world, 'I looked into Steven's eyes and saw the determination.' I craved the chance to lift the European Cup, to put Liverpool back where we belong – at the top. The thought of getting knocked out within touching distance of Istanbul and Chelsea going on to win made me almost physically sick. There was more than determination in my eyes. Staring back at Benítez was a burning will to win. Nobody was going to stand between me and the final. Not Lamps. Not JT. Not Makelele. I couldn't wait to launch into Chelsea.

A touch of arrogance accompanied Chelsea into Anfield on 3 May, and Benítez brilliantly played on it. 'Chelsea's players think they are in the final,' he told us. 'Chelsea think they have beaten you. Now go out and show them how wrong they are. And remember Xabi.' We also heard Chelsea booked a room, at a place called The Mosquito, for an after-match party. Chelsea's confidence was mentioned more than a few times before kick-off.

Chelsea did not just run into eleven stirred-up Liverpool players that night. The Londoners were hit by a whole wave of emotion rolling out from 40,000 fanatical Scousers, who could not have had a voice between them the following morning. They screamed themselves hoarse that night. They knew the team had a really good chance of going to the final. It was nail-biting – they wanted victory so badly it hurt. Liverpool fans are obsessed with Europe. Anyone can win a title, but only Liverpool had dominated Europe. Whenever I look at the Kop, I see all the banners reminding everyone of past successes in Europe. The European Cup glides through the dreams of every Red. I saw it in the faces of the Liverpool fans that night. 'Make Us Dream' ordered one banner. I heard it in their songs. Get us to the final, Stevie. Lead us back where we belong.

I have never, ever experienced an atmosphere like it. Celtic Park was massive when we visited, but this was bigger. Running out to warm up forty-five minutes before kick-off, I couldn't believe my eyes or ears. Anfield was three-quarters full. Usually when we warm up, Anfield's empty. Not that night. The fans were so impatient to slaughter Chelsea and praise us that they poured out of the pubs early and streamed into Anfield. The stadium was bouncing. As I stretched my muscles, I was mesmerized by the Kop. The fans sang all the Liverpool players' names individually. Straight away, Liverpool fans were right on Chelsea's back; straight away, they built us up.

We headed back down the tunnel for Benítez's final instructions, and to get our match shirts on. Back in the dressing-room, everybody talked about our amazing fans. It makes a huge difference, at home, knowing all the fans are completely, passionately with you.

Looking along the Chelsea line in the tunnel, I

realized they had some strong characters, men like Lampard and Terry, who would not be intimidated by the hostility directed at them. Then I wondered how their weaker team-mates might react. Would they hide? Abuse chased every Chelsea player around Anfield that night. Every time a Chelsea player lost possession, he was assaulted with insults. When me or Carra steamed into a Chelsea player, a roar went up. The Kop cheered every pass, every tackle. The fans' noise worked on my body like an endless injection of adrenalin. I was so pumped up. So was everyone wearing Liverpool red that night. We flew out of the traps, tearing into Chelsea, hammering at everything they stood for, turning them inside out.

That's why we scored so early. Four minutes! When Riise megged Lamps out wide, me and Milan ran into positions. If I got the ball to Milan, he was through on goal. With Terry in the way, I had to keep the ball off the floor, so I put some sting into it, slightly over-hitting it to make sure it got past JT. Baros was really brave and got a touch, taking it away from Petr Cech, who brought Milan down. 'Pen!' I shouted. Cech had to be off. Cast-iron penalty.

Everything happened in a split-second. As Milan fell, García appeared from nowhere, got this contact and put the ball in the net. William Gallas hooked the ball out. Was it in? Where's the ref? There he is. What's he doing, saying? Lubos Michel blew and pointed towards the halfway line. Goal! My arms went up. Celebration time. All Anfield shook. Liverpool fans went mental. Chelsea fans and players went into meltdown. 'It wasn't across the line!' they screamed at Michel. Chelsea moaned about it, but if it wasn't a goal, Cech would have been red-carded for bringing down Milan. Down to ten men, facing a penalty, probably down 1–0. Is that what Chelsea wanted? Liverpool could have gone on to win 4–0. Chelsea got off lightly.

I raced back to the halfway line, shouting instructions at the lads. 'Keep it tight. Give nothing away. Make every tackle count. Every pass.' I knew Chelsea would hit back. They were livid over the goal. Their blood boiled and they sought revenge. Time to stand firm. We were under siege, under attack from every angle. Chelsea had players everywhere, like it was thirteen against eleven.

We survived because of one man – Jamie Carragher. I looked at Carra and saw a man hell-bent on not letting the lead slip. He was prepared to offer the last drop of sweat and blood in his body to get us to Istanbul. Carra knows his history and knew what it meant for Liverpool to reach the final. He did everything to prevent Chelsea ruining Liverpool's dream. He tackled, blocked, headed. Carra was a Colossus at Anfield. In fact, he was awesome all the way through the tournament.

I began looking around for the fourth official. How much injury time would he give. Three? Four, tops. The electronic board went up. Six minutes? What was going on? I couldn't believe it. How can we survive? We are in trouble here. Running on empty. Shattered. I glanced at Carra. His face was stained with sweat and worry. Even heroic Carra had nothing left to give. He had dug deep so often. Liverpool were like boxers who had taken too many punches and now clung to the ropes. Those six minutes felt like sixty. Chelsea's pressure was like an electric drill, hammering away at the rocks of our defence. At some point an opening would surely appear.

With seconds left, the ball fell to Gudjohnsen close in. Not Gudjohnsen. Of all Chelsea people. That was it. Goal. He can't miss. Dream over. I couldn't bear to watch as he made contact. Then a roar swept around Anfield. He'd missed! And it's a goal-kick! I smiled at Carra. 'His shot touched my legs!' laughed Carra. 'It was going in. I was waiting for a corner!'

Then Michel blew for full-time. Bliss. Safety. We had hung on by the skin of our teeth. 'We're going to the final,' I said to Carra as we partied on the pitch, 'and we're going to win it!' Liverpool deserved to be in Istanbul. For all Chelsea's whingeing, we were the better side over the 180 minutes.

Back in the dressing-room, it went mad. Everyone was dancing, hugging, punching the air and shouting. Istanbul! Final! Brilliant! 'Right,' I shouted. 'Into town now. Everyone.' So off we went, the boys in their trackies, wives and girlfriends in their smart clothes. Carra, as usual, led the dancing and singing. People were bouncing off the walls. Adrenalin made up for the tired legs. We'd won nothing, just the right to compete for the European Cup, but the lads partied like we had won it.

Only in the cold light of day the following morning, when I leafed through the papers, did it fully sink in what we had achieved. Liverpool were back in the European Cup final.

That night, I met up with John Arne Riise in town to watch the second leg of PSV Eindhoven against Milan. 'I hope PSV go through,' I said to John Arne. 'We'd have a better chance of beating PSV than Milan.' The Italians had so many good players, like Andrei Shevchenko, Kaka and Andrea Pirlo. 'Don't fancy playing them.' Over the two legs, PSV deserved to make it, but Milan pipped them at the death. As I climbed back into my car, I knew one thing: Istanbul was going to be hellishly tough.

# 17
# The Miracle

Istanbul was madness, pure, utter, wonderful madness. Scousers everywhere. In the airport, in the hotel. In bars, up trees. Everywhere. We couldn't move. Even on the journey from Istanbul airport to our hotel, I kept looking out the window and seeing people I knew. Amazing. Kick-off was still forty-eight hours away! Whenever I stepped out of my hotel room, Liverpool fans were walking down the corridor, giving me the thumbs-up, slaps on the back. 'All right, Stevie lad? All the best.' Time after time. Fans booked rooms in Liverpool's hotel, others just blagged their way in. Every time we came down to eat, we weaved through masses of Liverpool supporters. Every time we went out to train, we got stopped for photographs, autographs. I love Liverpool fans, but their invasion of our hotel became a serious distraction. Every time I tried to catch some sleep, the fans' singing shook my room. I closed the window, pulled the curtains tight, and put the pillow over my head. Still it came. Song after song. It was like trying to sleep on the Kop.

Even when I managed to find some quiet in my room, my mobile went crazy. Mates and family kept calling to wish me luck and to check on tickets. Tickets were gold-dust; it was like a scene from *Charlie and the Chocolate Factory*. The whole world, and certainly half of Merseyside, hunted one of those precious, reddy pieces of paper with the Champions League logo and 'Atatürk Olympic Stadium' on it. Sorting out tickets proved a mental job, far more difficult and time-consuming than actually preparing for the final. 'You will each be allocated twenty-five tickets,' Liverpool told us. Brilliant. 'My list of names already runs to fifty,' I told Carra. He laughed. Carra was the same. He had a whole army coming out to Istanbul. With a bit of sweet-talking here and calling in favours there, I somehow scrounged the fifty.

Struan was busy. His phone was red-hot. Players kept calling him to pass on good luck messages. John

Terry phoned. 'Give Stevie all the best from me,' JT told Struan. When Stru passed on JT's message, I was genuinely moved. JT already had massive respect from me, but he went up even higher in my estimation. We'd beaten Chelsea, but JT didn't think of his own disappointment. Just of me. Another top man, Thierry Henry, also got a message through. Thierry and JT were my rivals, opponents I had torn into all season; now they showed their class as blokes. I'll never forget their calls of support before Istanbul. Never. When Arsenal reached the 2006 final, I was straight on to Thierry, wishing him all the best. I was gutted Arsenal never held on against Barcelona in Paris.

A year before that, Istanbul felt like a giant, over-crowded waiting-room for me and the rest of the Liverpool squad. We trained, we ate, we tried to sleep, but all we did was run down the clock until D-Day. Training was good, although we were all amazed at the Atatürk Stadium. We drove along roads into the middle of nowhere, and eventually the stadium loomed up in the distance, like a spaceship abandoned in the desert.

I had to attend a press conference at the stadium

with Milan's famous captain, Paolo Maldini. As I left the lads to make my way there, Carra shouted after me, 'If you see the European Cup, don't touch it.' All the boys yelled similar warnings. Footballers are a superstitious bunch. Sure enough, I walked into the press conference room and there it was, the silver trophy with the big-ear handles, standing in pride of place on a pedestal. I had to walk past it to reach my seat. 'Don't touch it.' Carra's words boomed in my head. Don't tempt fate. Maybe tomorrow I'll touch it, hold it and lift it to the heavens. Only then.

It was tough though. As I inched past the cup that fills the dreams of everyone at Liverpool, my palms flooded with sweat. I felt it call out to me. Touch me. Feel me. I was mesmerized by it. One glinting trophy, a million memories. I thought of all those great players who'd touched it before. Kenny Dalglish, Graeme Souness, Alan Hansen. Liverpool legends. European Cup winners. I wanted it so badly. I just wanted to take it home, back where the European Cup belongs. Anfield. Somehow, I reached my seat without touching it. Carra would never have forgiven me.

I sat down and turned to Maldini, all suave and Italian, he looked so relaxed. Been there, done that, got the T-shirt. I was a kid next to Maldini, an apprentice next to an experienced master. Maldini's all right, a decent guy, but he had been in this situation so many times. It was another season, another final for this Milan great. He smiled at me. I saw his perfect teeth, caught that look of confidence in his eyes. We shook hands for the cameras. I stared at him, and then at the cup. Which of us would hold it tomorrow? Which of us would take that cup home?

Maldini cut into my dreaming. 'Good luck tomorrow,' he said.

Milan were the favourites. History, the bookmakers and the pundits sided with them. Everyone expected Maldini to be the captain who touched the European Cup in Istanbul. I was desperate to say to him, 'Listen, Paolo, you've lifted this cup four times. Just let me lift it once.'

Lost in thought, I climbed back into a UEFA car to head back to the hotel. Tomorrow would be the toughest night of my life. Fears crowded in. Meeting Maldini reminded me of the quality of opponent barring our way to the European Cup. Images flashed up in my mind like penpix plucked from the match programme: Andrei Shevchenko, Cafu, Kaka, Hernan Crespo. My stomach twisted in knots.

Then my natural competitive streak quickly kicked in. Respect, but no fear. We're Liverpool. We're not here to make up the numbers. Carra, me and the boys have been through too many scrapes, passed too many tests. Olympiakos. Juventus. Chelsea. We'd taken the hard road to Istanbul. We have nothing to lose. Nothing. I looked out the car window and saw the thousands of Liverpool fans sitting in Istanbul's bars and cafés, singing and chatting away without a care in the world. So, Stevie lad, where's the pressure? No matter what happens tomorrow, we will return to Liverpool as heroes. Our fans love us. We got them to a final. They are having a party. At the start of the season, Milan expected to be in Istanbul on 25 May; Liverpool expected to be on holiday. The pressure was all on Milan, not Liverpool. Let's have a right good go and then go home.

The day of the game passed in a blur of nerves, snatched moments of sleep, and deep thought. Each player knew he approached the crunch-point of his career, when he could write his name in the history books. Time to go. Time for the bus. The adrenalin really flowed as we worked our way through the crowds outside our hotel. On the bus, sit back in the seat, breathe deeply.

The journey to the Atatürk was weird. Usually on the way to European away games, the sights and sounds are pretty familiar. Sirens, people hanging out of windows, giving us abuse. But this was bizarre. Because the Turks had built this new ground in the middle of nowhere there was just silence, until we started seeing our fans near the stadium. Playing a final miles from anywhere did not stop them. If Liverpool reached a final on the moon, our amazing fans would get there. The memory of all those supporters flocking to the Atatürk, walking across fields, on the hard shoulder, in the middle of the road, will never leave me. The scene resembled a pilgrimage, with 40,000 worshippers trekking miles to a steel cathedral. Liverpool fans waved at us, banged on the side of the bus. 'This means everything to the fans,' I shouted down the bus. 'We can't let them down.'

Passing Liverpool's support congregated on one side of the Atatürk, we drove around to the Milan side, to the main entrance. It was dead quiet there, no-one around – really weird. A few Milan fans were about, but they ignored the Liverpool coach. They were cool. Obviously, Milan fans thought they were going to walk it. I stole a last listen to my phone, read the final good luck texts from Michael and family, and switched it off. Time to focus. Time to exclude all other thoughts from my mind except beating Milan.

Rafa had not told us the team, so our dressing-room was racked with tension. About an hour before kick-off, he finally called for quiet and read out the starting eleven: 'Jerzy in goal; Finnan, Carra, Sami, Djimi at the back; Luis on the right, Xabi and Stevie in the middle, Riise on the left; Harry and Milan up front.' No Didi. That was my immediate reaction. I glanced across at him. Typical German, he showed no emotion. I really felt for him. He must have been devastated not to start. Instead, Rafa picked Harry Kewell, who had been injured. He wanted to attack AC Milan, using Harry's pace. Was he fit? No, not 100 per cent. All the Liverpool players knew that, but we also all had confidence that Harry could deliver.

Rafa was dead relaxed. The boss never came out with any great rallying cry, just some calm, last-minute instructions. 'Keep it tight,' he said. 'Make no mistakes. Let's settle and try to play our own game.'

It was time. I led the players into the tunnel, lined up, and nodded to Maldini.

I stepped out into the Atatürk Stadium, striding towards my destiny. This was it. I gripped the hand of the mascot. The Champions League anthem sent my heart racing even more. More handshakes, more formalities. I glanced towards the fans, looking for friendly faces, for reassurance before battle commenced with Milan. And then the huddle. Everyone gathered around, arms around each other, bonded together for death or glory. The noise from Liverpool fans was deafening, so I drew the players even tighter into the huddle so they could hear me. People like Carra understood how much this final meant to everyone at Liverpool. The years of waiting. The frustration at seeing other clubs dominating. I had to get this message across to the foreign lads. I'd been thinking about this speech all week, just getting the right words, and they all came flying out.

'We are Liverpool,' I told them, 'and Liverpool belong in the European Cup final. Just look at our fans. Listen to them. Look at how much this means to them. It means the world. Don't let them down. You don't realize the reaction you will get from these fans if you win. You will be a hero for the rest of your life. This is our chance, our moment. Don't let it slip. We have come this far, let's not give it up tonight. Let's start well, get into them, show them we're Liverpool. Lads, no regrets. Make every challenge count, every run count, every shot count, otherwise you will regret it for the rest of your life. No regrets. Let's win it.'

Enough words. Time for action. We broke away and sprinted to our starting positions.

So much for my gee-up. Milan were ready and waiting. We ran into a blizzard of white movement. Within a few seconds, Djimi Traore challenged Kaka. Andrea Pirlo to Maldini, slack marking, good volley, 1–0.

Gifted a goal, Milan then dominated. This was the half from hell. Harry snapped his groin and hobbled off, replaced by Vladi.

One down, Harry gone, Liverpool were in the grip of a worsening nightmare. Nothing went right. Alessandro Nesta blatantly handled a shot from García. 'Handball!' screamed Luis. 'Handball!' screamed the crowd. Penalties don't come more obvious, but Manuel Enrique Mejuto Gonzalez, the ref, ignored it. He waved play on. We were distracted, we struggled to get back, and Crespo tucked one away down the other end.

I looked at my team-mates. Stunned and dazed, we couldn't get near Milan. Five minutes later, Kaka conjured up more magic and Crespo poached another. 3–0. It's over. Surely. That's us dead. Never had I faced such a good side. Kaka was a great player, I knew that. Anyone who starts for Brazil must be special. But not until I spent that half running around after him, chasing his shadow, did I appreciate how quick he was in possession. Never in my career had I encountered anyone as fast with the ball at their feet. Kaka was lightning. I'm quite quick for a midfielder, and usually I reel in most players if they have the ball. Not Kaka. He was awesome, easily Milan's best midfielder. Gennaro Gattuso was also in midfield, and he was the one Milan player who had a smirk on his face leaving the pitch at half-time. That disgusted me.

I was steaming as I arrived in the dressing-room. 'They think it's over,' I said. 'It's not.' All words then left me. I was speechless, enraged by our display, my own performance and that smirk of Gattuso's. The dressing-room fell quiet for a couple of minutes. We sat there lifeless, our dreams seemingly shredded. Misery clung to everyone in that room.

Gradually, players began to speak. No recriminations. No blame. Just general laments. 'What's going on?' I said. 'Rafa told us to be compact, to not make mistakes. There is only one side in this. We haven't even started.' Some of the guys were in pieces. Surely there was no way we could score three goals against Milan, not after the way they played first half? 'Let's just stop this being 5–0,' said Carra. 'Let's not have a massacre here.'

We needed someone to shake us into life, to make us believe. Rafa stepped forward. The boss was brilliant, truly brilliant, at half-time. 'Silence,' he said. All the murmurings and the moanings ceased. We looked up at our manager, wondering how he was going to change tactics to perform a miracle. 'Finnan off, Didi on,' Rafa said, rattling out orders. 'Three at the back. Didi alongside Xabi, but more defensive. The two of you sort out Kaka. Vladi, play like a wing-back rather than right midfield. Steven, play a bit more forward. You and Luis link up with Baros. Get at their players. Close them down earlier. And keep the ball.' Just listening to the boss's escape plan lifted our spirits. Rafa was our leader, the man who could help us out of this mess.

Having sorted out the tactics, he went to work on our minds. 'Don't let your heads drop,' he said. 'You are playing for Liverpool. Don't forget that. You have to hold your heads high for the supporters. You cannot call yourself a Liverpool player if you have your heads bowed. The supporters have come a long way. Don't let them down. Believe you can do it and we will. Give yourselves a chance to be heroes.'

Rafa helped change our mood from defeat to defiance. Let's go out fighting, not with a whimper. Rafa kept mentioning the fans. Outside, that huge electronic scoreboard that read 'Maldini 1, Crespo 39, 44' stared at our fans. Proof of Liverpool's terrible performance was written large up there. Looking at that scoreboard, most Liverpool fans must have felt the race was run and lost. Deep down, the fans were simply buzzing we got to the final. They could see the quality of opposition we struggled against. Yet against all the odds, against all the evidence of Milan's superiority, our fans were singing loud and proud. 'Listen,' I said to the players. 'Listen to that.' The singing of 40,000 Liverpool supporters floated down the tunnel, into the dressing-room and into our hearts.

Unbelievable. Liverpool were 3–0 down, being thrashed by Kaka and Crespo, and our fans were singing 'You'll Never Walk Alone'. All the players looked at each other in amazement, and pride. 'They haven't given up on us,' I shouted, 'so we can't give up either.' By singing 'You'll Never Walk Alone', the fans sent a message to eleven shattered men in the dressing-room: the fans will be with you, through the wind and the rain, through times of adversity like this. No matter how much the players hurt, we'd never walk alone. Our fans were with us. Together. Their message was to play for some respect, play for pride in the shirt. 'The fans are with us,' I said. 'Let's give them something to shout about. They've spent loads of money. They're singing our name and we are getting stuffed 3–0. If we get one, they'll get behind us even more. That will help put another one in for us. Come on, let's have a go!'

As captain, the responsibility was on me to lead the fight-back. I came charging up the tunnel, staring at the Milan players as I raced past. I was determined to set a new tone: let's get on with the game, we don't believe it's over. Milan's players looked confused. They walked back out into a stadium where the only noise came from Liverpool fans. Even I was almost knocked over by the roar from our support. Milan's fans were overawed. Confidence seeped back into me. My natural instinct is to fight back anyway. Battered about by my brother's mates on Ironside, rejected by Lilleshall, pained by injuries, I was used to hard knocks. I'd recovered before. Why couldn't I recover now? Liverpool had forty-five minutes to get three goals. 'Come on!' I shouted at the team as the game restarted.

Immediately, we were reminded of the scale of the mountain we had to climb. Milan were pure class.

Within a couple of seconds, Shevchenko bent in a free-kick that Jerzy fisted away.

When the dust settled from that Milan chance, I took a look at their players. They seemed different. Complacency crept into their game. Milan felt the job was already done. Even if they lost one goal, Maldini and his mates clearly fancied themselves to see it through 3–1. Well, let's just test that. I was getting forward more, released from my anchoring duties by Didi. His arrival was key. Didi was brilliant second half.

With Didi patrolling behind me, I ripped into Milan. It was time to take some risks. I bombed on, racing towards Milan's area in the fifty-fourth minute as Riise got the ball on the left. His cross got blocked by Cafu. I checked, then went again. Just a gamble – the ball could come in again. Ginger delivered big-time, smacking the ball across before Cafu could close him down again. I was twelve yards out with a yard of space. Riise's ball was travelling in fast. 'Use its power,' I told myself. 'Direct it over Dida.' Milan's keeper put his arms out, but the ball was over him and in. Get in! Some header! I sprinted over to Liverpool's fans and gave them a geeing-up sign. Come on! We have a chance! More noise. Liverpool fans lifted the players, and I wanted to lift the fans. They reacted as I knew they would. The volume rose.

Milan would surely react. Their team was packed with winners, stars like Kaka and Maldini. Before they caught their breath, we had to go for their jugular. Keep pushing. Two minutes on, Didi got the ball and slipped it to Vladi, who was twenty-five yards out and not looking threatening. When he first hit the shot, I thought Dida had to save this. It wasn't that hard. But he flapped at Vladi's strike, and the ball wandered on into the net.

'We can do this!' I thought. 'Come on, let's get the third!' I yelled at the players once we'd finished congratulating Vladi. I was utterly convinced from that moment that Liverpool would not lose this European Cup final. No way. Milan had gone, their heads were down. No talking. No reaction. Milan were dead men walking. Let's bury them.

Carra, unbeatable Carra, my mate and Liverpool's magnificent servant, led another charge three minutes on, feeding the ball to Baros near the box. I was running in behind. I hoped Baros saw me. If he did, I was in on goal. 'Milly!' I shouted. 'Milly, Milly, Milly!' Baros heard me, heard my prayers, and found me with a spot-on touch. I pulled my left leg back to shoot, and then bang, Gattuso caught my back leg. I went down. 'Penalty!' everyone cried. I looked up to see Mejuto Gonzalez's reaction. He was surrounded by complaining players: Milan players claiming I dived and Carra telling the ref that the foul was a sending-off offence.

Xabi was the appointed penalty-taker. Cool as you like, Xabi took control, collected the ball from Carra and placed it on the spot. Talk about pressure. 'Put that ball in the net, please, Xabi,' I prayed. Xabi hit it hard and low. I started leaping into the air to celebrate. But Dida saved it. Yet the ball was loose. Xabi reacted quickest. Always the top pro, the Spaniard followed up, and his finish was exquisite. He smashed it in, left foot. Get in! Take that, Dida! Take that, Milan!

Relief, joy, every emotion was there as we chased after Xabi. It was a piley-on, Xabi disappearing under shouting, laughing, uncontrollable team-mates. What a turnaround! Six minutes that shook the world. Six minutes that broke Milan's hearts. The suddenness of our comeback killed the Italian side. If the goals had been spread out, Milan might have got their heads together, regrouped and composed themselves. It was the sudden impact of the goals that devastated them. Me, then Vladi, then Xabi. Bang, bang, bang. Milan's players looked like they had been in a car-crash. Staggering around. No direction.

Carlo Ancelotti tried to shake the corpse of his Milan side back into life. Seedorf was knackered, so on darted Serginho, who began flying down Milan's left. Rafa reacted immediately. 'Steven,' he shouted. 'Go right-back, Steven. You've got the legs to mark Serginho.' Vladi had been right wing-back, but Benítez didn't think he was good enough defensively to handle Serginho. So I got the right-back shout. Thanks, Rafa! Serginho was lively and I was close to cramping up.

As Mejuto Gonzalez blew for the end of normal time, my body was a mess. Cramp invaded my calves. 'Got nothing left,' I gasped to one of Liverpool's masseurs, who went to work on my legs. The Atatürk pitch was massive and the air really humid. I was drained. The thirty extra minutes stretched out in front of me like a life sentence. Moments like this are when a footballer discovers most about himself. I've dug deep once. Can I dig deep again? Have I anything left to give? Doubts briefly besieged me. I lay on my back, my socks rolled down, my shin-pads sticking out as the masseurs pummelled some life back into my legs. The cramp remained, eating away, but I could move and could definitely block the pain out. Thirty minutes remained. Give it all. And again. And again.

Extra time started and Serginho was coming at me again, all murderous intent and burning pace. I played from memory, somehow throwing myself into tackles on this Brazilian. From Ironside to Istanbul, I have launched myself into tackles all my life. My body is programmed to do it. So when I was at my most exhausted, my energy gone, my brain closing down, my body followed its natural instinct and kept challenging. My long legs stretched out to get some big tackles in on Serginho. Everyone in red pushed themselves to the limits and beyond. Don't let Milan score! Our so-called lightweight players, the flashy ones like García and Vladi, battled like lions. Backs to the wall. Everyone fought. Bonds of friendship kept us together. Inevitably, Carra was a commanding presence, putting his body in the line of fire, getting blocks in, even with cramp gripping him too. An incredible desire to win consumes every fibre of Carra's body. We needed him in Istanbul big-time. He gave everything. At one point, I saw him pushing against the post, stretching his calves to take the sting out of the cramp. Carra remarked afterwards that playing with cramp was worse than playing with a broken leg. I sympathized. We were running on empty, just relying on guts and a refusal to be beaten.

I wished I'd been near a post to ease the pain in my calves. I was out wide fighting a Brazilian fire-storm called Serginho. As I chased him, I remembered the agony of past defeats like the Carling Cup final to Chelsea. I wasn't letting this final get away. That medal was mine. Dead inside, I had to show strength to keep the team believing. Be strong. Be the captain. I kept urging everyone on.

Shevchenko is among the top forwards in the world, and when the ball fell to him two yards out with two minutes remaining, I thought, 'That's it. It really is over now. Shevchenko will never miss.' I couldn't believe what happened. No-one present in the Atatürk Stadium that extraordinary evening will ever understand. Shevchenko thought he had scored with a header. Jerzy blocked. Shevchenko then thought he had netted the follow-up, but Jerzy blocked again. These were freak saves, not technical ones worked on in training. Some extra force protected Liverpool in those moments. I really believe that. When Jerzy made that incredible double save, I felt someone upstairs was on our side. Milan felt that God and Lady Luck deserted them. Psychologically, the Italians were shot to pieces, and that is the worst frame of mind going into a penalty shoot-out.

When the final whistle went I was pulled all over the place by different emotions. There was relief and pride that we had fought back to draw. But I felt desperately nervous because pens awaited. Rafa marched across and looked at us, establishing who was confident enough to take one. 'No,' said Djimi. 'Yeah,' said Carra, typically. Carra always fancies himself at pens. Rafa also got a yes from Didi, Xabi, me, Vladi, Djibril, Riise and García. From those eight, Rafa chose his starting five. I looked at the order on his list: Didi, Djibril, Riise, Vladi and me. Fifth! Thanks. The pressure is always on the fifth penalty-taker as any mistake usually means oblivion. As I thought about the additional pressure on my kick, Luis badgered Rafa. 'I want a pen,' he said. I was proud that so many of our players wanted the responsibility. Inside, they may have been screaming 'No, no!' but they didn't hide when Liverpool Football Club needed them most.

As the ref called the teams together, the reality of pens began to sink in. Can't get out of it now. I began preparing myself, imagining where I was going to put it. When I missed against Spurs, I said publicly, 'I will never take a penalty again.' I lied. Penalties are a great opportunity to score. And as captain, I must take responsibility. I must step up. 'Fair enough,' I'd said to Rafa, 'I'll take the fifth penalty.' I'll go and score it.

First up, I had to go across to the ref with Maldini to toss. 'If you win the toss, go first to put the extra pressure on them,' Carra told me. Maldini won. 'We'll kick first,' said Maldini. They also had the end, which seemed a real advantage. Milan's fans would do everything to put us off. Flares, screaming abuse, everything.

But we had our own secret weapon: Carra. Just before Jerzy set off for the goal, Carra pulled him. 'Do the spaghetti legs,' he told him. Jerzy looked blank. Carra explained how Bruce Grobbelaar had done a wobbly legs routine in the shootout of the 1984 European Cup final to put off Roma. I'm not sure Jerzy was up for a history lesson at that particular moment, but he understood Carra's impersonation of Grobbelaar. My advice to Jerzy was simpler: 'Good luck.' Carra's words, though, clearly impressed Jerzy, who jumped around on the line like a scalded cat. We all watched from the halfway line, arms around each other's shoulders – a statement that we won or lost together.

Serginho was first up. Unnerved by Jerzy's dancing, he shovelled his kick into the crowd. Standing in the centre-circle, I felt the line of Liverpool bodies rise up and the hands of García and Riise grip my shoulders. 'Yes!' I shouted. 'Go on, Didi.' Didi untangled himself from our line, and stepped forward.

Some penalty-takers look like condemned men as they walk from the centre-circle to the spot. Not Didi. Didi is class, and I knew he would score. He never panics. He's so experienced. He's taken pens for Germany. And he nailed this one past Dida. Again I felt the ripple of joy course through the Liverpool line. Didi strolled back, towards his footballing family, to a row of smiling faces: Carra, Sami, Djibril, Djimi, García, me, Riise, Xabi and Vladi. All in it together.

We watched transfixed as the shoot-out continued. Jerzy saved Pirlo's penalty. Yes! Cissé scored. Yes! Jon-Dahl Tomasson then made it 2–1 to us, and it was Riise's turn. He's got one of the best left foots in the game, like a hammer. He ran in to hit the ball. Smash it. Bury it. Surprisingly, Riise placed it, and Dida pulled off a worldie save. My heart went out to John Arne. If he had the chance to take that penalty again, he would rip the net off, sending it flying backwards over the Milan fans. In training, if Riise ever takes a penalty or a shot from outside the box, he takes the net off. In Istanbul, he changed his mind during his run-up. When he returned to the line, looking shattered, I tried to console him. But there is nothing anyone can say in situations like that. Riise wouldn't have heard anyway. He was lost in his own grief.

When Kaka beat Jerzy to make it 2–2, it was Smicer's turn to leave the security of the Liverpool line and make that unforgiving walk. Go on, Vladi. Surprise still coloured my thoughts as I watched Vladi go. Why did Rafa pick him among the five? Vladi was leaving Liverpool after the final. Would he be right mentally? Again, Rafa got it right. My doubts disappeared into the back of Dida's net, along with Vladi's fantastic penalty. He strolled back kissing the Liverpool badge. How calm was that, sending Dida the wrong way with his last kick for the club? Top man.

Vladi's pen meant Shevchenko had to score. 'He will,' I thought as I watched him place the ball down. Usually, Shevchenko passes the ball hard into the net. Time after time. His finishing is up there with the best in the world. But Shevchenko looked to have the world on his shoulders as he took the ball from Jerzy, our new master of the mind games, who added to the great Ukrainian's sense of unease by staring him down, bouncing around on his line and then moving a yard off it. Shevchenko's kick was weak, placed down the middle, and Jerzy saved it.

Yeeeessss! All the nerves in my body disappeared in one long scream of delight. All my anxiety at having to take the next pen went. I don't have to take one! It's done! It's over! Go and party!

Looking back on the moments after Jerzy's save is like trying to recall pieces of a dream. I was so caught up in the emotion. But every day since 25 May 2005, little memories of that night have come back to me and I am now able to paint the picture of those precious minutes. Seeing a photograph around the house or at Melwood or Anfield triggers a memory. Did I really dance like that? Did I really sing like that? Whenever I hear 'Ring of Fire' I'm swept back to those delirious scenes of celebration. As the picture of that night becomes clearer in my mind, my pride swells even more about winning the European Cup.

When Jerzy made that save off Shevchenko, the sprint was on to reach our amazing keeper. Carra was supposed to have cramp, but it didn't look like it! He was first out of the blocks, followed by Finnan, Luis,

Riise, Xabi, Didi, then me and the rest. I then took off to the fans. This special moment was for them. Kopites had put up with so much, spent so much. We'd repaid them. I danced around on the running track, surrounded by photographers, screaming 'Yeeeessss!' I looked at the Liverpool fans and saw all the banners and joyful faces. I saw grown men crying, breaking down with the emotion of seeing Liverpool back on top of Europe again. I saw fathers hugging sons who should have been at school. I saw the best supporters in the world revelling in a moment that meant the world. We had five European Cups. Our fifth trophy meant we kept the cup for good. The European Cup was coming home, and it would never leave Anfield again.

When that thought hit me, it briefly knocked all the pain out of my battered body. I'm Liverpool captain, and I have just won the European Cup. Won it back permanently for the club I love. Tears rose within me, threatening to break out. I choked them back.

Slowly, I regained my senses. As people came back into focus, I noticed Shevchenko was still there on the pitch, stunned, as if turned to a statue by his penalty miss. One bad kick cannot destroy a forward of Shevchenko's qualities in my eyes. For me, he will always be a true champion. I hobbled over and embraced him. I looked into his eyes and saw the deep distress. Poor guy. He wore a hollow, haunted look. As I looked at Shevchenko, pictures of my own past disappointments came to mind: my own-goal in the Carling Cup final, the back-pass against France at Euro 2004 – moments when I died a sporting death. My dad and Steve Heighway always taught me to take it on the chin and be gracious in defeat, and some of the Milan players, like Shevchenko, were brilliant to us. 'Well done,' Andrei said as we agreed to swap shirts later. Amazing. He'd endured the worst night of his life, yet there he was congratulating the man who had just beaten him. He rose even higher in my admiration. Maldini was magnificent as well, shaking my hand and congratulating me. Maldini's class, on and off the pitch. 'Enjoy it,' he told me as we got ready for the presentations.

As Maldini applauded, we went up to receive our medals. As captain, I was last. When it was my turn, I collected my medal from the main men at UEFA, Lars-Christer Olsson and Lennart Johansson. I kissed the medal and thought of Dad. His pride. His smiling face. 'Thanks, Dad,' I thought. 'This is for you, for all the encouragement and the good advice.' I stood there on the podium, waiting while Rafa and the other coaches were presented with their medals. I had eyes only for the cup. There it was. On the pedestal. Closer and closer. Now I could touch it. No inhibitions now. No superstitions. I leant forward and kissed it gently.

'You must be happy,' said Johansson as he prepared to hand me the cup.

'It's for them,' I replied, pointing to our fantastic supporters.

I lifted the cup to the stars and the whole place went crazy. Players leaping up and down, red fireworks and streamers going off, the fans dancing madly. Magical. I held it in the air and felt at that moment everyone in the world stopping what they were doing and watching me.

Back in the dressing-room, everyone embraced, sang and carried on partying. Liverpool's chairman, David Moores, was in tears, unable to hold back the wave of emotion, his pride getting to him big-style.

The dressing-room was full to bursting. Gérard Houllier squeezed in, which surprised a few. Some people at the club muttered darkly about whether a former manager should join our moment of triumph. Not me. I was pleased. Gérard wasn't gate-crashing. He came down to congratulate the lads and the chairman. He had earned the right. Other managers with different characters might have got their jealous heads on and not wanted us to win. Not Gérard. He was buzzing for us.

When I got back to the hotel, I was shattered, and slumped into a seat. Some of the lads, like Baros, shot off down to Tacsim Square to party with the fans. Our hotel was crammed with fans. My bed called to me, but thousands of people wanted a word, an autograph, a picture. Fighting back the utter exhaustion, I went to the do Liverpool laid on at the hotel. Nothing wild. A lot of the players had their girlfriends and wives around, and we just sat about talking about the game, the emotions, still trying to take it all in.

I couldn't think any more. By now, bed screamed out to me. But my mates came into the hotel, so we had a few more beers, a few more laughs. Everyone raved about Kaka, who'd been sensational for Milan. 'He was the one Milan player I couldn't get near,' I said. Struan came in and we talked some more. 'I really wanted you to take the last pen, for the drama of winning the cup,' Struan said. I was confident I would have scored, but it was good not to have to find out. Struan ran through all the messages he had received, including one from John Terry. 'I'm buzzing,' said JT. 'Hairs out on the back of my neck. Tell Stevie, brilliant. I'm buzzing for him.' JT had seen me lift the European Cup knowing it could so easily have been him, and he still wanted to congratulate me. Top man.

Everyone was so happy and smiling. The room was packed. It seemed every Liverpool supporter had blagged their way past security. I didn't want to talk to people because I was that drained, but I did. I stayed on and talked and drank beer until it was light outside. I was one of the last out of the party. As I stumbled out towards my room, I looked back and saw my new best mate, the European Cup, just standing there on a table. I grabbed the cup and we headed off upstairs together.

Two hours later, I awoke with a start. Where the hell am I? My eyes struggled to deal with the daylight streaming in through the window. Gradually, the outline of something large came into focus at the end of the bed. It's the European Cup! It was just me and the European Cup. I gazed at it, and memories of the previous night came flooding back. For twenty minutes I lay there, just staring at the cup. Just the two of us. Then, I realized no-one will know where this cup is! Liverpool had waited twenty-one years to get their hands back on the cup and now it had gone. I'd better get down to breakfast.

I staggered into the meal-room.

'Where's the cup?' Carra shouted.

Everyone was there, looking concerned, as if they were about to scramble a search party.

'Don't panic,' I laughed. 'It's in my room. Come and have a look if you want!'

So all the boys piled upstairs and saw the cup again. Then we brought it down, had a team picture taken with it and the hotel staff, and said goodbye to Istanbul.

I hate flying, but the whole trip was heaven. The

second we landed at John Lennon International, it all went crazy again. Press and fans, questions and autographs. More pictures. Back at Melwood, we boarded an open-top bus and headed back into town. We had to do the parade that Thursday because all the foreign lads were flying off for internationals. On the bus, champagne open, good drink, good laugh. Brilliant. All the players took it in turns to lift the trophy, showing it to the fans, milking the moment, and deservedly so. The foreign lads were gobsmacked. They hadn't realized we had so many supporters. Only as the bus snaked slowly through the streets did they appreciate how big a club Liverpool is. I'd experienced it before with the Treble, all the passionate support lining the side of the road, but the European Cup tour was even better.

It was a scrum on the pavement, people often spilling off into the road. 'Someone could get seriously hurt,' I said to Carra. And the crush was worrying at certain points on the route. Police horses kept crashing into the side of the bus; fans were getting thrown back. People were a hundred feet up in the air, hanging off lamp-posts, out of trees and buildings.

Merseyside Police did a super job controlling all those people because really it was mission impossible. When we got into town, the bus didn't move for forty-five minutes. I kept catching sight of friends, waving, smiling, punching the air. The European Cup was home.

# 18
# Feeling Blue Again

In climbing to the peak of my club career in 2004/05, I endured moments of doubt. The thought of joining Chelsea still ate away at me. Liverpool might have won the Champions League, but the Premiership belonged to Chelsea.

Because honesty is a quality I prize so highly, I was always straight with Liverpool. In a press conference before the Champions League tie with Olympiakos, I was asked, 'What are you going to do if Liverpool don't get Champions League football next season?' I didn't flinch. 'I am going to have to consider my future,' I replied. No choice. So the crazy whirl of rumours intensified because I didn't come out and say, 'I'm not going to Chelsea or Real Madrid.' I didn't want to lie, or claim everything was all sweetness and light at Liverpool. I wanted to wait and see how the season panned out. Ideally, Liverpool would finish first or second, and I could announce, 'I don't have to move.' Sadly, we were soon fighting it out for fourth or fifth again.

On 10 December 2004, Rick Parry tried to calm the speculation by insisting Liverpool had 'no intention' of letting me go. 'If we can deliver top honours, I am convinced Steven will remain at Liverpool,' he said. More stories about me appeared during the winter transfer window. 'Is Gerrard Staying?' 'Is Stevie G-oing?' Headline after headline, more fuel on the fire. Again Rick emphasized how highly the club rated me. 'Steven is above money,' Rick told the press. 'He is the future of Liverpool. Even if it's thirty, forty or fifty million, we won't accept offers.' Privately, Rick also came to me twice during the season and said, 'We want you to extend your contract. We want you to stay.'

But I was confused. If they wanted me so bad, why didn't they put a contract on the table? Show me the deal. Show me you really want me. Rafa was also on at me to commit myself. But how could I without seeing what Liverpool proposed? They never contacted Struan, who sorts out all my deals. I didn't understand Liverpool's game-plan. Did they want to keep me?

The stand-off led to further speculation in the press. Chelsea, Chelsea, Real, Real. Non-stop. It was becoming a soap opera. Before our League Cup semi-final with Watford in January 2005, Benítez pulled me and said, 'Listen, you can put a stop to all this stuff in the papers by signing a new deal.' But there was no deal there! Frustration at the situation did my head in.

'You know where my agent is,' I told Rafa. 'Talk to him. He represents me with deals.'

The first time Rafa and Rick cornered me, I said, 'Look, how can I seriously sign a four- or five-year contract now when we are fighting for fourth or fifth place in the Premiership?' I needed to know what Liverpool were offering me financially, but most importantly I wanted Rafa and Rick to guarantee progress.

'Can't we just wait until the end of the season and find out if we are in the Champions League?' I asked. 'Let's see how we do from now until the summer, and then I will sign a deal. If this club goes forward and you bring success, I'll stay. You will have to trust me.'

My feelings towards Liverpool, and particularly some of the fans, darkened because of events during the Carling Cup final against Chelsea on Sunday, 27 February 2005. A day that began so full of hope ended in a mess. It was only the League Cup, but it felt special because it was the first time I had led Liverpool out in a cup final. The night before, I dreamed of lifting the trophy. Me. First with my hands on the cup. Holding it up. Liverpool fans going crazy. The reality, however, brought only misery. We were so close to winning, leading through Riise's early goal. But then I scored an own-goal, Chelsea won it in extra time, and the nightmare kicked in. I was torn apart emotionally. I'd let everyone down – the club, the fans, the players. Mourinho was very gracious in victory. I admired that, because I was a wreck. Devastated. Down. Lifeless. Even now, when I see pictures of that final, the hurt comes flooding back. The image of the Chelsea boys collecting their winner's medals is always there in my mind, a reminder of my failure that day in Cardiff.

After dragging my shattered body onto the team bus, I switched on my phone and went through texts from mates, trying to lift my spirits. Dad called. 'Keep your chin up,' he said. 'Forget about it.'

But some of the Liverpool fans were less supportive, slaughtering me for the own-goal, and claiming I did it on purpose because I was headed for Chelsea. I was fed up with the whole messy saga. I love Liverpool, and it hurt having my powerful bonds to the club strained by the speculation. When we beat Chelsea in the Champions League semis to reach the final in Istanbul, I couldn't hold back. 'All I wanted was to see the club going in the right direction, and this victory shows we are,' I said. And once we won that glorious final, I let rip again, pouring out emotions that had been building for a long time. 'How can I leave after a night like this, and all the nights I've experienced?' I said at the press conference in Istanbul, gazing at the European Cup and listening to our brilliant fans partying outside. 'I'm signing for Liverpool Football Club for four or five years,' I told the world. I'd been dying to get to this point, to blow away all the clouds of speculation and reveal my passion for Liverpool Football Club. Adrenalin rushed through me in Istanbul, but my mind was completely clear, totally cold in its analysis. I can't walk away. I want to stay.

Liverpool never truly realized how desperate I was to get it signed. I admire Rick Parry, who has been a fantastic chief executive for Liverpool Football Club, always acting with the club's best interests at heart. But he didn't seem to understand how battered my head had been over my future ever since Euro 2004.

A wave of doubt rolled through me again. All season, Rick had been saying that Liverpool wanted to keep me. Three times they approached me. I was a symbol of Liverpool Football Club, a hungry lad from Huyton, raised at Melwood and Anfield. Surely they wanted their homegrown captain to stick around? Didi signed a contract the day after Istanbul. Not me. Rafa asked for meetings with three or four players to sort out their futures. Not me. 'Steven, I'll see you when you come back after the summer,' Rafa said after Istanbul. What was going on?

I spoke to my family and to Struan, just to see if

they could throw up a clue over why Liverpool were going cold after months of being warm to me. No-one could understand it. Was it just part of their negotiating tactics? Liverpool sounded positive in public. On 19 June, Rafa was all over the papers, announcing, 'I am not in favour of selling Steven Gerrard.' Five days later, I picked up the papers to read Rick saying, 'We want Steven to stay. There is no delay on his contract.'

The speculation revved up again. Real Madrid were heavily tipped to buy me. I snapped. I fronted up the Boss on what was being said in the Spanish press. Man to man, face to face. Come on, talk.

'Listen, do you want to sell me?' I asked him.

'No,' Rafa replied. 'Do you want to go?'

I looked at Rafa in astonishment. How could the Boss say that after what we'd been through in Istanbul?

I walked out and called Struan. 'Is Rafa waiting for me to push off? Does he want me to say I want to go? What are Liverpool playing at?'

Amid all the chaos, on Monday, 27 June, just over one month after Istanbul, Struan and Rick arranged to meet. At last. Surely now we'd come to an agreement.

Surely now all the speculation would end. Struan walked into the meeting expecting an improved offer. After all, Liverpool had had enough time to draw up a deal. I waited at home, full of relief that the wheels were finally in motion. I gripped my mobile in my hand, poised to answer at any moment a call from a delighted Struan. I could already hear him talking me through how committed Liverpool were to me and how an agreement had been reached. Just a signature, and on we go. Bliss.

I waited and waited. When Struan finally phoned, his voice was studded with frustration. 'There's no deal on the table,' Struan said. 'Liverpool first want to know what we are after.'

The following day, Tuesday, Rafa called me into his office at Melwood and put a blank piece of A4 paper in front of me. 'There you are, Steven,' he said. 'Write down on there what you want.'

'With all due respect, Boss, that's what I have got an agent for. I just want to concentrate on my football. I have never talked to a manager about my contract before. That's my agent's job.' I was pretty steamed up. 'My agent knows exactly what we are after.

We thought you would have an improved offer for us.'

Rafa didn't reply immediately. After leaving a long pause hanging heavily between us, he finally said, 'We'll have to wait and see.'

That week, the tension between me and Liverpool doubled by the day. Throughout the week I read more headlines like 'Benítez Might Want to Cash In on Gerrard', and more speculation about what Chelsea would pay me – £110,000 a week, £120,000. I just wanted to sign a decent deal at Liverpool and stay. Sensing my darkening mood, Struan was keen to break the deadlock. On 29 June, he contacted Liverpool again and indicated what we were looking for in terms of wages. As all the papers reported, I was already making between £70,000 and £80,000 a week, depending on appearances, and now I was looking for £100,000. I had helped Liverpool win the European Cup, which gave us a chance of playing in the competition the following season, and that was worth a fortune to Liverpool. Anyway, other clubs were apparently going to offer me a stack more.

'Give me a couple of days,' Rick replied. 'I will go and speak to the chairman and the board.'

Any minute I expected a call from Struan to tell me that Rick had been on, everything was sorted, deal done, and all it required was my signature. Sadly, silence reigned again. Each day I went into Melwood and told Rafa, 'You can put a stop to all this rubbish. I am not enjoying it. I will stay if you give me the contract.' I wasn't confrontational. I admit my relationship with Benítez for that week was strained, but it never got out of hand or aggressive. I respected the Boss immensely. He was frustrated as well.

'If this delay by Liverpool goes on any longer,' I thought, 'I may have to leave.' The prospect hit me like a hammer-blow. Leave Liverpool? Yes, it was possible. The door out of Anfield was opened by Liverpool's hesitation: I inched towards the door. On 1 July, Struan called Rick. 'Stevie wants to go,' Struan said. 'I need a few more days,' Rick replied.

We still didn't have an answer from Liverpool by the weekend. Nothing. I'd had enough. As the weekend wore on with no word from Liverpool, Struan and I decided to break off contract negotiations. We were getting nowhere. Struan took a call from an agent asking if I had re-signed. 'The answer is no,' he replied. Chelsea took that as enough of a signal for them to have a go. On the Monday, with all the papers full of me heading out of Anfield, Chelsea made their move, faxing Liverpool an offer for me.

My head was in turmoil. On television, I listened to Benítez talking at a press conference to announce the signing of Bolo Zenden. All the questions were about me. 'I'd like Steven to keep playing for us for the next eight years, and there could be a role for him beyond that,' Rafa told the cameras. 'Maybe the boss does want to keep me after all,' I thought. But really, I just didn't know what to think. I was in that bad a state – worried, stressed, head all over the place.

A ray of light then appeared. Liverpool's brilliant chairman, David Moores, called a meeting at Melwood on that Monday afternoon. I know how much the chairman cares for me as a person, and as a footballer. Mr Moores had become concerned by the stand-off between Liverpool's captain and the club. So he decided to intervene. The chairman, me, Struan, Rafa and Rick sat around the table and talked through the situation. Nothing was agreed, but I came out feeling better. As I got into the car, I said to Struan:

'Maybe they do want to keep me'. I began blaming myself for the way I had been thinking. I felt guilty. I thought Liverpool wanted me out, but this meeting in Melwood gave me a different impression of the club's intentions. But I still wasn't sure.

Were Liverpool talking about a new contract just to keep the fans onside while they flogged me to Chelsea? I had to know, so I decided to force their hand. I rang Struan. 'Struan, I'm going to find out whether they want to sell me. Put in a transfer request.' Struan phoned Liverpool. 'Take this call as a transfer request,' Struan told them. 'We will back it up in writing if you need us to. But this is it.' Bang. In went the transfer request, a hand-grenade rolled into the Liverpool boardroom.

That Tuesday, 5 July, was mental, the longest, hardest, most emotional day of my life. Action was required. I was sick of all the speculation in the papers, sick of getting pulled into Benítez's office, sick of waiting on Liverpool for an answer on the new contract. I was annoyed with Liverpool for waiting so long after I told them in Istanbul I wanted to stay.

It was supposed to sort things out, but Liverpool

immediately made my request public. Rick had to. He had to be fair to the fans. Madness broke out. I sat at home, my phone in one hand and the TV remote control in the other, staring transfixed as the drama played itself out on Sky. I was the main actor, yet there I was, sitting dazed at home, watching all these people and pundits debating me and my future. When I saw fans burning an old GERRARD number 17 shirt by the Shankly Gates, it did my head in.

I called Dad and Paul. 'Can you get over here, please?' I pleaded. They raced round. We went into my bedroom and talked for twenty minutes.

'Steven, don't go,' Dad begged.

'But Dad, look at the TV. Fans are burning my shirt at Anfield. The club aren't stopping them. Liverpool don't want me any more.'

Dad and Paul couldn't believe that.

'Don't walk away,' said Dad. 'Don't leave the club you love.'

After Dad and Paul left, I talked to my girlfriend, Alex. She isn't a footballing person, she doesn't under-stand the game, but she was brilliant. 'Stevie, you have to decide,' she said, 'but whatever you choose, I'll support you. I will come to Chelsea, Madrid, wherever. Don't worry.' Alex was just worried about me. She knew I hadn't been the same person for almost a month. As we talked, our beautiful daughter, Lilly-Ella, ran around without a care in the world. If only my life was that simple.

Struan came flying through the door, trying to calm me. I stared at the rolling news through flowing tears. I was suffocated by stress. My head was banging. Why had it got so bad? I looked at Struan. 'A month ago, I'm lifting the European Cup in front of the whole world, Stru,' I said. 'Then I'm touring the city in front of half a million people. I'm celebrating the biggest cup with fans of a club where I have been since I was eight. Now I'm watching my shirt being burned live on television. How has it come to this?' It was the lowest point of my career.

I broke down. I was burning up, pulse racing off the scale. I managed to call Doc Waller. A friend, a doctor, a man I trusted with my life. 'Doc, I'm a mess,' I told him. He was straight round, and he calmed me down. Doc Waller has always done so much for me. I rely on him greatly. All the players do.

The sight of Liverpool's doctor looking after me made me realize that people at Anfield do care about me. I began to think about what I was in danger of throwing away. All that love, all that history between us, the years dreaming of wearing the Liverpool shirt. Could I hand in that Liverpool armband? Could I turn my back on Liverpool, the club and the city that raised and shaped me? Could I let down my dad and my brother? They were mad Liverpool fans; leaving would seem like betrayal in their eyes. Could I look myself in the mirror again? Could I really put on a Chelsea shirt and face Liverpool in front of the Kop? Just think, Stevie. Think hard. I had to get this decision right. Could I really leave?

No. No. No. I couldn't jump over the edge of the cliff. I could see the great possibilities of Chelsea, but my heart wouldn't let me leave Liverpool. My beautiful little daughter Lilly-Ella was happy here, with her cousins, her friends in playschool. Was it fair on Alex to drag her away from her friends and family, from the environment where she was happiest? I couldn't do it. I was scared to leave what I had at Liverpool. I couldn't cut my roots. The clouds of doubts and questions began clearing. Chelsea had ambition, but I had ambitions for Liverpool. I was the club captain. We'd just won the European Cup. Rafa could take us forward, make us even more successful, as he's the best coach I have ever worked with.

Finally, my mind was made up. I'd walked through the storm. At eleven p.m., I called Struan. 'Tell Rick I want to sign,' I told him. 'I want to stay.'

Struan contacted Rick. 'Is that offer still available?'

'Yes.'

'Stevie will sign it.'

Thank God it was over. My heart stopped racing, and I relaxed. I awoke on the morning of Wednesday, 6 July, with a smile on my face for the first time in weeks. I got in my car and sped into Melwood.

'Look, I'm made up I'm staying, but I'll hand over the captaincy if you think it's best,' I told Rafa.

'Keep the armband,' he said.

Thank God. Giving up the captaincy would have broken my heart, but I had to make the offer. I apologized to Liverpool, to Rick and to Rafa, for all the mess, and they said sorry as well. The blame lay fifty-fifty, I know that, and I hold my hands up to contributing to the mess, but Liverpool could have handled it better. They so nearly drove me out of Anfield. I still received a couple of nasty letters from Liverpool fans, but overall they were good to me. Most of those on the Kop knew how torn I was. Liverpool fans understand how emotionally I feel about the club. My previous contract had contained a clause so that if Liverpool were not doing so well, I could move on. I didn't need an escape clause in my new contract. When I put pen to paper on Friday, 8 July, it was like signing a love letter. I was so glad my brief flirtation with Chelsea was over.

# 19
# Three Lionesses

The Chelsea saga reminded me just how deeply I was in love with Alex Curran. Alex is never nosy, although she always knows when something's on my mind. She never, ever gets involved in football. That's my world. The only time I ever talked to Alex about football was over Chelsea. I had to. When I was on my own, it would have been my decision. But in the summer of 2005 I had been with Alex for four years, we were engaged, and we had a beautiful little girl, Lilly-Ella. I had responsibilities, family commitments.

Of course, Alex is interested in how well I'm doing with Liverpool and England, but her knowledge of the sport is not good enough for her to get involved in a football conversation. She's watched me for four years and still doesn't know what the rules are. She comes to Anfield to enjoy the atmosphere, and to see the other girls. When I get home, she never mentions the match.

Girls have always fascinated me. I would have liked to have had a sister. Through school and up until the age of twenty-one I had loads of dates, but nothing really serious. I was waiting for the right girl. I was twenty-one when I met Alex and ready to calm down. I also wanted kids. I so admire Alex for what she has been through for me. She was twenty-two, really young herself, when I told her I wanted to get on with having a family. I felt becoming a father would be good for my career, to get me even more settled. And I wanted to be a young dad, rather than wait till the end of my career to start having kids. Alex was brilliant. She agreed we should start a family, even though she was so young.

Before Lilly-Ella was born, I was really scared. I arrived at the Liverpool Women's Hospital not knowing what to expect. When Lilly-Ella appeared, I'd never felt such pride, elation and relief. My career has brought me many highs, but nothing has matched the sight of those tiny hands and feet, that sweet face, that little body entering the world.

Before England left for the World Cup in Germany, I experienced the same wonderful sensation when Lexie was born. Again I was choked up, a huge lump in my throat. A lot of men cry when they see their children born. I certainly could have, I was that emotional. I counted all the fingers and toes, and checked the babies were healthy. Always nagging away in the back of my mind was that something might go wrong. But Lilly-Ella and Lexie were perfect.

Alex is a brilliant mum to Lilly-Ella and Lexie, and always supportive to me. When Mum and Dad broke up, Alex was a rock. She was just there for me, letting me know how much she cared. All the boxes are ticked for me with Alex. I wouldn't change her for anyone. I love her. She doesn't get involved in my career and I don't get involved in hers.

Alex has a column in the *Daily Mirror* and enjoys bits and bobs of work when she gets some free time, but her main priority is to be a mum. And she does a great job. Alex is more into the celebrity world than me. I'm not one for premieres or photo-shoots. My priority is football. If I wasn't playing well, I wouldn't get the attention I do get off the pitch. My number one concern is delivering for Liverpool and England.

When I was younger, I went out golfing, and I hung around snooker halls, and with my mates. A lot of the Liverpool lads were gamblers. Training finished and, bang, straight down the bookies. But for me, betting is pointless. I can't watch a horse race. It doesn't interest me. If the racing is on the TV when I come in, it is bang off. At Melwood, I see players studying the racing pages, and I think to myself, 'What are they doing?' I wouldn't know where to start. Maybe that's a good thing, because betting can be a dangerous road to go down. Some players go racing after training, or do all that online gambling. Now, the first thing for me after training is race home, get to the girls.

I walk in through the door of our new house in Formby and Lilly-Ella races across the hall into my arms. We have a pool, so I take the girls swimming. I love those girls. I miss them so bad, even when I go away for one night. I pace around my hotel room, holding a photograph of Alex and the girls, thinking of the moment when I'll be back with them, holding them. The family. Together. It means everything to me. I dream of having a little boy as well some time in the future, a son I can take to the park and enjoy kick-abouts with. If I do have a son, I would love him to play for Liverpool one day. I want to get a Gerrard dynasty going at Anfield.

# 20
# Millennium Magic

The thirteenth of May 2006 was a day to tell my children about as they grow older. 'This is our FA Cup final,' I told myself as Liverpool's coach inched through the raucous crowd and into the fantastic Millennium Stadium in Cardiff. 'This is our moment.' I was Liverpool's leader, settled at the club I love. I had the respect of my peers, having just been named the Professional Footballers' Association Player of the Year – an unbelievable honour. I was ready for the 125th FA Cup final. My stage, my time. In the build-up to the clash with West Ham United, I played the match through in my head at least three times. I used up a lot of energy thinking about every possibility, reminding myself constantly of the need to take responsibility, to seize the moment. Liverpool expected me to deliver. So did I. Let's go to work.

I led Liverpool out onto the pitch and into an unbelievable scene. All the fans, from Liverpool and West Ham, were magnificent, cheering twenty-two players as we lined up. We were favourites, a strange sensation. In all our other cup finals, Birmingham apart, Liverpool had been underdogs. In massive Champions League games, against heavyweights like Chelsea or Juventus, Liverpool were never given much hope. I liked that. Going into a game knowing the pressure was on the opposition was fine by me. But this was different. Everybody thought we would steamroller West Ham. I certainly never under-estimated the Hammers.

West Ham were up for this final, all right, as I quickly discovered. Paul Konchesky and Carl Fletcher both clattered me early on. Straight through. Whack. Hide the pain, Stevie, don't complain. Get on with it. I picked myself up, raised also by Liverpool fans singing the stirring 'Fields of Anfield Road', and hurled myself back into the fray. Get stuck in. Had to. West Ham meant business. Early on we tried to dominate, but we got caught on the break.

Within twenty-one minutes, we were behind. Carra couldn't do much about the own-goal, diverted in from Lionel Scaloni's cross. Carra had to go for it, because Marlon Harewood was lurking behind him and would have stuck it away. I was gutted for Carra. I knew how much the own-goal would hurt him. Carra's dead proud. If Liverpool had lost that FA Cup final 1–0, he wouldn't have been able to live with it.

We had to pull Carra out of the mess, had to fight back. But West Ham were on fire, and when they scored again, through Dean Ashton, a fear kicked in that I was not going to get my hands on the FA Cup. Ashton's goal was a bad mistake by Pepe Reina, but none of us Liverpool lads would dream of blaming Pepe. Our Spanish keeper saved us so many times that season. But two mistakes meant we were 2–0 down. Come on, lads! Let's get going!

The players lifted themselves. As we started to play a bit better, inspiring thoughts of Istanbul crept in. Time for another great escape. Pulling one back just before half-time was crucial. I spotted Djibril's run into the box. I took aim and whipped the ball into the box, where Djibril's finish was sensational. He didn't get much credit that season, but he deserves massive praise for that volley, because it got us back into the FA Cup.

In the Millennium dressing-room at half-time, Rafa made his usual inspirational speech. When the boys went back out, we were even more fired up. Liverpool lagged one goal behind but we had our tails up – let's take West Ham now! But as the second half wore on I worried about whether it was going to happen. Whenever I received the ball in West Ham's half, I tried too hard to push for the breakthrough. That's natural, I know. I was desperate to get that equalizer. We cannot lose, must not lose!

It was Peter Crouch, big Crouchy, who rescued us. When Xabi lifted a nothing ball into West Ham's box, Crouchy, Fernando Morientes and Danny Gabbidon went up for it. The moment I saw Crouchy stretching his neck, I started jogging into an area where I thought the ball would drop, around twelve yards out. Crouchy got the knockdown; it was bouncing and perfect for a shot. 'Over!' I screamed at Sami, ordering him to leave it. The set was ideal, and I caught it sweetly. Bang. Back of the net, 2–2.

What a crazy final it was turning out to be. Liverpool were level for only twelve minutes. When Yossi Benayoun put Etherington in on the left, there seemed no danger, no problem. We can handle this. I was running in at a decent speed and stretched out my leg into the perfect position to block his cross. But Etherington mishit the ball. There were only two places it could go: over the bar or into the top corner. Pepe, off his line, was caught out badly. The ball sailed over him, a freak goal, but an utterly preventable goal. Pepe was really disappointed.

At that point, Liverpool looked doomed. Our fans were quiet; their supporters were in party town. A few of our lads' heads were down. West Ham's name was on the Cup. It's over. The clock ran down, and I prepared for the worst. We needed impetus from somewhere.

Rafa, always top man with the subs, sent Didi on, giving me licence to push further forward. We charged all over the place, desperate for the equalizer. I got the ball and found Riise, who drilled the ball into West Ham's box. I heard the Millennium announcer declare, 'There will be a minimum of four minutes stoppage time.' The countdown had begun: Liverpool were 240 seconds from oblivion.

I was cramping up, nothing left, but I had to be around for the scraps. As the announcer's words drifted away, I hobbled forward. Morientes and Gabbidon fought for Riise's cross and the ball flew back out. Towards me. I stood there, legs stiff as boards, tank empty, thirty-seven yards from goal with this ball coming my way. I was a long way out. Too far to shoot, surely? Be realistic! There had to be too many bodies in the way. But the cramp made up my mind. I looked at the ball. 'It's set decent,' I told myself, 'so have a go, try to hit the target. Nothing to lose, Stevie.'

I made contact, pouring my few remaining drops of energy into the ball, willing it on its way. People said the ball went in at a decent speed, but it seemed to take ages to travel those thirty yards. My senses were drained, the cramp and the tension taking their toll. Through blurred vision, I saw Shaka Hislop moving. Has he saved it? Has it gone in? Please God. Then I saw the net ripple and stretch. I saw the Liverpool fans leap up. I saw the West Ham fans and players collapse. It was in: 3–3.

My first reaction was of pure shock. I was surprised how well I hit it because of the mess my body was in. All my muscles were pulling. But there was no pain from hitting the ball so hard; there never is when you catch the ball so well. Those two strikes in the 2006 FA Cup final were the best I ever caught the ball. The feeling ripping through me matched the one after my Champions League header, although my second FA Cup final goal was better – my best ever goal. The brilliance of it still hasn't sunk in. I still can't believe I scored from so far out. On the Millennium pitch, I couldn't celebrate properly, I was too shattered. I just smiled and patted the GERRARD on my back. I don't know why, because the lads always cane me. 'Everyone knows who you are!' they shout at me.

Extra time felt like running through wet cement. Everyone was tired, yet West Ham could still have won it when Reo-Coker headed goalwards. Has to be in. Somehow, Pepe appeared from nowhere and pushed the ball away onto the post – an unbelievable save. That one in Cardiff and Jerzy's off Shevchenko in Istanbul were the best two I have ever seen. I was made up for Pepe. It would have been a shame if we lost the FA Cup final on his mistakes, because he had been one of our players of the season. Even then West Ham could have won it, but Marlon Harewood, hobbling badly, missed the follow-up. Football's a harsh business; there's such a fine line between success and failure. Harewood gets the shot on target, West Ham lift the FA Cup, and my heart gets broken. But I didn't feel sympathy for Marlon or West Ham. I couldn't. You have to be hard in football. I don't think Harewood, Reo-Coker or Konchesky would have felt sorry for Carra or Reina if Liverpool had lost.

Football is brutal, and nothing is more brutal than penalties. Such unforgiving tests of nerve. But the moment the final went to a shoot-out, I knew it would be me lifting the FA Cup, not Reo-Coker. No question. The pens were down the West Ham end, an advantage to them as we would get battered by their fans when we stepped up. No problem. Confidence and a feeling of responsibility surged through me. As captain, I wanted to set an example.

'Can I go number one, boss?' I asked Rafa.

'You are number three,' he replied.

As ever, our brilliant manager had a plan. Obviously, I accepted Rafa's instruction and joined my team-mates in the centre-circle.

When Didi strolled forward to take penalty number one, my certainty intensified that Liverpool were on course for a seventh FA Cup. Germans don't miss from twelve yards. Didi is made for big games, daunting occasions, anything that challenges a man's mettle. Nothing fazes him. Ball down, step back, run in, goal. Hislop, no chance.

West Ham had no way back from that, I was sure. Reina would see to that. Pepe arrived in England with an astonishing record of saving pens back in Spain. In two seasons at Villarreal, he stopped twelve out of eighteen penalties, and a keeper doesn't save that many unless he's a master. West Ham's first taker, Bobby Zamora, was up against a goalkeeper with the quickest of reactions, a top professional who had done his research on his opponents. Zamora hit his kick hard and low towards the corner, but Reina read it. He stretched out his right hand and the ball was stopped. West Ham hearts must have stopped as well.

If Zamora could take such a good kick and still not beat Reina, what chance did they have?

Hope then smiled briefly on West Ham. Next up for Liverpool was Sami, which surprised me. Our giant Finn has never been a penalty-taker and his kick was pretty disappointing. At least he showed the bottle to go up there. That's why all the Liverpool lads stood in the centre-circle, arms around each other, showing our unity: we were all in this shoot-out together. Win together, lose together – the Liverpool way. Teddy Sheringham then strode towards the spot, and I knew West Ham would draw level. Teddy's as nerveless as Didi. Bang: 1–1.

Numbers three and four for Liverpool were me, then Riise. We were ready, confident. The pair of us had put in some serious shifts on our penalty technique at Melwood. I just worked on the same corner, over and over again. Same height, same spot. Through that practice at Melwood, I kept hitting the mark regularly. That ball was getting buried, just as at Melwood. Bang, past Hislop, job done.

When Konchesky missed, Riise had the chance to make it 3–1. He went for power down the middle. It went like a bloody missile, a bit too close to Hislop's feet for comfort, but still into the net. Brilliant!

All we needed was for Pepe to save from Anton Ferdinand and my hands were on that lovely Cup. I've met Anton a few times, and he seems a decent guy, but I certainly wasn't thinking 'Poor Anton!' when he missed. I was too busy hugging Steve Finnan and the rest of the team. Despite the brutality, penalties are the best and only way to settle finals. We can't go having replays at that stage of the season. Fans would hate it, too. It would be unfair on them to fork out for another expensive ticket.

When Anton missed, Carra was the first to take off in celebration. Winning trophies means everything to him and he never hides the emotion. Once he'd waved to his family, he came looking for me. It's a Scouse thing. Sharing the moment of glory means everything to two kids from Scouse estates. After I collected the FA Cup off Prince William, it was a case of you grab one handle, Carra mate, I'll hold the other, and let's go and party.

After I finally laid off spraying people with champagne and was leaving the Millennium pitch,

Alan Pardew stopped me and shook my hand. 'I'd hoped you were saving that for the World Cup,' he said with a smile. Top man. Pardew's players were also first-class. They came across, man after man, concealing their agony to say, 'Well done.' Everyone associated with West Ham behaved with real dignity in Cardiff, just like the way I try to be in defeat. It really moved me that in their hour of utter desolation, West Ham fans stayed behind to applaud as I lifted the FA Cup. I'll never forget that sporting gesture. I'm Liverpool through and through, head to toe, but I have a place in my heart for West Ham supporters after Cardiff. Fans like West Ham United's make football special. Usually when we do a lap of honour with a cup, the opponents' section is empty. The fans have disappeared, dragging their heartache with them. Not in Cardiff on 13 May 2006. The West Ham fans were tremendous, clapping us as we paraded the cup. Both sets of fans were brilliant, which made it such a terrific occasion.

Everyone raved about the match. The 125th FA Cup final was called the greatest ever, even 'The Gerrard Final'! That meant the world to me. I love the FA Cup. It has taken a few knocks over recent years, and Premiership clubs are perhaps more focused these days on the Champions League, but Liverpool and West Ham put the shine back on the trophy that day in Cardiff.

After the FA Cup final, Liverpool threw a party for the players and families, and Rafa was there. I wandered across to him, buzzing with our victory. 'Next season,' Rafa kept saying. 'Next season, we have to do better in the Premiership.' Typical Rafa, always looking forward, never revelling in the moment like me and Carra. Rafa never even mentioned my two goals. Top goals, great goals, rescue-act goals. Not a squeak! I smacked in twenty-three goals that season for Liverpool – not bad for a midfielder. Any other manager would have been all over me. Not Liverpool's gaffer. 'You never hit twenty-five,' he remarked. 'You missed the target by two!' But, a smile! Amazing! Rafa actually smiled! Thank God. I wandered back to the lads, thinking, 'My word, that was a compliment off Rafa.'

There I was, on top of the world after the FA Cup final and having scored twenty-three goals over the season, and there was Rafa bringing me back down to earth. Even his tiny compliment was an encouragement to improve. But that's Rafa, always challenging me to push myself higher. Go for twenty-five goals. Go for thirty. Don't relax. And Rafa has helped my performances go to another level. He's such a hungry manager. 'Small details, Steven, small details' is one of his biggest shouts. Leave nothing to chance, even the tiniest detail. I'm getting to like this Spaniard more and more, and my aim is still to get a 'well done' off him before I retire. His hardness drives me on. I must crack it, though. I want to deliver in games to impress Rafa. I dream of that 'well done'!

# 21
# Frustration in Germany – the 2006 World Cup

Winning's an addiction. As I gently placed my FA Cup medal in the trophy room at the top of our new house in Formby, another burning ambition confronted me. Space was set aside in the room for an even more precious medal.

Three weeks after Cardiff, England landed in Germany as one of the favourites for the greatest prize on earth. This was meant to be England's World Cup, the moment when the so-called Golden Generation ended forty years of hurt and brought the trophy home. Me and Becks, JT and Lamps, Michael and Ashley: England's players were better than at Euro 2004, more experienced and more determined. We arrived in Germany convinced we could win. England expects.

Everything seemed in place for a successful tournament. Our coach from Baden-Baden airport eventually pulled up outside a castle called Bühlerhöhe, our secluded base, with magnificent views over the Rhine Valley.

It was perfect. The Football Association had done us proud. They'd even got longer beds in for lanky lads like me, Rio and Crouchy. The food was outstanding, the kit ideal. Nothing was left to chance. When we drove down to the training pitch at Mittelberg the following morning, we found a surface better than any of the World Cup pitches. Determined to give us the very best, the FA borrowed Wembley's top groundsman, Steve Welch, to put in a fantastic new pitch. It was watered every morning, so no wonder our passing was good in training. That Tuesday, 6 June, I glanced around Mittelberg and all the players looked terrific. No excuses, no regrets. Everything was geared up for England to deliver.

We just needed Wayne Rooney fit after his metatarsal break. 'Give us Wayne,' I thought, 'and we'll give you the World Cup.' Manchester United's manager, Sir Alex Ferguson, kept saying England must be careful with Wayne. But England weren't rushing him, he was just healing quickly. Wazza and I are big mates and I talked to him all the time at Bühlerhöhe. 'I'm ready,' he kept telling me. 'I'm ready for Paraguay.' Paraguay! That was our first game, on 10 June.

Speculation about his return was crazy. Every day, Wayne was on the back pages. Will he? Won't he? The saga wasn't fair to Wayne or the other England players, but that's the country we live in. We know what our newspapers, radio and TV are like. Mad at times. Wayne is England's most important player so the attention was bound to be on him, but it was a distraction. Every time we went to dinner, turned on the TV or picked up a paper, there was Wayne. We did lose some of our focus.

Sven was right to take a gamble on the fitness of someone as special as Wazza. If England were to bring back the World Cup, we needed Wayne Rooney. The mistake Sven made was that he should have picked five forwards in his World Cup twenty-three – Wayne plus four others. For a tournament as big and demanding as the World Cup, every team needs five strikers. Sven talked about midfielders operating further forward, but that's too specialized. I was gutted when I walked in the Old Trafford dressing-room before the World Cup warm-up against Hungary on 30 May and saw the number 9 shirt hanging on my peg. I'm an attacking midfielder, not an emergency striker. England required real strikers, footballers comfortable with number 9 on their back, like Wazza, Michael and Crouchy. Sven named them in the squad, but it was his fourth striking choice that stunned me. Not only were England embarking on an arduous World Cup campaign with only four forwards, one of them was Theo Walcott. I almost fell over when I heard.

I felt sorry for Theo, but more so for Jermain Defoe and Darren Bent. Jermain and Darren worked hard all season to go to a World Cup, then a kid comes out of nowhere and takes the place they were after. It didn't look right. Darren stayed at home, but at least Jermain came to Germany on stand-by, just in case Wayne didn't recover. Defoe was unbelievable. From the moment England joined up, he was probably one of the best in training. His finishing was sharp. His attitude was spot-on. He never once mentioned any grievance over a kid like Theo being in the twenty-three. When Wayne was confirmed in the squad after flying back for that final scan, Jermain hid his heartache well. Before heading for the airport and a flight back to England, he shook hands with all of us and wished us all the best. Top man. He must have been boiling inside. On the surface, though, he was fantastically professional. Good for him. Jermain went up massively in my estimation as a bloke and a player.

Still, I was punching the air with delight that Wazza was cleared for action. As poor Jermain was upstairs packing his bags that Wednesday, 7 June, Wazza marched back into the Bühlerhöhe, stood in reception and declared, 'The Big Man's back!' Typical Wazza! He wasn't being cocky. Wayne just has so much belief in himself. Even before his scan he knew he would be all right. The overhead kicks in training were a statement of intent. The scan was simply a doctor's note confirming what all the players and Wayne knew. He was welcomed back into training on Thursday like a returning hero. But he was still prevented from playing against Paraguay, and it almost killed him to watch it. Football is to Wayne Rooney what oxygen is to everyone else.

Along with all the talk about Wazza, other issues occupied my thoughts. I was just hours away from my World Cup debut, my supreme test. I was desperate to take my Liverpool form into an England game. Everybody was watching. Could I cut it? Could I do in the World Cup what I had done in the FA Cup and European Cup? Questions crowded in on me. Climbing on board the plane out of Lisbon after Euro 2004, I carried a kit-bag full of regrets. Flying into Germany, I kept telling myself, 'No regrets this time, Stevie.' I cranked up the pressure on myself. I paced around my room at Bühlerhöhe, saying out loud, 'First World Cup game – make sure it goes well. Remember France at Euro 2004: you were OK until the last five minutes. Have a solid game this time. Ninety minutes, no mistakes.' *No mistakes*.

I couldn't really sleep that week. My mind was jumping with too many concerns to close down for an hour or two. And another worrying distraction soon affected my preparations. I went into a tackle with Joe

Cole at Mittelberg. Whack. Joe's elbow banged into my hip, and my back went into a spasm. All the old fears tumbled back into my present. 'That's me out of the group games,' I thought. 'That's another tournament gone.' Thank God I was in good hands. England's physio, Gary Lewin, examined my back and said, 'It will settle down quite quickly.' Fingers crossed. Touch wood. The doc, Leif Sward, agreed. The next morning an osteopath called Carl Todd arrived from England, and he manipulated my back four times that day. 'You'll make the Paraguay game,' Carl insisted, filling me with belief. But I carried a back problem for the rest of England's stay in Germany.

All that mattered was that the medical lads got me on the field against Paraguay. My instructions were simple in Frankfurt: to hold back when England bombed on. Sven had us playing 4–4–2 without a holding midfielder, so someone had to take responsibility in case Paraguay broke away. 'You are a little bit more defensive than Frank,' Sven told me, 'so don't go up as much as him. Be more cautious.' That sacrificed one of my strengths – storming forward. I craved to play my Liverpool role for England. But Frank Lampard had the attacking licence. Lamps was worth his place in the World Cup starting eleven. In fact he was one of the main reasons England reached Germany: he'd been immense in qualifying. I had no complaints. Just get on with it, Stevie lad. Frankfurt was my first World Cup match and I was aching to play. Right-back, left-back, anywhere – just let me taste the World Cup atmosphere. I'm twenty-six, it's been too long, let me out there.

The mood in the dressing-room before the game was good. Everyone was up for it. Everyone buzzed with anticipation. This was it. The World Cup. Our time.

When we walked out of the tunnel, the home of Eintracht Frankfurt belonged to England. What a sight! England flags everywhere. Our fans everywhere. The ticketing problems never affected England. Our boys were out there in force. I wasn't surprised. England fans are unbelievable; I knew they'd pack out the ground. I'd switched on the TV the night before and seen them partying all over Frankfurt, all over Germany really. I'd opened my hotel window in

Frankfurt and heard them running through their song-book. Football's Coming Home! Us players now had to make sure it did come home.

We started well. Becks forced an own-goal from Carlos Gamarra early on and we should have made it three or four, but the heat seemed to come straight from the Sahara. My mouth felt like it was lined with sandpaper. Yet the sweltering conditions affected us only towards the end. Eintracht's pitch was the real reason we never played well. On our beautiful Mittelberg surface, our football was quick. Not here. Frankfurt's pitch was too dry, the grass too long. England tired after the break and Paraguay kept the ball better than us. Yet apart from an unfair booking, I was really, really happy with my individual perform-ance. Collectively, though, we all knew we'd face criticism for our second-half display. But so what? Three points meant one thing: England were up and running.

Next up were Trinidad and Tobago in Nuremberg on 15 June. 'England should win this no problem,' I told myself. Again we failed to impress. In the second half, particularly, I got really frustrated and some of my passing went astray. England did not have the look of potential world champions. For eighty-three minutes, the so-called Golden Generation were held by a team of players from Wrexham, Port Vale and Coventry. We could not break through, until Peter headed in. At last we led. We could relax, and I could take a few more risks. Go on. Push on. Get a few shots in. Back at Melwood I work on my left foot all the time, so when I created a chance in the ninetieth minute I did not hesitate to use my left. I caught the ball really sweet and knew it was destined for the net. In it went. Unstoppable. The feeling of scoring in a World Cup was magical. There was relief, too. People see me hitting the target for Liverpool week in, week out. I felt under a lot of pressure to score for England, so seeing that ball flash past Shaka Hislop was wonderful. As it flew in, all the frustration over missing the 2002 World Cup finally disappeared as well.

Two games, six points, Wayne now back in action – it should have been all sunshine and smiles for England, but the clouds of concern persisted. This time, the press had a go at us for too many long balls.

Rubbish. England were not a long-ball side at the World Cup. Sven's tactics were not the problem. It was us, the players, simply not performing as we should do against lesser opposition.

Some tension began to creep into the England camp, partly because we could not spend proper time with our families after each match. The paparazzi and reporters who dogged us in Baden-Baden were a disgrace. So much rubbish was written about the WAGs, as the players' wives and girlfriends became known. People claimed they got more attention than the team.

A lesser frustration surfaced as we prepared for our final Group B match, against Sweden in Cologne on 20 June. One afternoon, after training at Mittelberg, Sven pulled me aside. 'Keep doing what you are doing, Steven,' he began. 'You are doing really well. But I'd like to rest you against Sweden. We're already through. You have a yellow card, and I can't afford not to have you in the last sixteen. What do you think? I think it's for the good of the team that you are on the bench.'

I returned to my room and thought hard about

the situation. My hunger for involvement against Sweden was immense. Why did that ref book me for nothing against Paraguay? Without that I would be starting against Sweden.

I was torn, so I decided to wait and see what Sven had to say the next day. The boss came straight to the point. 'I'm resting you, Steven. I can't risk losing you for the last sixteen. I know how much you want to play, but I have no choice. We want to finish top of the group. If we need to use you to make sure we get that point, we will.'

I understood completely. Sven's concern over my booking was really a compliment to me.

Reluctantly, I took my place on the bench in Cologne and watched team-mates like Michael Owen line up. Michael had been subjected to some flak for his first two performances, so he was right up for Sweden. A feeling swept through me that Michael would score. Definitely. I caught that determined glint in my mate's eye. Been here before, seen it before: Michael means business tonight. I thought back to the Euros where there'd been similar pressure on Michael and he hit back with that great finish against Portugal.

He looked focused, sharp and ready to remind everyone of his class.

But then he smashed up his knee barely seconds after the first whistle. I was devastated for Michael, as a friend and also as a player. Michael's accident exposed the boss's crazy decision to take only four strikers. If only England had travelled to Germany with five forwards.

England's fans clearly wanted Theo on. Sven was having none of that. His sole aim was to top the group so he couldn't risk anything. There was no possible way the kid from Arsenal was ready. Crouchy came on, and England looked good for a while. Joe Cole gave us the lead with an absolute worldie, definitely a contender for goal of the tournament. At last England were playing good football, living up to our billing as one of the World Cup favourites. Thoughts of Berlin and the final filled my mind. The medal, the parade, the glory.

My day-dreaming was suddenly interrupted when Sweden equalized, through Markus Allback, and we were under real pressure. Sitting along from me was Sven, wearing a worried look. How would he react?

England must hang on to the draw to guarantee an easier last-sixteen game.

Sven turned to me. 'Are you ready?' he asked.

What was all that about not wanting to risk another yellow? 'Yeah,' I replied. 'Of course I'm ready.'

We had to re-impose ourselves. Come on, Stevie lad, get busy. With Owen Hargreaves buzzing around in midfield, I roamed forward. Look for a goal, look for the win. With five minutes remaining, Joe Cole cut into the area on the right and I made a diagonal run into the box. His cross was perfect, lifted over on time and right on the money. Heading is not my strongest point, but I made great contact with Coley's cross. The ball flew in. Yes! At last, England seemed destined for a first win over Sweden in thirty-eight years. Now we were really on the move in Germany. Just watch us go now!

Then, stupidly, we conceded a goal from a set-piece. We failed to cut out a long throw-in, Henrik Larsson pounced, and victory was snatched away. In the dressing-room, Steve McClaren was livid with us. He'd spent hours organizing the players for set-pieces.

Every session he'd drummed into us the importance of concentration, and we'd dozed off for a split-second in Cologne and been punished. 'If we defend like that again at set-pieces we will be out of the tournament before we know it,' Steve told us. I felt the mistake was a one-off; we'd actually defended well at set-pieces during the World Cup. Losing Rio to an injury hadn't helped, because he's a big presence at set-pieces. Come on. Be positive. Yes, it was disappointing not to finish the group with a third victory, but we had booked a last-sixteen place against Ecuador rather than in-form Germany. The quarter-finals beckoned.

The knockout rounds now awaited England and we were back at Mittelberg, preparing for our bout with Ecuador. All the players knew we must raise our game. We spoke about that in team meetings with Sven and also among ourselves. During the group stage we showed only in flashes how good we were: first half against Paraguay, last twenty minutes against Trinidad and Tobago, and first half against Sweden. For all the criticism, we still believed we'd go all the way to Berlin.

Stuttgart was the next stop, and Sven gave us a new shape. After starting three games with 4–4–2, England now switched to 4–5–1. It was a big leap. Me and the other players arrived in Germany thinking we would play 4–4–2 all the way through, but after Michael's injury we went 4–5–1. Even though we'd prepared for 4–5–1 we were still not familiar enough with such a different system. Other World Cup teams stuck with one formation they spent ages fine-tuning. Not us. England changed for the knockout stage of a World Cup, and you cannot expect it to work immediately. Players need time to adapt from 4–4–2 to 4–5–1.

We were still too good for Ecuador, though. Becks whipped in one of those trademark free-kicks on the hour to see England into the quarter-finals. Thank God for David. He had been slaughtered in the media, many critics questioning his right to a place, but that goal in Stuttgart showed why David must start. Becks's set-pieces are brilliant, and he offers much more than that. He is so gifted technically, and so competitive, that he can change a game's fortunes in a split-second. Without his stunning free-kick we were destined for extra time and pens. I admire Becks. It's good to play alongside someone who ignores all the criticism and just gets on with helping the team he loves to victory. Other players would collapse under that weight of pressure or simply hide. Not Becks. No chance. He thrives on it. All the players were surprised and disappointed that David got stick at the World Cup. We love him, and respect him. Ecuador confirmed Becks's importance. We need experienced players out there, particularly those like Becks with such an amazing desire to deliver.

When we knew we had Portugal in the quarter-finals, all the players thought, 'Last four. We're on our way.' Of course we were worried that we weren't yet firing, but our confidence never dipped. Portugal were nothing special. They'd hardly set the World Cup alight. 'We can beat them,' I told the guys up at Bühlerhöhe. Portugal had lost Costinha and Deco to suspension, and those two were big players for them. We had more time to work on 4–5–1 down at Mittelberg, too, and slowly the new system was getting better.

As we kicked off in Gelsenkirchen on Saturday,

1 July, all the lads were convinced the evening would end with England in the World Cup semi-finals. But almost immediately we had a reality check. Portugal surprised me with how well they kept the ball. They seemed to glow with a belief in their tactics, and their touch. Even without Costinha and Deco, they looked a really settled team. Each player knew his role under Luiz Felipe Scolari. Facing Cristiano Ronaldo and Luis Figo was a nightmare: they were so elusive, so quick at picking up very clever positions. Now you see them, now you don't. It was like chasing ghosts. But Ronaldo didn't hurt us with the ball; he only played in flashes.

Sadly, a dark side stains Ronaldo's game. His part in Wayne's dismissal in Gelsenkirchen was a disgrace. All the Portuguese players should hang their heads in shame for their ambush on Wayne midway through the second half. When I saw the incident, I thought, 'Well, that's a free-kick for us.' The Portuguese were obviously fouling Wayne. Blatant. Wayne came deep to collect the ball and they were pulling his shirt, pushing him, banging into his ankles from behind. If Wayne had fallen over, England would have got the free-kick. But in the end, Wayne was punished for being too honest. Wazza's strong, and he always tries to stay on his feet, even if defenders like Ricardo Carvalho are fouling him 24/7. It's not in Wayne's nature to go down.

Then I saw Carvalho writhing around on the ground as if his life was coming to a sudden and brutal end. What was going on? The referee, Horacio Elizondo, had blown his whistle. Commotion raged around the Argentinian official. I saw the red card raised. He's sent one of the Portuguese off. About time. They've been fouling Wazza all game. Tiago even kicked Wayne in the face in the first half. Then, to my horror, I realized it was Wayne walking slowly off. FIFA are always banging on about fair play, but the English are the only ones behaving properly. The world's governing body want footballers to stay on their feet. Wayne did. Yet he's the one who got sent off in Gelsenkirchen.

Of course Wayne had become frustrated. Up front on his own, he hadn't received the service he expected. He was desperate to score in the World Cup. But the real frustration was having Carvalho and his partners in crime constantly pulling and pushing him. FIFA should be embarrassed about what the Portuguese did to Wayne. Crowding round Elizondo, trying to influence him, calling for a card against an opponent. It angers me. Portugal's deviousness got one of my best mates sent off in the World Cup. England would have won if Wayne had stayed on.

The ten Englishmen who remained on the field in Gelsenkirchen seethed at the injustice, which doubled our determination against Portugal. You can cheat us, but you can't beat us. That was the message coming out from me and JT, Rio and the rest as we resisted everything Portugal threw at us. 'Stick together!' came the shout. Everyone was stirred up. Everyone was screaming encouragement, particularly JT and Rio. Ashley too. I went over to the left to help Ashley as Portugal tried to open England up by going wide. No chance. Ashley and I would not let anyone through. All ten of us were helped by the positive approach from Sven and Steve. I thought the order would be 'hold out for pens'. Sven and Steve thought differently. 'Push on!' came the instruction from the bench. 'Go and win it on the break!'

But as soon as we reached extra-time, my mind turned to pens. I knew I'd be on one. Sven had indicated his main penalty-takers in training. So as extra-time went on around me, I spent half an hour worrying about the only kick that counted – my penalty. Sweat poured even faster off my forehead. Stay calm. Focus. You must get through extra-time. But I was already distracted, the clock only showing how long it was until I had to make that soul-destroying walk from the centre-circle. Nearer and nearer. My pulse raced madly. My head was pound-ing. Penalties, penalties, penalties. 'Where am I going to put it?' I thought. 'Has their keeper seen my Liverpool pens? Soon find out.'

Elizondo's whistle went, and the teams gathered in two tense groups in the centre-circle. I wish I was first up. Get it out the way. The wait's killing me. I envied Frank, taking penalty number one for England. Standing in the line, given support by team-mates, I felt weak with nerves, expectation and pressure. I could hardly watch as Simão scored. Don't worry, Frank will get us level. Go on, Lamps. In training, Lamps had been lashing them in. No problem. He stepped up. Ricardo saved. The knot in my stomach tightened. I had never felt this bad on a pitch in all my life.

The shoot-out continued its grim course, making heroes and villains. Viana and Petit both missed, Hargreaves stuck his away. Now the spotlight burned on me. Here goes. I broke away from the safety of my friends in the centre-circle. Suddenly I was alone, making my way towards the penalty spot, towards my fate. The journey was only forty yards, but it felt like forty miles.

As I neared the spot, my body went numb. I wouldn't wish that walk on my worst enemy. Yet even with all the doubts building, I had belief in my technique. That penalty was going in. I will score. I went through my penalty routine. Set the ball right? Yes, done. Remember all the good kicks in training? Yes. I had hit the target nine times out of ten at Mittelberg. Know where you're going to place it? Yes. Ricardo's good, but if I place the ball exactly where I want, at the spot where Robbo, David James and Scott Carson told me about in training, Portugal's keeper can't stop it.

I was ready. Elizondo wasn't. Blow the whistle! Get a move on, ref! Why the wait? I'd put the ball on the spot, Ricardo was on his line. Why do I have to wait for the whistle? Those extra couple of seconds seemed like an eternity, and they definitely put me off. Doesn't he know I'm on edge? I was screaming inside. In training, it seemed so easy: ball down, step back, run in, goal. No wait, no tension. Not here. Not with Elizondo delaying everything. At last he blew, but my focus had gone. The moment I made contact with the ball I knew it wasn't going where I'd planned. It was eighteen inches away from my chosen spot, making it easier for Ricardo. Saved. Nightmare.

A feeling of utter helplessness washed over me. The walk back to the halfway line was really, really bad. Question after question ate away at me. My FA Cup final penalty had been so good a few weeks before, so where had my accuracy gone? The pressure just got to me. For months, now, it had played on my mind that I would have to take a penalty in the World Cup. I knew we would come up against a shootout in Germany. My nerve, and my accuracy, just went. But wait. There's still hope. The lads can get me out of this mess. Surely? Even when Helder Postiga tucked his away, I felt Carra could make it 2–2. Sven brought Carra on with a minute remaining simply because he had been deadly in training: one miss from thirty. Carra is not one for hanging about, so he quickly took his pen, which flew past Ricardo. Elizondo hadn't blown, and he pulled Carra back. That was out of order.

When Ricardo got to Carra's second kick, my heart sank. England were going out of the World Cup. Ronaldo would finish us off. The story was set. It had to be Ronaldo, the kid involved in Wayne's sending-off, one of the best foreigners in the Premiership, sending us back home. Empty-handed. Broken-hearted. Ronaldo showed no mercy.

England were down and out. I collapsed in the centre-circle, my body shutting down. I've never experienced such depression on a football pitch. That own-goal against Chelsea in Cardiff was bad, so was getting knocked out of Euro 2004 in Lisbon, but Gelsenkirchen was much, much worse. I sat there with a lump in my throat, fighting back the tears. A few got through. People came across to console me, first Sven, then Steve and Gary Lewin. Becks tried to pull me up. Thanks, guys, for your support, but leave me to my pain.

Eventually, I climbed to my feet and joined the rest of the England players in a slow, mournful lap of Schalke's ground to thank our brilliant supporters. They stood and gave us a salute we did not deserve. I felt bitterly that I'd let every one of those magnificent fans down. Every one. They followed us across Germany, lifted our spirits during dark moments. Before each match, when we drove from our hotel, they would be there in their tens of thousands, lining the route, waving at us. We love you. We believe in you. Every game felt like a home game. And how had we repaid them? More heartache.

Why did England mess up? It cannot have been simply down to Portugal's gamesmanship. Everyone called us the Golden Generation. We should have coped. I hate using the word, but we failed. England went out of the World Cup in the quarter-finals, and that stinks. The reasons are scattered around: we didn't keep the ball well, we didn't take our chances, we took some poor penalties.

The real reason behind England's short stay in Germany is simple. It pains me to admit this, but it needs saying. We were just not as good as we think we are. On arriving in Germany, England were guilty of over-confidence. It was ours for the taking. No-one better than us. Me and the other players placed too much pressure on ourselves by constantly claiming we could win the World Cup. Stupid. We talked ourselves up too much. Never again. In future tournaments, we must learn to be humble. Be calm. We went around Germany blowing our trumpet and returned home mute with embarrassment.

Sven was deeply upset. The media paint him as a cold, unemotional man, but that's wrong. He hurt badly in Gelsenkirchen. The media heaped the blame on Sven, but that's unfair. The players who crossed the white line must share the responsibility with him for England's failure. But I will have another chance with England. Sven won't. That was it. Game over. I was sad to see him go. I loved working with him. He was always constructive. Sven definitely improved me as a player, developing my positional play and stressing the importance of retaining possession. He always believed in me, and for that I will always be in his debt. I have so much respect for him. Sven kept leading England to quarter-finals but not beyond, and that's one of my biggest regrets. I let Sven down. I just wished I could have scored the goal, or hit the pen, that got England into the semi-finals in Germany. I would have loved to see Sven's face as I scored the winner because he is a great guy.

Of course we knew Sven would get coated for England's failure. He knew it as well. I don't think he was too cautious, as many people claimed, but I did understand some of the criticism towards him. A few decisions were wrong, like not taking five strikers. He certainly shouldn't have brought Theo to Germany. As well as Theo, Sven also didn't seem to have any intention of using certain players. In midfield we had three or four guys who were really, really similar. Sven never showed any interest in playing some of them, so why bring them to Germany? Take those who are going to play. And another forward would have been nice.

The retreat from Germany took us first to Bühlerhöhe to pack. It was late when we arrived at the hotel, but Sven immediately gathered the staff and players together and spoke for fifteen minutes. 'Thank you all for your support,' he said. 'I really believed this was our year. I can't believe we have gone out on penalties again. We should have been last four at least. All the best.' Sven then turned to Steve McClaren, his successor. 'Steve, I wish you all the best.' Sven was all dignity. He went round and shook each player's hand.

Sven was off, and Becks was stepping down as captain. It was the end of an era. I had no idea David was thinking of giving up the armband. I was in my room at Bühlerhöhe on the Sunday morning, getting my stuff packed and thinking about holidays, when Becks came on the telly at a press conference. I assumed he was just going to say a few words, expressing the players' disappointment. I was stunned when he announced he was finished as captain. But, looking back, I feel Becks resigned at the right time. He'd led England at three tournaments and was under a lot of pressure. I'll always remember him as a great captain. Becks loved the job, and I know how much it hurt him to hand over the armband. Watching him read his statement, I was just pleased to hear him say he would carry on playing for England. Becks has so much to offer the squad, whether he is in the starting eleven or not.

But that's now Steve McClaren's decision. I'd watched the FA's hunt for a new manager with interest. I'm happy the FA decided on Steve. I just hope he believes in me as Sven did. Steve certainly knows my game. He can get the best out of me. I respect him. All those who doubt his credentials should give him a chance. As he tries to steer England towards Euro 2008, people should judge Steve on his ideas and what changes he makes, not on what happened under Sven. Sven made all the big decisions, while Steve did his job really well as coach. Under Sven, Steve took a lot of training, which was second to none. His coaching's top class. I'd come off the training pitch thinking, 'I really enjoyed that.' He tried to improve me as a player, tried to improve the team shape in certain situations. Having worked with McClaren, I'm convinced England have the right man. I listen closely to Steve, and 99.9 per cent of what he says is right. He knows his stuff, and he's more in your face than Sven. Noisier. Livelier. He's excellent at speaking in front of the England squad and also very good at one-on-ones. He deserves a go at being England manager. If he hadn't become manager, we might have missed out.

Steve will improve this England team but I'm not making any predictions about Euro 2008. Germany taught me to be more cautious in public. Defeat in the World Cup hit me hard. I had to get away quick. I took Alex off to St Tropez. Just the two of us. Five days' complete break; just what the doctor ordered, although nothing could cure the frustration I felt over England's World Cup display.

On our last night, Sunday 9 July, I couldn't help but turn on the telly to watch the final. Alex didn't mind this intrusion into our romantic break. She was busy packing. So I sat there, and watched France lose to Italy. I was stunned by Zinédine Zidane's head-butt on Marco Materazzi. Even though I idolize Zidane, and understand he got provoked, you simply can't do what he did. It was crazy. France could have done with him in the shoot-out. Watching the pens brought painful flashbacks for me. When I then saw the Italians celebrating, I thought: 'That could have been us.' Neither Italy nor France produced anything special, certainly nothing that would have scared England. It reinforced all my regrets over England's 2006 World Cup campaign.

## 22
# Athens, Andorra and the Altar

As the 2006–07 season unfolded, it felt like Liverpool's destiny to reach the European Cup final again. When Liverpool were drawn against Barcelona in the last sixteen, many people thought that was it. Season over. My first reaction when we were drawn against the European champions was excitement. Bring it on. Soon, though, that initial buzz faded. The reality kicked in over what a tough draw this was.

The first leg was at the Nou Camp on February 21. Rafa's game-plan was to shock Barcelona. Do the unexpected. Stand firm. Get stuck into them. Even when Deco scored early, we stuck to our tactics. Our plan was to hurt Barcelona down the sides, in the full-back areas. Craig Bellamy's job was to race down the channels, either side of Barcelona's centre-halves,

Carles Puyol and Rafael Márquez. When Craig scored, drawing level, and Riise had scored the winner off a Bellamy pass, we were laughing. We had just beaten the European champions 2–1 at their place.

What made victory particularly special is that Barcelona were a class side. For the first 20 minutes, they made us really sweat. That was the first time I had run into Ronaldinho in a competitive game, and the Brazilian didn't disappoint. I felt that when he was in possession, anything could happen. But he never got a chance. Carra was fantastic against Ronaldinho, getting blocks in, blotting him out.

Back in the Nou Camp dressing-room, Carra, me and all the lads were buzzing. Liverpool had beaten Barcelona. But we couldn't risk any complacency. 'It's not over,' I warned. 'Barcelona will come at us at Anfield. They've got the quality to destroy us.' But they didn't. Eidur Gudjohnsen scored but it was too little, too late. The away goals took us through.

Next up were PSV Eindhoven, and we were really shifting now: 3–0 in Holland, 1–0 at Anfield. Job done. The semi-final draw brought familiar faces: Chelsea.

José Mourinho. John Terry. Frank Lampard. Joe Cole.

Having to overcome Chelsea's 1–0 first-leg lead, the Kop played their part again, big-time. Chelsea walked into another wall of noise. Mourinho's players were caught completely cold by our goal, when I knocked a free-kick to Daniel Agger, who scored from the edge of the area. Chelsea were stunned. Simple as that. It was off to penalties. We held our nerve, Chelsea didn't, Pepe Reina was sensational and we were off to Athens. Brilliant.

One area where Chelsea cannot touch Liverpool is in the amazing noise generated by our fans. I'm not worried that the new stadium planned in Stanley Park will lose that atmosphere. No chance. It's the people who make the atmosphere, and those supporters will never disappear. I know how much Liverpool means to the fans. If the new stadium is built right, the noise and intensity will be unbelievable. It has been delayed an extra year because the club want to build a Kop, recreating the best parts of Anfield. If Liverpool do have a Kop, with more people in, the atmosphere on big Champions League or Premiership occasions will be out of this world.

Liverpool's new American owners, Tom Hicks and George Gillett, are doing things the right way. The first time I encountered them, I was bowled over by the enthusiasm pouring from the pair of them. I saw the ambition in their eyes, heard it in their words.

When the party finished on Merseyside that night, our thoughts turned to Athens, to another final. Again our opponents were AC Milan.

Liverpool's tactical preparations were perfect. As against Barcelona at the Nou Camp, Rafa came up with the right game-plan in Athens on May 23. We all knew Milan's strengths, the class they had in midfield. We swamped the middle, Javier Mascherano got tight on Kaká, doing a really good job at keeping him quiet. Liverpool still controlled the final, without really creating chances. Many of our best moments in the first half flowed from Jermaine Pennant out on the right. He got in one great cross that I just failed to convert. Jermaine finished the season strongly, showing his terrific potential.

For all the efforts of Jermaine and the other players, we couldn't break through. Milan took a flukey lead on the edge of half-time, the ball catching Filippo

Inzaghi and sending Pepe the wrong way. How unlucky was that? I couldn't believe it. Early in the second half, I missed a chance which I'm still gutted about. Cutting in from the left, and through on Dida, only one thought hammered through my mind: don't waste the opportunity. I didn't want to shoot with my left foot and regret it. I must use my right, my stronger foot. So I opened up my body to try to pass the ball around Dida with my right. Sadly, I never made a good enough connection. Dida saved. When Inzaghi added another, I felt the spirit of Istanbul desert us for good, even when Dirk Kuyt made it 2–1 in the 89th minute. The final whistle blew through me like a vicious wind. I looked around at my devastated Liverpool team-mates, and at our wonderful fans who sang to the end and beyond, and my heart broke in two.

Having congratulated Gattuso, Paolo Maldini and the rest of the Milan team, I retreated to the dressing-room. It was grim in there. The players were shattered emotionally and physically. I had to behave as a captain and not as a heartbroken player. 'We can be proud of ourselves,' I told the players. 'Look to the future.' For all the frustration raging in me in Athens,

I believe Liverpool are heading in the right direction.

I have to. Putting all the agony of Athens to one side for a moment, the reality is that Liverpool reached two finals in three years, which is terrific. The future looks bright for Liverpool: we've got a good team, an outstanding manager in Rafa, a new stadium being designed and brilliant new owners.

Athens left a bad taste in the mouth. The moment I turned my mobile back on, calls and texts came thudding through from family and friends who were at the Olympic Stadium and were horrified by the behaviour of the Greek police. What I heard shocked me. My family and friends were caught up in minor incidents trying to get into the stadium; they were pushed, shoved, and tear-gassed.

The Olympic Stadium in Athens was too small and too poorly prepared for clubs the size of Liverpool and Milan. Such a showpiece game as the European Cup final must be in a larger arena than Athens, with fairer and bigger ticket allocations, proper turnstiles, and double the security.

Frustration became a constant companion for a while. Seeing Steve Heighway leave his post as

Liverpool Academy director was particularly disappointing. Steve is impossible to replace. No one works better with kids from eight to 18. Liverpool Football Club, and I personally, will miss Steve Heighway.

Disappointment dogged me during 2006–07, for country as well as club. England enjoyed a good start under Steve McClaren but we soon ran into some stormy weather. By the time England came away from Israel on March 24 with a 0–0 draw, we were beginning to feel the anger of England's supporters. As we left the field in Tel Aviv, England's fans showed their frustration, giving us a taste of the treatment in store in Barcelona four days later for the tie with Andorra. On the Tuesday, the day before the game, I did a press conference with John Terry and the questions were really, really difficult. The mood was dark and against us. Stepping out in the Montjuic against Andorra felt like climbing into a pressure cooker. As we struggled to break down Andorra, the abuse was incredible.

With every scoreless minute, the boos worsened. At half-time, England needed inspiration. 'Try to raise the tempo,' Steve told us. He was really good at half-time. He used his experience to help the young players. 'Ignore the atmosphere,' Steve told them, 'concentrate on the football.'

'Keep going, don't hide,' I told the team. 'Be patient, blank the noise out.' Action was needed to match my words. I had to make something happen myself, so I drove into Andorra, scoring twice, and taking the sting out of the fans' venom. For my first goal, set up by Wazza, I made good contact with a half-volley. The moment the ball hit the grass I knew it was in. Relief seeped into our bodies. But England needed another goal. I played a one, two with Stewart Downing and then Jermain Defoe, and produced a good finish. David Nugent's late goal made it 3–0, and the storm subsided. After surviving that, the only way was up for England.

England's next Euro 2008 qualifier came in Estonia on June 6. Again, pressure mounted on McClaren, and the players, but England had too much for Estonia. Joe Cole scored the first and Becks then created finishes for Crouchy and Michael. Becks' return lifted us. I was pleased to see him back. Definitely. He puts quality balls into the box. He's a danger at set-pieces. Becks has achieved so much in life, and in his career, that everyone should look up to him and learn from him. I do.

I did get one medal while on England duty that season: an MBE off the Queen. From where I come from, a housing estate in Huyton, I never, ever thought I would be walking up to Buckingham Palace to meet the Queen. I was really flattered and shocked to be invited. I must admit to feeling nervous stepping through the gates of Buckingham Palace. Luckily enough, it went perfectly. I bowed in front of the Queen. 'All the best with England,' she said. A sense of pride filled me.

Afterwards, I got a picture of me and Alex outside Buckingham Palace. It was a great day, particularly for Alex. I am not one for all this attention but I'd do anything for her. We got married on June 16, a magical day, and it felt so right.

The future looks bright. There are more chapters to be written in my life-story. I've not finished yet. No chance.